NEW DEVELOPMENTS IN URBAN GOVERNANCE

Rethinking Collaboration in the Age of Austerity

Jonathan S. Davies, Ismael Blanco, Adrian Bua,
Ioannis Chorianopoulos, Mercè Cortina-Oriol,
Andrés Feandeiro, Niamh Gaynor, Brendan
Gleeson, Steven Griggs, Pierre Hamel, Hayley
Henderson, David Howarth, Roger Keil,
Madeleine Pill, Yunailis Salazar and Helen Sullivan

BRISTOL
UNIVERSITY
PRESS

First published in Great Britain in 2023 by

Bristol University Press
University of Bristol
1-9 Old Park Hill
Bristol
BS2 8BB
UK
t: +44 (0)117 374 6645
e: bup-info@bristol.ac.uk

Details of international sales and distribution partners are available at bristoluniversitypress.co.uk

British Library Cataloguing in Publication Data
A catalogue record for this book is available from the British Library

ISBN 978-1-5292-0582-4 hardcover
ISBN 978-1-5292-0587-9 paperback
ISBN 978-1-5292-0584-8 ePub
ISBN 978-1-5292-0583-1 ePdf

Cover design: blu inc, Bristol
Front cover image: JR Korpa – unsplash.com

Contents

List of Figures and Tables

Figures

Tables

Acknowledgements

Delivering a large-scale international project requires great commitment from many people playing different roles. Immense thanks for assisting with the research underpinning this book are due to Naya Tselepi (Athens), Kristin Smith (Baltimore), Iolande Bianchi (Barcelona), Eamonn McConnon, Nessa Ní Chasaide, Valesca Lima and Morina O'Neill (Dublin), Ed Thompson (Leicester) and Grégoire Autin (Montréal). Our project consultant, Paul O'Brien played an invaluable role, creating vital channels for communicating the research to stakeholders in his role as Chief Executive of the Association for Public Service Excellence. We are also very grateful for support from colleagues at De Montfort University, including the Research Services Directorate and staff in the Faculty of Business and Law. Jan Holland, Tom Moore, April Perrie and Suzanne Walker played a central role in supporting the administrative and financial sides of the project. We are very grateful for the immense patience and support from publishing and marketing staff at Bristol University Press, especially to Caroline Astley and Stephen Wenham, and also to anonymous reviewers who wrote invaluable comments on the initial proposal and draft manuscript. Sincere thanks are due to the UK Economic and Social Research Council (ESRC) for generously funding our research, under the title *Collaborative Governance under Austerity: An Eight-case Comparative Study* (ES/L012898/1). Above all, finally, we thank the hundreds of respondents across the eight cities who gave valuable time and invaluable insights to the research.

Introduction

The 2008–2009 Global Economic Crisis (GEC) created an opportunity, eagerly seized by many national governments and international organizations, to impose a prolonged, and widespread period of austerity. Austerity is widely recognized to have done enormous damage to social, cultural, political and economic infrastructures in cities and larger urban areas across the globe (Davies, 2021). As the GEC was also the first such crisis in what is widely considered 'the urban age' (Brenner and Schmid, 2015), (COVID-19 merely the latest and most intense), austerity measures were chiefly administered through municipal and regional mechanisms. A great deal has been written since the crisis, about the way austerity was experienced, governed, resisted and urbanized. This volume considers these issues anew, by reflecting on the multi-faceted and shape-shifting concept of 'collaboration'. It draws from research funded by the UK Economic and Social Research Council titled *Collaborative Governance Under Austerity: An Eight Case Comparative Study*, led by the Centre for Urban Research on Austerity at De Montfort University in the UK City of Leicester.[1] Research was conducted over three years (2015–2018) in the European cities of Athens, Barcelona, Dublin, Leicester and Nantes, North American cities of Baltimore and Montréal, and the Australian City of Greater Dandenong, part of the Greater Melbourne metropolis.

Our objective in this volume is to reflect on the theme of collaborative governance, considering this from the perspective of resisting austerity, or otherwise finding ways to circumvent or move beyond it. As a research team, we have a range of political views, but all share egalitarian sympathies articulated in the following chapters. None of us are convinced of conservative, neoliberal or neoclassical justifications for austerity, and we deplore the assault on public goods and social solidarities that have occurred because of them. Many sources attest to the way austerity intensifies a spectrum of inequalities (Hastings et al, 2017). Nor are we convinced of the economic dividends meant to flow from austerity. These either did not materialize at all after the GEC, led to renewed and unsustainable speculative

1

bubbles, and/or further amplified disparities. With respect to our views on austerity, we are also guided by the perspectives of respondents in the eight cities, as well as the recent discursive turn away from austerity on the global stage, accelerated by the imperatives of COVID-19 (e.g. United Nations, 2020). Accordingly, the insights we draw about collaboration throughout the volume are directed towards locating agency found or created in urban arenas, for resisting or transcending austerity.

Why is it useful to explore austerity through the lens of collaborative governance? The study was initially motivated by the question of how robust state-led participatory governance mechanisms created in previous decades would prove to be, when exposed to austerity. Read from the standpoint of the 'global north', recent history falls into roughly four periods (although these categories are too neat to be applied without geographical nuance). In schematic terms, the Fordist or Keynesian Welfare National States of the post-war period (Jessop, 1999) were followed by the rise of the new right, represented by figures like Pinochet, Reagan and Thatcher and dominated by 'rollback' neoliberalism; the creation of markets by withdrawing state support from 'uncompetitive' parts of the economy, alongside internationalization of production, increasing unemployment, lowering labour costs and confronting adversaries with force. This phase was marked by widespread conflict, the destruction of old industries and institutional settlements, and defeat for organized worker struggles. After the tumult of the new right, the third period was marked by reduced turbulence, and became associated with the term 'rollout' and 'roll with it' neoliberalism, or the 'third way' (Keil, 2009). With centre-left national governments taking the reins in Germany, the US and UK and similar policy regimes rolled out by the European Union (EU), the United Nations (UN) and the Organisation for Economic Co-operation and Development (OECD), resources were invested in constructing institutions of a different character than in the Fordist-Keynesian period, more closely aligned with cultivating an ethos of personal responsibility and competitive individualism. It is here that our interest in collaboration begins, with the significance it acquired for governmental and non-governmental actors during what might be termed the neoliberal boom years preceding the GEC. As Davies (2021: 4) put it,

> International organisations and governments sought to construct state-market-civil society partnerships, focusing particularly on the mobilisation of business and civil society actors. They privileged collaboration variously as a necessity in dealing with 'wicked problems', as a rapidly proliferating phenomenon, and as enacting a new and virtuous form of sociability in de-traditionalising, post-scarcity and knowledge-rich societies.

Then came the GEC, and the dark clouds of austerity. We were motivated, in part, to consider what happened to this collaborative mood or ethos in the aftermath of the crisis and as austerity was introduced, or further intensified in the fourth period. Davies (2021) suggests that harsher cases of austerity led to a dramatic rollback in the participatory institutions that had been constructed in the 1990s and 2000s, with accompanying tendencies towards centralization, authoritarianism and democratic disempowerment. These tendencies were noted particularly in Athens, Baltimore, Barcelona, Dublin, Leicester and Montréal. However, the research disclosed a multitude of other ways to think about collaboration, not only as a means of governing and delivering austerity, but also as a way of mitigating and resisting it, while advancing other agendas. The chapters in this book explore collaboration from this perspective, asking 'who does politics with whom', to what ends and how effectively?[2]

The book is based on research in the eight cities between 2015 and 2018. In each, inquiry was led by a local investigator with support from research assistants, with more than 20 people involved in collecting and analyzing data across the project as a whole.[3] We explored how cities navigated the 'age of austerity', looking at how it was governed, deflected, resisted and showed glimpses of alternative ways of living and governing. Over the timeframe of the study, some 320 interviews were undertaken across the eight cities together with observations, focus groups and stakeholder workshops. The research was initially written up in a series of 26 unpublished project working papers. These papers, cited in the text where appropriate and referenced in a separate bibliography, form the basis for our published work. Issue 42(1) of the *Journal of Urban Affairs* (2020) was one major output from the project, with essays on each of the eight cities, and a thematic overview by Nik Theodore (2020).[4] These papers are also cited and referenced in the bibliography. *Between Realism and Revolt: Governing Cities in the Crisis of Neoliberal Globalism* (Davies, 2021) is a companion volume recording the Principal Investigator's thoughts on the project, while a stakeholder-facing report published in 2017 can be downloaded from the Centre for Urban Research on Austerity.[5] The chapters in this volume articulate our collective perspective on collaboration, in the context of strikingly diverse and uneven austerity challenges.

What is 'austerity'?

Austerity is a simple idea, here referring to the purposeful withdrawal, curtailment and reorganization of public goods by 'the state', by which we mean a multi-scalar set of institutions that spans the local/municipal to regional and national territories and beyond. States are different in centralized and federal systems and complicated by historical specificities and path dependencies (such as Catalunya or Québec) (see Chapter 4 for more detail). Proponents of austerity believe it is necessary to correct the perceived economic malady of state over-spending, and virtuous if frugality is associated with the good life or fiscal and moral rectitude. As we explain later, the idea of austerity can serve many different political ends. However, after the GEC, it became indelibly associated with a raft of measures to change the relationship between state, market and civil society by exposing states and citizens to and re-educating them (more-or-less successfully) for, the rigours of competition and self-reliance. Core austerity justifications were that government should spend less on public goods and redistribution ('free stuff' in the vernacular of conservatives) and more on supporting and extending the market economy, with the effect of redistributing wealth upwards. The mission of government in this worldview is not merely to cut the cash and wean people from public services, but also to refit its institutions and train its citizens for life competing in a society where market relations extend into previously sheltered areas (Theodore, 2020).

This kind of austerity is commonly branded, usually by critics, as 'austerity urbanism', 'austere neoliberalism' or 'neoliberal austerity' (Peck, 2012). In part, this is because it captures and radicalizes the spirit of the often-violent revival in free market capitalism after the development of modern welfare states began to falter in the 1970s, in parallel with the end of the post-war Keynesian boom. But the 'neo' in neoliberalism also highlights the central and active role of states in fitting themselves, citizens and civil society organizations for competitiveness and self-reliance. The reality of neoliberalism is that it contrasts sharply with the classical liberal idea that the state should confine itself to strict limits and respect the private domain. For all that free marketeers want a smaller state, their predicament is that they need governmental mechanisms: to drive through reforms, roll out seemingly endless surveillance and direct repression, when necessary, regulate market exchange, cultivate ideas and instincts capable of holding society together under market rule and facilitate extraction and upward redistribution to elites. Some critics have gone further, arguing that austere neoliberalism isn't really about the market at all, and certainly not for those who benefit economically from it. Market rhetoric rather conceals a deeply authoritarian concern with instilling household discipline and control, maintaining systemic inequalities and facilitating the upward transfer of wealth (Bruff and Starnes, 2019). Therefore, on the pro-austerity right, free market rhetoric is often accompanied by apparently contradictory conservative commitments to 'family, faith and flag' and an ever-growing edifice of rules and regulations. Anyone working in a public body (or British university) will be wearily familiar with this ever-extending 'utopia of rules' (Graeber, 2015). As the political scientist Andrew Gamble observed (1994), despite liberal protestations to the contrary, the 'free economy' simply cannot thrive without a 'strong state'. In fact, it is often argued that the state at various scales has been a central agent of globalization and neoliberalization (Rosenberg, 2000). In contrast with the public welfare goods associated with strong Keynesian or social democratic states, the particular strength of the neoliberal state is its moralizing, marketizing and disciplinary capacities. As we suggest in several chapters, inter-dependence between markets, marketizing states and civil societies has been very prominent throughout the age of austerity.

Yet, important as the politics of austere neoliberalism have been, this is not the only story of the post-GEC period. Much of the scholarship about neoliberalism, particularly in cities, accentuates difference, complexity and hybridity to search out grounds for hope that another world, or at least a different politics, might be possible (Davies and Blanco, 2017). The urbanist's fascination with cities arises from their centrality in human development over thousands of years (Childe, 1950), but also their dynamism in generating, shaping and sometimes repelling forces operating at larger scales and, in the modern era, burdens imposed by higher tiers of government. Big ideas like austere neoliberalism are usually driven by national and supra-national elites and institutions, but urbanists draw attention to the many ways in which they accentuate, warp, diminish and transform as they encounter cities, sometimes from the bottom-up. Each city has its own economic configurations, political cultures, traditions, institutions, geographies and struggles. This means that while there are many commonalities in the 'planetary' urban experience (Brenner and Schmid, 2015), there are also important differences and counter-currents, which we attempt to capture.

Austerity itself is also replete with commonalities and differences. There are very few, if any political traditions that do not have some place for economizing, thrift and sacrifice. When soon-to-be British prime minister David Cameron announced what turned out to be a prolonged and internationally widespread 'age of austerity' in 2009, he was borrowing the idea from post-war Britain where severe privation preceded the boom-years of the 1950s and 60s. But, in this 'age of austerity', welfare states were being constructed, exemplified by the 1945–1951 UK Labour government's commitment to equalization through collective consumption goods, including the national health service, public housing and universal education, higher taxes on income and wealth, and the creation of workplace bargaining mechanisms involving state, employers and unions. The work of Esping Andersen (1990) charts the development of different welfare state models in post-war capitalism.

The most recent age of austerity reversed much of what was started in the last. The motivation in the post-war period was not marketization and individualization, but rather the collective endeavour and sacrifice to re-build nations and construct institutions to give a voice to worker representatives and allocate public goods. This understanding was articulated by one of our interviewees in Ireland (Gaynor, 2016):

5

As I understand it the word austerity would go back to the period around the Second World War and austerity under the British wartime government and subsequently because of rationing etc went on way into the 1950s. And that meant equal rationing for everybody. And that meant tax at 19 and 6 in the pound. That meant an attempt to share the burden of war time and post-war time fairly equally. What has happened since then, certainly in Ireland, and I suspect in other countries, is not that.

Keynesian economics were popularized during the post-war period throughout much of the North Atlantic region and parts of the southern hemisphere, including Australia and New Zealand. The Keynesian approach to austerity differs considerably from austere neoliberalism. Neoliberal economists argue for austerity in response to recessions, to cut business costs and stimulate investment. Keynesians think restraint should be employed when the economy is booming. Governments save during boom times for recessionary periods, when savings can be deployed to stimulate growth (Konzelmann, 2014). Other philosophies espouse moral and political imperatives to frugality and periods of self-imposed deprivation linked, for example, to religious traditions of fasting and self-sacrifice. Even some expressions of communism share an ethos of austerity, linked to revolutionary asceticism. Austerity philosophies, rooted respectively in notions of economic necessity and moral virtue, are by no means mutually exclusive and often reinforce one another.

The geographer Jamie Peck popularized the term 'austerity urbanism', as a way of thinking about the diverse urban political economies that emerge from the encounter between cities, austerity and its counter-currents (Peck, 2012). Chapter 1 begins by looking at one aspect of this encounter, exploring what the term 'austerity' evokes for our eight cities, and how it influenced approaches to governing in the post-2008 period. This exercise is instructive, because it draws attention to what muddies or subverts austerity in its conventional neoliberal guise, as well as the experiences of cities exposed to the full force of 'austerity urbanism'.

Austerity in the city

Although city leaders can certainly be enthusiasts for austerity, depending on their politics, it is more commonly driven by international, national or regional actors. It is by no means a uniquely urban problem, and rural or peripheral urbanizing areas lacking services and infrastructure are particularly vulnerable. So, why focus on the urban experience? In this volume, we are concerned with the politics of austerity governance, rather than with its immediate economic and human impacts, which demand as much attention to non-urban as to urban areas. The primary rationale, explained earlier, is that cities have been dynamos of human development for thousands of years, driving forward both economic and cultural development through antiquity, renaissance and modern times, and political development as new ideas incubate, movements arise, and great national and international transitions are inaugurated. Moreover, while the digital age might have shifted the dynamics, cities are still 'zones of intensity' where interactive or collaborative politics proliferate. They are laboratories for top-down and bottom-up experimentation around governing mechanisms, and – unlike rurality or the scale of the nation state – are places where state, market and civil society actors come into close and routine proximity, whether as allies, instrumental partners, or adversaries (John, 2009). Moreover, at a very practical level, austerity creates major stresses and strains for political actors in the urban arena. Cucca and Ranci explained in relation to European local government (2017: 267) that 'the capacity of urban governments to carry out effective policy has been substantially reduced by a three-fold dynamic: state delegation of responsibility for local economic development as well as social integration, strong cuts in central funding and tighter constraints on local budgets'. An irony, then, is that the great planetary wave of urbanization in recent decades occurred in parallel with the widespread weakening of local state and place-based institutions. Thus, municipalities feel compelled to collaborate with other state and non-state actors, whether this is to mobilize policy and resource coalitions, for example at city-regional scales and beyond, or find ways of resisting and working around this relentless dynamic.

Governance, collaboration and resistance

How, then, do we frame the nebulous question of collaboration addressed through the remainder of the volume? In recent political science and public policy, the term has been associated with the way states attempt to form alliances and coalitions with other states and non-state actors, often operating across scales. It is conventionally framed via the question of how social forces located respectively in the profit economy, civil society and the state pull together around common, or at least overlapping agendas and activities, to deliver goods valued by the contributing parties. Collaboration in this sense can be traced back at least as far as the formal or *de jure* detachment, from the state, of economic and public spheres that occurred with the rise of capitalist modernity. The volume looks at state-corporate-civil society collaboration as it reinforces (or undermines) alignment between different social spheres, but also in the wider sense of what political forces collaborate, and how, to resist austerity and transform cities.

As explained earlier, collaboration as an idea or norm became especially popular in the reconstructive period associated with the terms 'rollout', 'roll with it' and 'social neoliberalism', particularly at the local and urban scales. For this reason, collaboration in the governance of cities became prevalent in discourse and practice and prominent in academic literatures from the 1990s, and not only in the global north. The concept is fluid in origin and use, reflecting both aspects of neoliberal thinking (Davies, 2011) and mounting demands for transparent and participatory forms of policy and decision-making (Davidoff, 1965). In its most ambitious expressions, collaborative governance is understood as the 'formal, consensus-oriented, and deliberative' processes created to enhance relations within the triad of state-market-civil society forces (Ansell and Gash, 2007: 544). In the thinking of Sørensen and Torfing (2018), governance in this sense is now a fully mature paradigm, capable of both analyzing social complexity and improving economies and societies.

The substantial attention given to collaborative governance in both academic and governmental spheres highlights many nuances in understandings of the concept. For example, it reveals the ubiquity of closely related concepts such as joined-up or network governance and variations in theorization, including the differing role that state actors can play (Korfmacher et al, 2010), the extent to which citizens are involved and the possibility of collaboration being initiated and led by actors outside the state (Agranoff and McGuire, 2003). There are many different focus points of collaborative institutions, for example on specific issues like environmental management or disease control, and collaboration can occur at different stages of policy or project development. Others have brought attention to different qualities of collaboration, such as the dynamics of inclusion (for example, Ansell, Doberstein, Henderson, Siddiki and 't Hart, 2020). It is sufficient here to point out that the purported shift from 'government to governance' (Rhodes, 1997) was largely construed as a positive development in the political mainstream, though it is far from a fixed idea or precise practical method.

While collaboration is often treated as a desirable approach to solving urban problems through 'consensus-building' or for delivering services in cities, attention has also been drawn to weaknesses and counter-intuitively coercive applications, for example through 'dark' networks, elite or clientelistic networks and network closure (Davies, 2011). Some of the problematic aspects of collaboration include the lack of recognition given to the value of conflict, arguably just as important to creative processes as deliberation (Dickinson and Sullivan, 2014). The potential for state-led collaboration in 'invited spaces' to suppress dissident voices and selectively co-opt interests in pursuit of pre-established policy goals can also be overlooked. Critics suggest that collaboration attracts participation by citizens and community organizations to channel efforts into pre-established priorities, to depoliticize (Gough, 2002) or corral alternative perspectives into forums and processes managed by the state. Collaboration is therefore a construct common in policy and scholarly usage, but one that is multiply defined and contested in much the same way as austerity. The following chapters engage these debates and go beyond them in employing the term 'collaboration' creatively and openly to explore alliances in and against austerity urbanism.

Eight cities as case studies

Though we expected experiences to be diverse in the eight cities, they turned out to be far more so than initially anticipated, partly on account of changes occurring between submission of our grant application to the Economic and Social Research Council (ESRC) in late 2013, and the commencement of research two years later. Each city tells a distinctive story, though there are also many commonalities. Written in light of the COVID-19 pandemic, the Afterword, at the end of the book reflects on what transpired in each city since the study concluded.

Athens

Athens is the capital of Greece and the epicentre of European austerity. The city grew in an unregulated fashion, via self-built constructions on the urban fringe, while informal social support networks and irregular employment opportunities in small businesses shaped the backbone of its socio-economic traits. Informality, in fact, is one of the city's known and fairly appealing qualities, noted primarily in respect of the vibrancy of its social fabric. But informality also suggests that the city lives relatively on the edge, lacking structured welfare support responses and adequate social safety nets. More so, since local authorities were, up until recently, excluded from social welfare, operating in a strongly centralized administrative system with limited competences and meagre funds (Hlepas, 2020). In such a context, the economic downturn brought about by the 2008 global economic crisis, and the seven-year long recession that followed the implementation of austerity policies from 2010, was bound to have severe socio-economic consequences.

As elsewhere, the impact of austerity was predominantly noted in urban areas. In Athens, deteriorating socio-economic indicators exceeded averages, calling for urgent intervention measures. In parallel, an austerity-driven local authority reform (2010), transferred fiscal, developmental and social welfare duties to cities, amidst budget paring, impelling municipalities to address local challenges in collaboration with civil society. The neoliberal 'rescaling' goal, promoting local policy spaces that fend increasingly for themselves, was put forcefully into practice via austerity (Chorianopoulos and Tselepi, 2019). In an attempt to secure funding and respond to acute social need, the city of Athens endorsed the governance shift, opening up its policy-making structures to the influence of corporate and third sector organizations. Austerity was not contested by the local state, as stringent fiscal administration became an explicit partnership prerequisite. The city's collaborative quest also stretched to the informal associational realm but was not taken up by the grassroots. The numerous informal solidarity networks that sprung up in Athenian neighbourhoods after 2008 echo the city's past. Unlike the post-war era, however, current informal collaborative vehicles are overtly contentious, defined in respect of their firm avoidance of austerity-related agents, policies and institutions (Chorianopoulos and Tselepi, 2020).

Baltimore

Baltimore sits at the southern end of the mega-region stretching several hundred miles from Boston to Washington DC in the USA. In the realm of urban policy, Baltimore is known for its Inner Harbor redevelopment of the late 1970s, which became a blueprint for waterfront regeneration around the world, from Sydney's Darling Harbour to Cardiff Bay). But the Baltimore as immortalized in the HBO series 'The Wire' is better known for its concentrated poverty and racial injustice, which focus attention on the stark power imbalances of state-society relationships and their spatial manifestations. Indeed, Baltimore is a textbook example of a deindustrialized city, which was an early adopter of what David Harvey (1989) termed strategies of the entrepreneurial city, or the pursuit of wealth creation rather than equality. Baltimore therefore punches above its weight as an example of the changes wrought under neoliberal urbanism, with de facto federal withdrawal in the US from the 1970s onwards presaging state restructuring and changed priorities elsewhere. The divided city of Baltimore is extreme by the standards of our other cities. It can be perceived as a salutary warning of the extremes of austerity and its related coercive and carceral tools, which were prevalent in the city long before the global economic crisis of 2008.

But Baltimore is a rich research arena for other reasons. The city gained worldwide attention in 2015 when there was an uprising following the death of a young black man, Freddie Gray, due to injuries sustained in police custody. The research we document here was phased over the following two years, drawing specific attention to what has changed, and what hasn't, as a result of what became known as 'The Uprising' (Pill, 2020). Studying Baltimore affirms the salience of the city as a political realm, given the importance of everyday struggles about public services, especially policing, housing and education, together with conflicts about urban renewal and redevelopment, such as the distribution of tax subsidies, which reassert the dominance of the waterfront and of major non-state actors in the city (notably its powerful 'ed and med' institutions). These struggles focus attention on the governance of the city, and the scope for more equitable alternatives which can disrupt the normative power of neoliberal ideologies and redress the iniquitous divisions with which Baltimore is synonymous.

Barcelona

Barcelona is the capital of Catalunya and, in terms of size and stature, Spain's second city. Like the rest of Spain, the city was hit hard by the effects of the economic and social crisis that began in 2008. The growth of unemployment and economic and residential precariousness among large segments of the population led to a period of profound political and social change. After three decades of electoral hegemony by the Socialist Party of Catalunya (PSC), the 2011 elections gave victory for the first time to the conservative Spanish nationalists of Convergència i Unió (CiU). The imposition of harsh austerity measures on local governments thus coincided with the formation of a conservative minority government that accelerated the privatization of public services, strengthened collaboration with large economic agents, and reduced the political influence of the institutional mechanisms of citizen participation. Interestingly, however, CiU attempts to undermine the city's elaborate participatory mechanisms in the city came to nothing.

Meanwhile, urban social movements gained momentum as a result of the confluence of different social struggles culminating in the emergence of the national 15M movement in 2011. During this period, there was an explosion of cooperative social initiatives aimed at exploring and promoting new ways of living in common (Walliser, 2013). The new political formation, Podemos, aimed at articulating and representing the spirit of the new social mobilizations in the institutional sphere at the national level. At the same time, local political actors began to forge new coalitions between left political organizations – including Podemos – and urban social movements. The resulting political platforms achieved historic electoral results in the 2015 municipal elections, enabling them to govern in five of the six largest cities in the country, including Barcelona. The electoral victory of the political platform Barcelona en Comú (BeC), led by social activist Ada Colau, became the icon of a new municipalist political movement that claimed the municipal arena as a space for building progressive alternatives to neoliberal austerity. The case of Barcelona therefore exemplifies the intensification of the tensions and contradictions between alternative urban political projects during the years of the GEC. On the one hand, it provided an excuse for the acceleration of public sector cuts, the privatization of services and the strengthening of urban technocracy against the collaborative traditions of the city. On the other hand, the same economic and social context stimulated the construction of radical alternatives and opened a window of opportunity for the electoral 'assault' on the institutions, making cities a critical arena for the development of progressive alternatives to neo-liberal austerity and novel forms of collaboration.

Greater Dandenong

Greater Dandenong is a relatively small city within the south eastern area of the Melbourne metropolis, with minority ethnic communities constituting a large majority of the population. Melbourne itself is the major city-region in the Australian State of Victoria, comprising over 75 per cent of the state's population. The context informing this study was very different from that of counterparts in the northern hemisphere. Though this is an area subject to economic restructuring and de-industrialization, Dandenong provided a much more positive context for revitalization. As Henderson, Sullivan and Gleeson (2020: 129) put it, 'Australian cities have not experienced the material crises visited upon other cities in recent decades, with urban rioting, extreme social dislocation, deprivation, or fiscal default'. Consequently, although we thought that austerity was looming, on account of the soon-to-be replaced government of Tony Abbott, our research in fact records the collaborative politics of market-led revitalization in a deprived, multi-cultural city centre and showcases significant differences between austere and non-austere forms of urban governance.

Dublin

Dublin is Ireland's capital and, like Athens, dominates the political economy of its host country, accounting for forty-seven per cent of its gross domestic product (GDP). Between the 1990s and the beginning of the GEC, it was a major driver of Ireland's so-called 'Celtic Tiger' economy, attracting high levels of global capital investment, notably from US multinationals, with much of this investment concentrated in and around the city. A wide range of international corporations including Amazon, Facebook, eBay, Google, LinkedIn, Microsoft, PayPal and Twitter have their European headquarters in Dublin's hi-tech 'Silicon Docks', where they enjoy a series of generous tax breaks including one of the lowest rates of corporation tax in the EU.

Like Baltimore, this strategy of urban entrepreneurialism resulted in growing inequality and social tensions as its inevitable segregating effects led to rapid escalations in land and property prices and widespread displacement of local use values (social housing, community facilities, small businesses etc.). The associated banking crisis and property market collapse in the GEC left the city with a major housing crisis. Meanwhile, the extensive period of austerity – which governmental elites attempted to represent as payback, not for corporate or speculative excess, but for the excessive spending of citizens – severely depleted social services. Dublin attests to the contradictory impacts of austerity and its implications for both collaborative governance and urban resistance.

Leicester

Leicester is a medium-sized city in the UK context (some 342,000 people), located in the East Midlands region of England. On some measures, it is the poorest in the UK. Like Greater Dandenong, it has a very ethnically diverse population and is known as 'Britain's multicultural city'. The Labour Party dominates city politics, with the City Mayor, the overwhelming majority of city councillors and three members of the UK Parliament. Historically, Leicester is considered to have been a prosperous city, but with industrial decline in the 1970s and 80s it entered a labour market crisis from which it has never fully recovered. Poverty and deprivation in the city were intensive and extensive even before the GEC, and Leicester's predicament only deteriorated as austerity was implemented, first by a Conservative-Liberal coalition and latterly by the Conservatives governing alone from 2015. As of 2020, the municipal budget had declined by 39 per cent, leading the City Council to slash 63 per cent from its discretionary spending in order to concentrate investment in threadbare statutory social services (Davies et al, 2020).

In a country where collaboration developed significant normative appeal for governments in the 1990s and 2000s, Leicester shows the impact of austerity on urban governance and the spaces and potentialities for state-civil society partnerships. In the New Labour years between 1997 and 2010, and often at the behest of national government, local collaborative institutions proliferated at city and neighbourhood levels. These mechanisms were often held in poor regard by local politicians, community activists and researchers alike as 'talking shops' (Davies and Thompson, 2016). Others, however, regretted their disappearance in the Conservative age of austerity, particularly at the neighbourhood scale. Inadequate as they were, 'talking shops' were seen as having provided a space of interaction and communication between community facing public officials and citizens.

Montréal

Montréal is a large metropolitan area in the predominantly French-speaking nation of Québec, currently a province of Canada. The 2008 economic crisis did not hit Montréal directly but had a secondary economic impact due to a drop in international tourism and a decline of foreign investments. However, although the impact of the 2008 financial crunch was rather muted, Montréal has undergone a series of consecutive and on-going crises since the crises of 'Fordism' in the 1970s. In Montréal, austerity was not understood as a necessary policy in an exceptional time, as it was in Europe, other parts of North America, and in regions and cities across the rest of Canada. It was rather understood as an ideological choice, a conservative approach to state restructuring in the context of a historic and enduring crisis of the welfare state. This style of politics was pursued at the federal level by the Conservative Harper Government until the election of the Liberal Justin Trudeau in November 2015. Local government in Canada, however, is subject to regulation by the regions. It enjoys very limited autonomy and municipal power is weak. For that reason, it is necessary to understand urban issues and urban governance from the standpoint of the local state in its more expansive sense, which always involves more than just local or municipal actors (Magnusson, 2015). In other words, it is a combination of interventions from three different tiers of the state – federal, provincial and municipal – that have to be taken into account for understanding past and future orientations of urban development and collaborative governance. The programme of cuts and restructuring pursued by the Québec government led by Philippe Couillard (2014–2018), perceived by many as centralizing and authoritarian, led to a significant reduction in support for the community sector. At the same time, Montréal has a vibrant civil society, capable of initiating collaboration with the state and other civil society actors, resulting in significant – if fragmented – expressions of resistance.

Nantes

Nantes is situated near the eastern coast of France and the Loire Valley and is of similar size to Leicester. The city represents a paradigm case of decentralized collaborative governance – the so-called 'Nantes Model' – which is explicitly understood by its proponents and practitioners as a form of pragmatic-collaborative governance (Griggs, Howarth and Feandeiro, 2020). The rhetoric of pragmatic-collaborative governance, which brings together commitments to citizen dialogue, neighbourhood renewal, sustainability and attractiveness has continued to frame the politics and policies of Nantes municipality, and the metropolitan combined authority, Nantes Métropole. In other words, community collaboration remains the foundation of the city's internal and external branding. Indeed, following on from its Green Capital 2013 award, Nantes was named in 2019 the European Capital of Innovation, with the jury declaring that Nantes demonstrated how 'a city can harness democratic participation to tackle challenges like energy, ageing, the digital transition and social inclusion'.[6] At the same time, the research charts tensions and potential contradictions in the Nantes Model, also explored in the following chapters.

Book structure

The diversity of the eight cities discussed in the remainder of the book was approached from the very beginning as a valuable challenge, capable of shedding new light on the themes explored. A snapshot of the diversity is provided in Table 1.1, which captures data about population, economic

Table 1.1: Urban populations, economies and municipalities

	City population (2019)	Metropolitan population (2020)[1]	Metropolitan per capita GDP (2015) $[2]	National per capita GDP (2015) $[3]	Political leadership (2015–2018)
Athens	664,000	3.153 m	32,167	22,615	Centre-left platform. Mayor Georgios Kaminis. Lost to Conservatives in 2019.
Baltimore	619,500	2.325 m	69,590	52,099	Democrat. Mayors: Stephanie Rawlings Blake (to 2016), Catherine Pugh (2016–).
Barcelona	1.61 million	5.586 m	45,752	30,595	Barcelona en Comú. Mayor Ada Colau.
Greater Dandenong	169,000[4]	4.968 m[5]	41,062	55,183	Labor (Victorian Government). Non-executive Mayor elected annually.
Dublin	554,000	1.228 m	55,909 (2011)	50,304 (2011)	Centre-left coalition. Non-executive Lord Mayor.
Leicester	348,000	0.552 m	33,355	41,756	Labour. Mayor Sir Peter Soulsby.
Montréal	1.78 m	4.22 1m	35,498	50,255	Centre-left platform. Équipe Denis Coderre pour Montréal. Projet Montréal (2017–). Mayor Valérie Plante.
Nantes	306,000	0.678 m	38,736	41,765	Socialist Party. Mayor Johanna Rolland.

[1] Data from Macrotrends at: http://www.macrotrends.net. All metropolitan areas, bar Athens (99.3 per cent) saw significant population increases between 2008 and 2020.

[2] Data drawn from the Regions and Cities section of OECD. Stat: https://stats.oecd.org. Stat includes data and metadata for OECD countries and selected non-member economies.

[3] Data drawn from Trading Economics' website at: https://tradingeconomics.com

[4] The figure for Greater Dandenong is downloaded from: https://www.planning.vic.gov.au/__data/assets/pdf_file/0009/11106/Greater_Dandenong_VIF_2016_One_Page_Profile_Output.pdf

[5] This figure is for the urban area of metropolitan Melbourne.

Source: adapted from Davies (2021: 48–9).

Table 1.2: Growth and recession in and after the global financial crisis

	Per cent: National peak-to-trough GDP in/after GEC[1]	Per cent: Metro peak-to-trough GDP in/after GEC[2,3]	Per cent: municipal budget real terms growth/fall 2008–2018[4]	Per cent: metro GDP growth relative to pre-GEC peak[5]
Australia/Melbourne	+4.2 (2008–2009)	-0.96 (2007–2008)	+15.4	+24.2
Canada/Montréal	-4.6 (2008–2009)	-1.23 (2007–2008)	+20.5 (2019)	+15.6
France/Nantes	-4.0 (2008–2009)	-2.4 (2008–2010)	-7.5	+13.0 (2015)
Greece/Athens	-29.5 (2008–2013)	-26.3 (2008–2015)[6]	-28.4	-26.3 (2015)
Ireland/Dublin	-13.6 (2008–2013)	-7.2 (2007–2009)	-20–25 (no data)	+24.1 (2014)
Spain/Barcelona	-10.3 (2008–2013)	-9.0 (2008–2013)	+0.25	-3.4 (2015)
UK/Leicester	-6.4 (2008–2009)	-5.3 (2007–2009)	-39.9 (2020)	+16.4
USA/Baltimore	-5.1 (2008–2009)	+7.3 (2007–2010)	-2.2	+12.24

[1] Data from Trading Economics: http://www.tradingeconomics.com

[2] Data drawn from the Regions and Cities section of OECD. Stat: https://stats.oecd.org. Stat includes data and metadata for OECD countries and selected non-member economies.

[3] Data for Baltimore from US Bureau of Economic Analysis (BEA): https://www.bea.gov/data/gdp/gdp-metropolitan-area

[4] Author's calculation taking account of compound inflation rates. The raw figure should be treated with considerable caution, as it takes no account of changes in tax base or levels of demand that might arise from population change, or administrative restructuring and downloading.

[5] 2016 data from OECD. Stat https://stats.oecd.org, at 2010 prices. Data for Baltimore from US Bureau of Economic Analysis (BEA): https://www.bea.gov/data/gdp/gdp-metropolitan-area – 2009 prices, 2017 figures.

[6] 2015 was the most recent data for Metropolitan Athens, where GDP decline had yet to reach its trough.

Source: Adapted from Davies (2021: 48–9).

performance and political control. Table 1.2 provides proxy figures for four economic outcomes of crisis, recession and austerity in the eight cities: national GDP trends, metropolitan GDP trends, real-terms municipal budget growth and metropolitan GDP growth relative to the pre-GEC peak. Given the multiplicity of variables unaccounted for in these data, they should be treated only as a very rough indication of austerity.

Written as a collective endeavour, the volume presents a series of reflections on the theme of collaboration and its intersections with austerity. The first chapter sets the scene, exploring the histories, diverse experiences and understandings of austerity in the eight cities. Chapter 2 expands on the central theme of the volume, exploring how collaboration was conceptualized and practiced in the eight cities. Chapter 3 further considers the politics of collaboration, in particular the means by which it forecloses and opens up spaces for urban actions and strategies beyond austerity. Chapter 4 explores a pivotal theme in global austerity governance, the question of re-scaling. In many ways, this chapter highlights the limits of collaboration most of all, as the discipline and control regimes of austerity drive retrenchment and restructuring from the top-down. Chapter 5 examines the composition and politics of the local state and its traditions in greater depth, while Chapter 6 considers what local state, local policy and civil society interactions contribute to racial diversity, equality and justice in a dangerous conjuncture. The concluding chapter draws salient lessons and insights together, focusing on the kind of practices that might plausibly result in more authentically equitable and inclusive governance. The Afterword following the concluding chapter reflects on changes in the cities since the research concluded in 2018, including emerging implications of the COVID-19 pandemic. A key message from the Afterword, and from emerging research, is that the pandemic was much worsened by legacies of austerity, particularly as a disease of urban peripheries and deprived neighbourhoods. Even if, for the time being, austerity has fallen into disrepute as a governing ideology, amid calls for new social contracts, and to 'build back better', its pandemic legacies have been dire (Biglieri, De Vidovich and Keil, 2020).

1

Crisis and Austerity in Eight Cities: An Overview

Chapter 1 focuses on how the eight cities encountered, worked with and against austerity in the period after the GEC. It begins by providing a flavour of the histories and traditions which contribute to explaining how austerity was experienced and mediated. It then turns to a discussion of Athens, Baltimore, Dublin, Leicester and Montréal, where more-or-less harsh forms of forms of austerity were implemented in the decade after GEC. It then looks at the three cities which, in different ways, provide a contrast with the story of austerity. These are Barcelona, Melbourne and Nantes. It is from these cities, primarily, that positive lessons emerge for charting governing directions beyond austerity. Chapters 2 and 3 build further on these reflections.

Urban histories and traditions

The eight cities are rooted in very different political systems and traditions. For example, the military coup in Greece (1967–1974) and the Francoist dictatorship in Spain (1939–1975) created highly centralized administrations characterized by repression and the suppression of civil society, which nevertheless survived underground and played crucial roles in the democratic transitions of the 1970s. In contrast, the modern welfare state elsewhere emerged much earlier, for example in Australia or in the United Kingdom after the Second World War, to prevent recurrence of the Great Depression and in response to political demands raised by the working class. While we do not analyse governance trends through the twentieth century, these examples capture something of how the scope for democratic practices, like participation, varied in the aftermath of the war.

By the late 1970s and early 1980s the cases had converged to some extent, fitting the model of contemporary capitalist welfare states in different ways (for example Fordist, neo-Fordist or peripheral Fordist). At different points in the 1980s and 1990s, they all experienced periods of retrenchment and restructuring, pursuing marketization agendas that clashed with previous welfare policies and institutional settlements. Some pursued structural adjustments to financial and governance systems in concert with multilateral organizations like the EU and others were influenced by the close ties between Ronald Reagan (USA) and Margaret Thatcher (UK), who enforced (and encouraged abroad) policies of industrial retrenchment, weakened the powers of unions, restructured state apparatuses at all scales (see Chapter 4) and squeezed municipal resources. The growing emphasis on collaboration after the Reagan-Thatcher shock politics can be understood as part of ongoing global trends in Western models of governance, predominantly the consolidation of market-based approaches, increasing demands for citizen participation and the partial dismantling and reconstitution of welfare states in favour of outsourcing, privatization and partnership delivery models.

Notwithstanding some shared conditions and storylines associated with the crises of welfarism and neoliberalization, national and local conditions powerfully shape governance practices and purposes, everything for instance from macro-economic circumstances to the personal qualities of local leaders, like the inspirational Mayor of Barcelona, Ada Colau. As Brenner and Theodore captured in coining the term 'actually existing neoliberalism' (2002: 349), top-down pressures to marketize cities are 'defined by the legacies of inherited institutional frameworks, policy regimes, regulatory practices, and political struggle'.

Athens and Barcelona have taken very different paths since emerging from dictatorship in the 1970s, exemplifying the potential for local conditions and traditions to shape the meaning and content of governance and collaboration (a theme developed further in Chapter 5). Both cities were sites of major anti-austerity struggles after the GEC and subjected to disempowerment by centralizing forces at national and European scales. The City of Athens ultimately eschewed collaboration with anti-austerity activists (and was in turn eschewed by them), instead soliciting alliances with transnational civil society actors, like Bloomberg and Rockefeller foundations, to cultivate cultures associated with good neoliberal governance: retrenchment, competitiveness, resilience and entrepreneurship (Chorianopoulos and Tselepi, 2020). The city of Barcelona, on the other hand, under the leadership of anti-austerity activist Colau, sought alliances with grassroots activists. Many activists, in turn, maintained a critical and sceptical distance, and saw their own movements and actions as the source of more radical policies and initiatives taken up by the city (Blanco et al, 2020). Moreover, the extent to which welfare policies and institutions have been dismantled or sustained since this time varies greatly across the cases, which in turn set different stages for perceiving and responding to the GEC.

We now explore the localized interpretations and mediations of austerity, what they reveal about the politics and governance of each city, and the potential for differentiation in urban responses. We first discuss five cities in which variants of austerity were present, but in interestingly different ways. We then look at three distinctive cities, Dandenong (Melbourne), Nantes and Barcelona, which position themselves as outside, against or subverting austerity.

Between idealism and realism: varieties of austere neoliberalism

We coined the term 'austerity realism' in the study of Leicester, but it resonates widely as a political logic capturing the way governance actors, some of whom oppose austerity on principle, feel dutybound to cooperate or implement it as efficiently as they can, given the perceived lack of alternatives (Davies and Thompson, 2016). Austerity realism is a governing characteristic we associate primarily, but not exclusively, with left-of-centre cities. It contrasts with 'austerity idealism', where downsizing the local state, balancing budgets and eliminating borrowing is deemed good economic policy by local leaders, regardless of pressure from upper tiers. Austerity realism, discussed here and in Chapter 3, is important both in muting anti-austerity politics and as a vehicle for shaping the forward trajectory of cities in the post–GEC period.

We first discuss Leicester, the city from which the term 'austerity realism' was initially derived. Leicester City Council (LCC) is overwhelmingly comprised of Labour Party councillors and has a Labour supporting City Mayor of considerable renown. As indicated in Table 1.1 earlier, it was subjected to a major squeeze in government funding, amounting to a reduction of 39 per cent overall and 63 per cent of its discretionary spend between 2010 and 2020. Nearly all respondents, across all groups, opposed austerity – not only cuts to local government, but also the draconian squeeze on public welfare entitlements. This was administered directly by a central government department with local offices, but completely beyond the control of the municipality.

Yet, Leicester City Council saw no choice but to deliver austerity. Its variety of austerity realism was concerned with avoiding conflict with government, ensuring that spending reductions were delivered optimally and employing resources to mitigate the impact on those rendered most vulnerable, particularly by welfare cuts. Austerity realism conjures memories of militant municipalities defeated by Margaret Thatcher's government in the 1980s and the folly of embarking on such a venture again. As one respondent put it, 'when diehards tried in the past, it hasn't succeeded really. It's ended up losing what power it had, so that's like picking a fight with no chance of winning it' (Davies et al, 2020: 68). This ethos was very influential: not only within the city council, but also the voluntary and community sectors and among anti-austerity activists.

Among Leicester's political leadership, the financial squeeze and restructuring, mediated by austerity realism, created a very clear growth imperative. The city mayor commented at a council meeting that while his administration continued to invest in public services,

> I make no apologies for investing ... in what is almost literally our shop window which is our city centre. Investment in the city centre is something that has been a major magnet attracting private sector investment into the city centre, a major factor in ensuring that our retailing in the city centre continues to prosper when many other city centres are dying as a result of changing shopping patterns and shopping online and so on. Ours does not face that bleak future.[1]

Sir Peter Soulsby was re-elected for a third term in 2019, with the Labour Party taking 53 out of 54 council seats. Those seeking to oppose austerity, or advance alternative strategies, operated at the political margins with occasional successes in preventing or deflecting specific cuts. As a discourse and practice, then, austerity realism had a significant influence on the prevalent tone and style of governing in and beyond the state itself. It was effective in mobilizing at least tacit consent among key business and civil society actors, and in keeping alternative worldviews at bay. For example, councillors resigning from Labour because of austerity, and sitting as independents, did not hold their seats at subsequent elections.

Athens has, for more than a decade, been exposed to the combined shockwaves of recession and austerity. Amidst the immense social crisis in the city after the GEC, grants to the municipality from government were cut by more than 60 per cent. Municipal staffing fell by nearly 50 per cent from its peak, and the municipal budget was reduced in absolute terms by some 21 per cent, unadjusted for inflation (Chorianopoulos and Tselepi, 2020). The Greek party-political left was deeply implicated in austerity, and as in France and Spain, support for the traditional party, Panhellenic Socialist Movement (PASOK), plummeted after the crisis. In Athens, however, the PASOK worldview survived the demise of the party itself. Former PASOK supporter, Georgios Kaminis (2010–2019), ran successfully for the city mayoralty as an 'independent', drawing support from his former party and other forces on the 'pragmatic' centre-left. Unlike the Mayor of Leicester, and despite hailing from the centre-left, Kaminis's discourse had distinctly ideological overtones. He claimed proudly in 2012 that his administration had eradicated borrowing in its first year and reduced municipal debt. Kaminis supported 'Nai' (Yes) in the July 2015 national referendum on whether to accept a third austerity memorandum with the Troika (European Commission, European Central Bank and International Monetary Fund). He viewed austerity through the lens of his attempt to promote the city on the international stage, envisioning a self-sustaining city-region with administrative and fiscal independence, within the European Union. The imagined remedy was not conflict, sovereignty or 'Grexit' but a strong, integrated, fiscally prudent and thereby competitive city-region.

While Kaminis embraced austerity in almost visionary terms, officials closer to the ground had a more pragmatic outlook, resonating with the idea of austerity realism. For example, developing public–private–civil society partnerships was perceived as the only viable way forward. Said one local politician, 'it's not the memorandum or austerity: it's necessity that drives us ... we made a choice' (Chorianopoulos and Tselepi, 2019: 89). This pragmatic outlook led the City of Athens to enter a range of partnerships with transnational organizations, like Bloomberg Philanthropies and the Rockefeller Foundation. They were embedded within the local governmental machinery, which emphasizes the benefits of prudential financial management as a vehicle for building 'trust' and attracting investors. Collaboration around austerity governance in Athens was therefore two-tone: an instrumental response to the pressures of austerity, but also strategic coalition building with international elites to change the direction of the city. However, as we explain in Chapter 3, austerity realism had minimal traction as a governing ethos in oppositional strands of Athenian civil society, even as they themselves embraced pragmatism in the battle to help Athenians survive the crisis.

It was impossible to obtain quality data on financial trends at the city level in Dublin. This was partly because austerity itself eroded the capacity to collect it and partly because funding mechanisms were complex and difficult even for local politicians and officials to unpick. We were informed anecdotally that there were nationally mandated spending cuts of 20 per cent between 2008 and 2015, partly on account of the bailout agreement with the Troika. Municipal staffing was cut from 6,800 in 2010 to 5,000 at the most recent count (Gaynor, 2020a). In Ireland, the politics of austerity were entwined with the influence of conservative traditions rooted in Catholicism. In transferring responsibility for the crisis from financial institutions and speculators to citizens, as mandated by the bailout agreement, the government sought to instil a politics of collective guilt and shared responsibility. According to the late former PM Brian Lenihan, speaking in 2010: 'Our problems are not just banking problems, we developed a serious problem as a state. We began to spend far more on ourselves than we could afford. ... Let's be clear about this, I accept that there were failures in the political system ... but let's be fair about it, we all partied'.[2]

This narrative of collective excess, together with its realist correlate 'we are where we are' (Gaynor, 2020a: 79) permeated state and media. With the

EU heralding Ireland as a role model, austerity was effectively de-politicized within the state apparatus, and for a time in much of civil society. In the years following the crisis and bailout agreement, austerity governance appeared to have been effective, not so much in mobilizing the public behind an austere vision for the future, but in maintaining the compliance of a feeble, fatigued municipal bureaucracy and an array of exhausted civil society organizations struggling to cope with rising social need, falling grant-income and an increasingly coercive approach to managing the grants system. One respondent commented on the political impotence of local councillors: many 'will tell you that you might as well be sitting at home as voting against the city manager because he gets his way every time. So … they've been in the business of frustrating the popular will for a very, very long time' (Gaynor, 2016).

Ireland was seen as having had an extremely passive and compliant civil society – a powerful cultural stereotype (Hearne, Boyle and Kobayashi, 2020). As one respondent commented, 'the cloak of austerity, as we described, is absolutely tearing our communities asunder. Right? For people, the sense of apathy now is incredible' (Gaynor, 2016). Elements of Dublin's civil society conformed with this worldview, and austerity certainly contributed to it, in debilitating the third sector. Both the trade unions, and professionalized civil society organizations were preoccupied with defensive strategies for survival and sought to sustain social partnership working. To this extent, pragmatism at the grassroots combined with the austerity idealism of the Irish government and the relative political impotence of the city council to create an enabling environment for austerity. However, the wave of anti-austerity mobilizations over water charging transformed the politics of Dublin, with a more quarrelsome strand of civil society making its voice heard and shattering the stereotype of passivity (Chapter 3). The politics of collaboration around austerity were therefore, once again, multi-tonal. The Irish government attempted to conjure the vision of collective guilt to unify the nation, while it then embarked on a series of measures that shattered institutional platforms for collaboration built up over preceding decades. The rollback of the collaborative institutions, including urban partnerships for social inclusion, signified the return to a more centralized and authoritarian mode of national and local politics.

In many ways, Baltimore is an exemplary austerity city, with a more-or-less permanent squeeze on municipal finances over decades, aggravated by debt-servicing obligations. Yet in spite of or perhaps because of the longstanding and normalized politics of austerity, the vocabulary scarcely featured in the city's governance. Despite the severity of the GEC in the USA, respondents in Baltimore did not see it as a decisive moment. One reason, as a respondent put it, was that 'Baltimore is used to austerity and functions like that all the time' (Pill, 2020: 146). They talked about a long-standing 'culture of scarcity' dating back to 'Reagonomics' in the 1980s. The most severe reductions to the budget since the millennium occurred under Mayor Martin O'Malley in the early 2000s. When we talk about the 'age of austerity' in a European context, it denotes a specific, clearly delineated period after the GEC. In Baltimore, the years before 2008 were more significant in terms of fiscal retrenchment, and the experience of 'austerity' is now so familiar as to be unspoken and for this reason largely absent from public discourse, despite healthy economic growth in the city throughout the post-GEC period (Table 1.2).

The 'naturalization' of austerity in Baltimore derives in part from a durable, informal governing system, which gives ideological priority to balancing budgets and enticing business investment into the city centre and its waterfront, while dismissing investment potential in the city's poor, predominantly black neighbourhoods. Priorities for the city are set by an alliance of municipal leaders and local non-profits, notably philanthropies and 'ed and med' institutions – the latter sometimes called 'anchor institutions', a term with more positive connotations in UK community wealth building discourses (Guinan and O'Neill, 2020). Unlike the Transnational Organizations (TNOs) gaining influence in the politics of Athens, Baltimore's were more locally-based. Baltimore's 'ed and med' network is seen very much as a driver of the city's iniquitous development policies. Following the 2015 Uprising in response to the death of Freddie Gray in police custody, it has done more to develop local hiring and procurement policies in support of dispossessed neighbourhoods, but these are not coupled with community ownership and control of the kind envisaged in research on radical municipalism and community wealth building (Russell, 2019; Thompson, 2020).

The dynamics of collaboration in the city therefore produced what Chorianopoulos and Tselepi (2020) called an 'elite pluralist' formation, based around the city council, the State of Maryland, and prominent policy-setting non-profits driving forward a developmental agenda. Though not generally construed as 'austerity', this coalition delivered and sought to normalize a politics of retrenchment, while diverting enormous resources into downtown development, and marginalizing the vast majority of the population, both economically and politically. Austerity was the default sensibility, what the philosopher Foucault would call its 'governmentality': an unspoken, unquestionable ethos of governing.

Although Montréal was not subjected to stark forms of austerity found in cities like Athens, Dublin or Leicester, a wave of what could be called austerity measures was driven by the Liberal government of Québec under the leadership of Phillipe Couillard (2014–2018). However, Couillard's preferred term was not *austérité*, but *rigueur*, which translates into English as rigour, but also connotes terms like 'truth', 'reality' or 'stringency' (Hamel and Keil, 2018). Couillard cut taxes and funding to health, education, welfare programmes and government salaries and ran a surplus budget. But again, his administration preferred the euphemism of a common 'effort' (the same in English and French), rather than the politicized language of cuts.

This exercise in wordcraft sought to de-politicize and make common sense an otherwise controversial and provocative approach. Indeed, it proved highly controversial in Québec. Respondents in our study thought that the policy was borne of idealism rather than necessity, a mission to downsize and transform the state. In this instance, discourses that we might associate with 'austerity realism' were employed in pursuit of an agenda more closely linked to 'austerity idealism'. Couillard himself made this very clear in insisting that the balanced budget, the cornerstone of austere neoliberalism, was 'an absolutely fundamental principle' (MacPherson, 2014). Indeed, we note that balancing recurrent spending is a fundamental principle of international municipal finance – the so-called 'golden rule' (Davies, 2021: 73).

As in Australia, discussed later, and the USA, Canadian local government is characterized as the 'creature' of its provincial government. This means that the regional, provincial or state tier plays a very powerful role in the governance of cities and creates major challenges for those wanting to pursue a different agenda. The position of the city council in Montréal was somewhat ambiguous. Throughout most of our study, it was governed by a centrist coalition led by Mayor Denis Coderre. On one hand, city government ran a significant budget surplus, suggesting adherence to conservative spending principles. But on the other, like Leicester, it sought to manage and mitigate the effects of cuts imposed from the state level. According to one official, the task for colleagues was to 'manage those changes that happened, and then try to bypass them because they have their own social consciousness' (Hamel and Keil, 2018). Municipal officials sometimes tried to deflect, impede or cushion the impact and sometimes re-interpreted it as prudence, or efficiency.

At the same time, there was little in the way of a direct challenge to the dominant ethos within the municipal tier. As one respondent said of *rigueur*, 'if it means a good public budgets management, I'm in. If it means cutting public action as a pretext so that the State has less of a role in society and that it serves an ideology, then I have more problems'. At the city level, then, the governing ethos was closer to 'austerity realism' than 'austerity idealism'. Widespread acceptance of the idea that public spending should be managed rigorously and prudently, even among those opposing austere measures from the state government, meant that to an extent, social actors had lost the perspective of a potential outside to neoliberalism, a viable alternative worth struggling for. At the same time, the proximity of municipal officials with activists, voluntary and community sectors led them to make efforts to mitigate, and even subvert top-down imperatives. And, as subsequent chapters show, these practices were supported by an ethos of collaboration linked to the traditions of the Québec Model, a collaborative approach to governing around a widely shared egalitarian and solidaristic ethos that emerged in the 1960s.

Cities beyond austere neoliberalism

When we first selected the city of Greater Dandenong (Melbourne) as a promising location for our study, it was considering the commitment by then prime minister, Tony Abbott to deliver austerity. However, for a variety of reasons, this did not happen, and Abbott was removed from office. Greater Dandenong was not a city in the grip of austerity. On the contrary, municipal budgets increased, as did municipal staffing between 2008 and 2014. According to one respondent,

> Austerity is a term that is talked about by people in Europe, we think about it more as a heavily constrained fiscal outlook where there is largely a flat line or negative growth in discretionary spending because revenue isn't growing. This combines with increasing service delivery pressures [for example with aging population] to create the constrained fiscal environment. (Henderson, Sullivan and Gleeson, 2020: 128)

Though with different emphases, particularly on the role of the state, governments of both colours in Australia (Labor and Liberal-National) pursued a policy of 'fiscal conservatism'. This is not austerity in the sense of an ideologically driven programme, or 'austerity realism' understood as pragmatic adaptation to austerity imposed from above. It reflects a widespread concern with efficiency and prudence in the context of flat-lining revenues. Fiscal conservatism is rooted in a neoliberal economic ethos, advocating a range of familiar reforms to the public sector, retreat from comprehensive approaches to urban planning, and a privileged role for the private sector in driving growth (see Chapter 2).

Nevertheless, Greater Dandenong showed that concerns dominating the governance of European and US cities do not always reflect the experience in other parts of the world. The very existence of a major government-led revitalization programme (Revitalize Central Dandenong, from 2006) attested to a distinct urban political economy compared with, say, Britain, where 40 years of area-targeted regeneration initiatives came to an end with the 'age of austerity'. The sense of a major socio-economic crisis linked to the concept of austerity prevalent in our northern cities was absent in Dandenong. Crisis talk existed, but was future-oriented, referencing potential threats associated with 'debt crisis' or 'budget crisis' – a tone that reinforces the sense of a city situated in a different political time, where a growth-oriented social investment dynamic prevailed. As Sullivan,

Henderson and Gleeson (2019: 10) summarized, 'What is abundantly clear is that Central Dandenong has maintained or improved a range of economic and social outcomes, which stands in stark contrast to many international cases of crises and decline associated with the Global Financial Crisis (GFC) and, in many cases, austerity policies'. As subsequent chapters show, this climate fostered a more constructive environment for collaboration than in some of our other cities and sought in turn to leverage the idea of a plural, inclusive, multi-cultural city.

Nantes was a different kind of outrider to the austerity norm and also, perhaps, something of an outrider in the French context. For many years it was led by Mayor Jean-Marc Ayrault, who built a powerful governing coalition around the objectives of public participation, sustainable development and enhancing the city's attractiveness to investors – the so-called 'system Ayrault' (Griggs, Howarth and Feandeiro, 2020: 97). It was affected by centrally mandated cuts and tax reforms, as shown in Table 1.2 earlier, but the political tone was strikingly different. Respondents were not comfortable with the language of austerity, but rather articulated a sustainable growth agenda, reinforced by the award of European Green Capital in 2013 (followed by European Capital of Innovation in 2019). They emphasized the city's capacity to employ counter-cyclical financing to mitigate the impact of national government cuts, following Keynesian principles.

Local officials were determined to differentiate Nantes from its French context, not only in terms of the ability to navigate austerity, but also in the sense of crisis engulfing the country; rather presenting it as an island of strength and cohesion in a turbulent ocean. They pointed to various maladies afflicting the nation, including crises of its political system, of public services and of social exclusion, building perhaps towards a crisis of the French Republic. This sense was somewhat validated after our study concluded, by the rise of the Gilets Jaunes. Nevertheless, local officials also recognized that in Nantes itself, the worst effects of crisis and stagnation had fallen on black and minority ethnic neighbourhoods such as Bellvue (Griggs and Howarth, 2015).

Nantes was the only city in our sample where leaders exuded such confidence in the inclusionary potential of urban development, in the face of mounting internal and external stresses. At the same time, there were signs that the power of System Ayrault was beginning to wane. Subsequent chapters explain how the major, ultimately successful, struggle against a new airport at nearby Notre-Dame-des-Landes (NDDL) became a vehicle for challenging both the 'Nantes Model', and the developmental goals of the French state. Perhaps the most significant lesson from our study of Nantes, however, was that with a modest degree of fiscal autonomy, a city can differentiate or even contrast itself politically with the national situation. Distancing itself from the language of austerity was a strategically meaningful manoeuvre.

The City of Barcelona, finally, takes austerity into more overtly politicized territory. As we commenced this study, Barcelona was locked into a three-tier system with pro-austerity or austerity compliant leaders: Xavier Trias, Mayor of Barcelona (2011–2015), Artur Mas, President of Catalunya (2010–2016), and Mariano Rajoy the Spanish PM (2010–2018). Trias and Mas were members of the conservative nationalist Convergència i Unió (CiU), while Rajoy led the national Spanish conservative party, the Partido Popular. During this period, the city pursued a vigorous austerity and surplus budgeting agenda, in which our respondents echoed several themes in both the austerity idealist and austerity realist vocabularies. At the same time, the Trias administration pursued an aggressive city branding policy, building on the 1992 Olympics and the renewal of the port area, attracting an international yachting class of multi-millionaires and billionaires.

Central to the story of austerity governance in Barcelona was the collapse of the Partit dels Socialistes de Catalunya (PSC) which dominated the city for more than 30 years after the end of the Franco regime, and the recomposition of the Spanish left into anti-austerity movements and eventually radical electoral platforms (Blanco et al, 2020). Barcelona, and other parts of Spain, witnessed mass mobilizations against neoliberalism and austerity in the years before and after the GEC.

After the seminal anti-austerity mobilizations of 15-M (15th May 2011) the city was one of several where street movements became part of radical left platforms to contest municipal elections, bringing together elements of the traditional left with new anti-austerity forces. Many of the diverse citizen movements involved in 15-M and minor left wing political parties, together with some cultural institutions and academics, formed Barcelona en Comú in 2014 with the explicit objective of working together to run for municipal elections in 2015, in pursuit of a 'democratic rebellion' and the 'reappropriation' of public institutions. In May 2015, the Barcelona en Comú coalition won the municipal election, forming a minority administration with the PSC and handing Ada Colau the Mayoralty. Under the banner of the 'new municipalism' (Russell, 2019; Blanco, Salazar and Bianchi, 2020; Blanco and Gomà, 2020; Thompson, 2020), Barcelona City Council developed many initiatives in support of economic justice, participatory democracy, women's liberation and the feminization of politics, anti-racism and radicalized, empowered co-production.

However, Barcelona City Council continued to operate under severe financial and legal constraints. It did not attempt to confront them directly or suggest that it had brought austerity to an end. However, it did emphasize the levers of power and influence at its disposal, and particularly the capacity to alter the terms of debate. One of the strategies it employed was to turn the politics of austerity against the right. It did this by highlighting its own integrity and governing competence, in contrast with the corruption of the right and wealthy governing classes. This turned out to be a common theme in the 2015–2019 'new municipalist' cities, emphasizing their competence in reducing debts, as well as rolling out progressive economic development, social and environmental policies and defending refugees from the far right (Russell, 2019). The exemplary case of Barcelona is discussed further in Chapter 3.

Conclusion

In Athens, Baltimore, Dublin, Leicester and Montréal variants on the neoliberal theme of 'austerity realism' were embedded in urban governance, alongside more aggressive forms of 'austerity idealism', and with strikingly different fiscal impacts. Neoliberal austerity assumed a variety of situationally contingent guises, and sometimes met stiff resistance, together with other forms of mitigation. The degree to which Dandenong, Nantes and Barcelona escape the austerity predicament should not be exaggerated, but the three do showcase a diversity of approaches in more-or-less trying circumstances and they reinforce the message that austerity can be challenged and circumvented at the municipal scale and through judicious state-civil society collaborations.

Greater Dandenong had constitutionally weak local government, but given relative financial stability over the past decade, and sound leadership and administrative capability, was able to pursue a positive and collaborative revitalization agenda in the city centre, related but not exclusively aligned with neoliberal development. Nantes was by no means exempt from austerity, or from the neoliberal growth agenda. Yet, through a combination of relative economic resilience, brand-confidence and the application of modestly counter-cyclical fiscal measures, it insulated itself to some extent from national trends, and downplayed the local significance of crises that respondents attributed to the national malaise. Under Barcelona en Comú, Barcelona was enormously inspirational on the international stage, in trying to move away from neoliberal austerity towards a different mode of municipal politics rooted in democracy, equality and solidarity.

The lesson we draw from all the case studies is that austerity was a political choice made by national and sometimes local elites, deriving from the ideological fetish for balanced budgets in neoliberal doctrine. This conclusion is retrospectively validated and contrasted by the ostensible turn against austerity among international actors and national governments in the aftermath of COVID-19, discussed in the concluding chapter and Afterword. It remains to be seen how Spanish 'new municipalism' will evolve after disappointing results in the 2019 local government elections – some successes were achieved for similar platforms in the French municipal elections of 2020. Yet, Barcelona remains a source of inspiration for the municipalist left, and shows that where resistance is strong it can be translated into alternative governing agendas in which 'austerity' can be confronted, subverted or turned to different ends.

2

Collaborative Governance After the Global Economic Crisis

Introduction

As the introductory chapter explained, collaboration was popularized as an idea across much of the globe in the 1990s and 2000s, including the Global South, and was considerably influenced by international actors and donor non-governmental organizations (NGOs) as well as ideas circulating through nation states about modernizing public governance and management. From the basis of multiple definitions and mixed practices of collaborative governance, this chapter explores trends found through the comparative study of our eight cities, in the decade after the GEC. We aim to examine the impact of austerity on localized collaborative structures of policymaking. Specifically, the chapter elaborates three dimensions where interesting comparisons and contrasts were identified: in discourse, in agency and in the spaces utilized to facilitate alliance building and joint working. Trends in discourse, agency, and spaces of collaboration after the GEC are linked to the historical events and traditions highlighted in the introductory chapter.

Collaboration as a state-led discourse

With the exception of Baltimore (Pill, 2020), the state played a leading role in fomenting collaborative governance discourses across the cases, though not necessarily an exclusive role. There were three cases in which the dominant discourse about governance was crafted strongly at the national level: Athens, Dublin and Leicester. All three cities had a heavily centralized mode of governance which defined local relational dynamics more compared with the other cities in this study. While local democracy rescaling and devolution of responsibilities have been part of reform programmes across these centres stemming back to the 1980s (see Chapter 4 for more detail), budget cuts have at the same time meant that local governments were not equipped to absorb new responsibilities, including the leadership of participation. In turn, the weak position of local governments meant that national governments (and their financiers) continued to set policy parameters and collaboration was narrowly conceived at the local level as a necessary mode of policy delivery, though not of policy definition.

Post-GEC, austerity provided an opportunity to reframe governance discourses in a way that consolidated and extended the reach of neoliberal restructuring, including accelerating processes of decentralization, wage freezes, employment terminations and greater emphases on partnering with NGOs with an ability to attract resources and deliver services with efficiency dividends. In this way, collaboration was used as a vehicle to discursively manage austerity in the same yet deeper way it has served functional logics of neoliberal structural adjustments since the 1980s.

Across these three contexts, where collaboration was identified during the study period it was piecemeal; it was discursively and practically concentrated on finding non-government delivery partners for basic services in the context of reform and austerity. Local level policy objectives, for example set by the EU or in following international trends, introduced some regulations to include consultation. While governance language has been modified as a result, our research suggests these schemes were followed as rubber-stamping exercises. For example, in Dublin collaboration initiatives such as the Participatory Public Networks, were characterized by respondents as 'talking shops' that functioned 'top down rather than bottom up ... I mean, where there is lip service paid to engage with the community ..., in reality, there's a scramble between officials and political parties to essentially get their people onto these things' (Politician cited in Gaynor, 2017). Overall, where links were made between the local state and non-state actors it tended to be with select and major corporates or Community Sector Organizations (CSOs) out of fiscal necessity to deliver on the contractual model of service provision.

Second, in Melbourne (Henderson, Sullivan and Gleeson, 2020) and Montréal (Hamel and Keil, 2020) urban policy and governance were led by state/provincial governments (The State of Victoria and The Province of Québec), though national and especially local governments also played important roles. In both cases, governance discourse relating to collaboration developed in the spaces of vertical coordination between the three levels of government. In this regard, and more so compared to the other cases, interjurisdictional joint working was emphasized, however a perennial problem was also recognized in terms of shaping governance language and practices: the diminution of other voices in favour of Québec or Victorian government priorities. Additionally, reforms since the 1990s in both cities led to the multiplication of stakeholders operating in urban governance – from privatizations and internal restructurings to the introduction of increasing engagement requirements – leading to policy fragmentation and coordination challenges (Gleeson, Dodson and Spiller, 2010; Bherer and Hamel, 2012). Institutionalized spaces of collaboration with non-state actors, such as formal advisory boards that provide strategic advice to state departments on policy matters, are also discursively formative. While collaborative modes of governance operate more often and through more mediums in these contexts, urban governance is more complicated due to its multi-actor character than it was prior to the 1990s. In this regard, while the provincial governments set the tone for collaboration, many other actors contribute to the way collaborative governance discourses evolved.

The remaining group of cases can be characterized by a leading role for local government in urban policy: Baltimore (paired with powerful 'ed and med' institutions), Barcelona and Nantes (Blanco, Salazar and Bianchi, 2020; Griggs, Howarth and Feandeiro, 2020; Pill, 2020). In Barcelona, the model of governance has historically placed great importance on collaboration between public, private and community actors, particularly since the mid-1980s to support the Olympic project (1992), which materialized in a range of mechanisms for collaboration, from public–private partnerships (PPPs) in urban regeneration to neighbourhood level citizen participation – the so-called 'Barcelona Model'. Barcelona entered a period of deep crisis following the GEC which rocked political and social relations. Traditional coalitions and the main political parties were weakened, and new political subjects emerged across Spain like Podemos on the left, Ciudadanos attempting to claim the centre ground and later Vox on the far right, leading to myriad anti-austerity platforms and social organizations as well as reactionary mobilizations. The anti-austerity mobilizations and, in particular the 15-M movement (2011–2015), delivered incisive changes to discourse and politics. In fact, the rise of Barcelona en Comú in 2015 rested on strong public-community collaboration and the political agenda since has been marked more by collaboration reflected in discourses of localism, co-production and 'commoning', issues discussed further in Chapter 3.

Collaboration has also been a central part of the construction of the 'Nantes Game' since the 1980s with labels used such as 'co-governance', 'co-construction' and 'participatory governance'. There are firmly embedded practices of participation which provide spaces for citizen commentary and required responses by the government in explaining decisions made. However, at the time of this study, it was clear that decision making ultimately resides with politicians and participatory spaces do not include some important actors (for example from the private sector, vulnerable groups and trade unions) and are not conceived as spaces of contestation or genuine co-creation (Griggs, Howarth and Feandeiro, 2020). In this sense, fundamental discourses and decisions do not appear to change as alternative views often become absorbed and transformed in the active participatory process or marginalized from it. Positive language used to describe a governance approach, like 'co-governance', can obscure views of how deep collaboration is in practice.

Finally, while the role of local government in Baltimore is broad in theory, the reality is that its weak fiscal position next to the strength of the 'ed and med' local industry anchors has led to uneven partnerships where the local state is accused of forfeiting its leadership role. In this regard, and increasingly like Athens and Dublin mentioned previously, collaboration is between the city's governing elites and non-profit organizations, in this case in a context of perma-austerity and continuing racial discrimination against the mass of the population:

> There's always a rub across the city. Like, who's calling the shots? ... It's like who has more influence? Is it the City? Is it a giant institution like Hopkins that has tremendous resources? They have a lot of these impressive initiatives. Is it the philanthropic community? I definitely get that sense they want to be the ones that are leading this work, they want to be the ones that are setting the agenda. ... But we also get it from the business community as well ... there are some giant businesses in the city that want to tell the City what to do. It's across the board. (Public official cited in Pill, 2017)

Here, austerity was already 'normalized' (Peck, 2012) and post-GEC it continued as part of an entrenched neoliberal approach to urbanism. In this regard, collaborative governance processes continued to be predicated on ongoing initiatives, like the role of its 'ed and med' anchors and quest to 'deconcentrate' poverty by attracting the middle class to the city through better services, a better quality of life and less 'fiscal stress'. Over the study period, however, though not directly related to fiscal tightening, the April 2015 Uprising and the Black Lives Matter movement, as well as new organizations like Baltimore United for Change (BUC), were pivotal in expanding spaces of joint working, demonstrating the capacity for resistance movements to influence collaborative governance discourses within civil society through calls for racial equality and social justice. Proposals from city hall in response to The Uprising, like the 'One Baltimore' initiative, were touted as a 'comprehensive and collaborative public-private initiative to support ongoing efforts to rebuild communities and neighbourhoods' (Pill, 2015). While the durability and authenticity of this rhetoric was unproven, it highlights how non-state actors can influence governance discourses on the need for collaboration, from the position of resistance.

Overall, the GEC and ensuing austerity policies in some contexts had less of a structural influence on governance discourses than we expected. The GEC, succeeding recession and fiscal restraint certainly affected economic performance indicators, while unemployment and poverty soared. However, most cuts and modes of working post-GEC mapped neatly onto existing governance discourses, serving to deepen trajectories of neoliberal reform already in place – especially in Athens, Dublin, Leicester and Baltimore.

In Melbourne, Montréal and Nantes the effects of the GEC were not felt as strongly and austerity discourses were not prominent at the city level, as Chapter 1 explained. Nevertheless, the fear of an amorphous 'crisis' was used by some political leaders, for example in Melbourne, and in media outlets as one reason to continue 'balancing budgets' and minimizing public debt as part of the ongoing erosion of the welfare state. At times, state intervention was justified in Keynesian terms, as operating in areas of clear market failure or as a stimulus to private development. For example, in the Melbourne case, interview participants explained how urban revitalization programmes were couched as necessary for responding to market failures and designed to be 'fiscally responsible,' spend 'public money in a commercially responsible manner' or 'to stay within your means'. Barcelona was the only case to demonstrate transformative change in governance discourse over the study period, precisely in response to fiscal tightening post-GEC and precipitated by the agency of social organizations working together through anti-austerity mobilizations.

Together, the cases demonstrate the established and taken for granted idea of collaboration has a significant influence over urban governance. They also demonstrate collaboration discourses can be used to describe genuine joint working as well as to label collaborative processes that are heavily one-sided or tokenistic, suggesting the need for careful and precise use in theory and practice. While collaboration is a primarily state-led discourse, it is also subject to the influence of others who modify conceptions incrementally through dialogue in spaces of joint working. Less often, though importantly, discourses can become radically changed through resistance movements, such as those in Barcelona or Baltimore. The latter city at this stage is yet to see the effect of discursive change in practice relating to race equality, social justice and collaboration, while the former continues to be influenced by expanded principles of collaboration, like co-production and commoning. In this regard, changes pursued in Barcelona are at times discursively framed in terms of reclaiming the radical origins of the 'Barcelona Model' from its incremental neoliberalization in the past 30 years (Blanco, Salazar and Bianchi, 2020: 27).

Agency in collaborative urban governance

While dominant discourses about collaboration in urban governance are state led, our research also demonstrates the potency of organized social movements, civil society organizations (CSOs), private organizations, foundations, networked sector interests and other non-state actors in driving collaboration and delivering urban projects and services. It uncovers some of the new social forces that have emerged, or the way networks have become consolidated in contexts of decelerating economic growth and austerity politics. It also highlights a contrary trend whereby the organizing capacity of some social and other grass-roots organizations have been diminished, including the tenuous links to state authorities built prior to recent crises and the introduction of austerity policies.

Where non-state actors play an instigating and central role in collaboration, they can be found to act 'together with the state, despite the state or against the state' (de Souza, 2006: 327). While Marcelo Lopes de Souza originally characterized only social movements as agents of urban planning through this tripartite framing, it can be used to broadly understand the way different types of non-state actors conceive of their role in collaboration. For our research, it illuminates how organizations may form and operate initially, despite the state, in contexts of tightening fiscal settings and then evolve either together with or against the state. At times non-state actors might operate simultaneously in these ways on different issues.

Despite the state

We found three main scenarios in which non-state actors operate in sync with others on urban projects or services, despite the state, in contexts of hardening austerity. The first relates to an ideological breaking point between the state and its partnering organizations: for many organizations in places like Athens or Dublin, austerity politics represented a loss of space for meaningful dialogue and partnerships: these organizations saw the state as apathetic or antagonistic to their aims and were no longer interested in partnering (to govern austerity) even though their organizing and financial capacities were sustained. In response, some of these civil society actors joined others with a tradition of resisting and disengaging from the state for lack of operative platforms for genuine dialogue and collaboration, most notably in Athens though also for example between activists in social housing in the Nantes case.

Second, many organizations not only lost hope in formal institutions, but also suffered funding cuts by the state because of fiscal tightening. From places hit hardest by austerity, like Dublin, to those in continued patterns of the ideological influence of 'fiscal responsibility' or 'economic rationalism', like Melbourne, funding cuts typically affect smaller and politically active organizations, reshaping the landscape of civil society along the way. In these instances, many smaller CSOs ceased operations. Where possible, others turned to mitigating the worst effects of funding cuts on marginalized people and optimizing minimal resources on direct service provision rather than advocacy. Sometimes the most effective way to so this was by working together with other organizations in similar positions, giving way to new collaborative initiatives despite the state. Some of the negative consequences of this breakdown reported in collaboration between governments and non-state actors include:

- the interruption to the slow relationship-building necessary in effective joint working, like the development of trust;
- the loss of joint problem solving between state and non-state actors; as well as; and
- the loss of experience gaining skills through joint working that have the potential to help solve complex problems.

Third, new organizations and groupings between them have emerged despite the state and directly in response to austere conditions to address unmet basic needs. Building on a tradition of collaboration and cooperativism, the 2008–2009 crisis in Barcelona led to the expansion of solidarity practices promoted by social movements like cooperative housing, self-managed centres, sustainable energy cooperatives, cooperatives of agroecology food consumption, and community gardens. Athens is another extreme case where new CSOs proliferated following the crisis, for example in running social medical centres, alternative currency initiatives, education collectives, cooperative enterprises and 'no middlemen' markets. While diverse in purpose, two common traits among these collaborative initiatives were their informality and suspicion of state institutions associated with austerity. As one respondent in our research described:

> These are groups that operate informally on principle, and only a few turn into NGOs. They don't want to have any dealings with the state or with handling funds. They just want to offer a way out to the crisis. That means a lot as we see a different civil society emerging; different from the one that surfaced in the 1990s because of EU funds. (Community activist, cited in Chorianopoulos and Tselepi, 2020: 48)

We also observed rapidly growing organizing capacities among the collectives during the crisis in Athens where decision-making bodies, like 'workers' assemblies,' were built around principles of self-management, equal pay for members and the redistribution of profit to support other cooperative initiatives with a similar logic. This organizing capacity led to the creation of the 'Athens Network of Collective Initiatives' in 2012 which not only set out to foster co-operation amongst these enterprises and collectives in the city, but also became a platform to establish political presence at the urban level, and therefore through collective action, a new positioning to engage with the state and in political action. While some of the Athenian solidarity networks have asserted themselves in the political landscape, their efforts are limited to small-scale schemes to address specific issues rather than focused on confrontational and transformative politics: 'when the "what can we do" issue comes up, the answer is "small things, small acts", and the reason is a very pragmatic one. We don't have the time and the energy for anything more; we try so hard on a daily basis to simply make ends meet' (cited in Davies, 2017: 9).

Compared with Barcelona or Athens, Baltimore has persisted much longer under 'perma-austerity' and therefore actions taken by large businesses and CSOs have been more embedded locally in terms of acting despite the state. On the one hand, the 'ed and med' sectors make investment, expansion and policy decisions that shape the city's development. On the other hand, there are old and new coalitions formed between CSOs working despite the local state to improve living conditions for marginalized groups, for example through affordable housing. One Baltimore United, a coalition of community and faith organizations and labour unions formed in 2014 focused on developing alternative solutions for affordable housing and job creation. Some of the longer standing social organizations in Baltimore, like Baltimoreans United in Leadership Development (BUILD) established in the late 1970s, work through both protest and advocacy, for example on the Living Wage campaign with local unions or on neighbourhood improvements, though at times also in collaboration with the City, for example to support a bottle tax to keep recreation centres open. These examples show how collaboration among social actors occurring outside the state, as a form of self-help or to help others, can erupt into action against the state when considered necessary. Over time these eruptions can also lead to engagement with public institutions in sporadic ways on specific issues where there is clear mutual interest, such as the case of BUILD (Pill, 2020).

Together with the state

Non-state actors operating despite the state can be found to work together with the state intermittently, as moments of alignment and opportunity emerge. However, the geneses of many collectives that operate together with the state is often precisely because of spaces created for collaboration by the state. For example, the cities of Melbourne, Montréal and Nantes have been governed by strong provincial and/or local governments that have been working in connection with non-state actors in urban policy development and delivery since the 1960s in the case of Montréal, and the late 1980s for the other cities. These well-institutionalized practices, from community consultation in urban policy development to partnerships in service delivery, have produced a diverse ecosystem of non-state actors and collectives with an operating logic that corresponds to state-led cycles and arrangements of collaboration. While there may be episodes of fracture between the state and non-state actors, on occasions where disagreement occurs (for example over proposed mega infrastructure) or crises lead to more oppositional relations (for example over homelessness), state-led modes of collaboration are generally supported and upheld by non-state actors.

On the one hand, the ongoing support for state-led engagement and relative absence of insurgency means that public institutions in these contexts have become comparatively apt at coordinating, mediating, and responding to the demands that arise among non-state actors. These forums institutionalize collaboration in complex ways that have the potential to co-opt alternative citizen viewpoints and actions (mentioned earlier in the Nantes case), as well as provide space for citizens and organizations to both challenge and contribute to state policy.

Furthermore, as our research highlights for example in the Melbourne or Nantes cases, over time collaborative structures can become more sophisticated. This is true both of state-led initiatives, such as the cooperative structure established to run the fresh produce market in Central Dandenong, as well as among non-state actors interested in influencing urban policy, for example business representatives in establishing lobbying networks like the Committee for Dandenong, which advocated for investment in major infrastructure to support local commercial and manufacturing activities during the later period of the Revitalising Central Dandenong initiative between 2011 and 2021. The Committee for Dandenong was established in the same tradition as other committees of businesses in Australia, which bring together representatives across major sectors to work together in a way that optimizes their shared interests and minimizes potential disadvantages through coordinated planning and lobbying. Like multi-sector collaborations, business representatives cooperate to identify common interests, which often require negotiation and compromise to reach agreements. The sophistication of these processes reflects learning through trial and error, as well as an interest in innovating from the foundation of established practices of engagement led by the state and mutual trust built between actors over time.

While the public sector can be recognized as the protagonist in these contexts, fiscal tightening weakened collaboration in some instances. For example, cuts were made to asylum seeker and former refugee settlement services in the Melbourne case, which reduced their participation in collaborative institutions and had the knock-on effect of generating more service demand for public agencies and CSOs. In Montréal, funding for public services as well as CSOs was cut by the provincial government, which increased workloads and reduced capacities. These cuts left less time for focusing on governance structures and processes. Furthermore, in managing the effects of budget cutbacks, CSOs become weakened and less able to resist deepening austerity in a strategic and coordinated way (and more likely to be placated by state-led collaborative institutions). Nevertheless, in these contexts, reduced spending undermined collaborative governance as a practice, though it did not alter formal structures or the primary agents behind them.

There is an important characteristic shared by some of the case experiences which has served to sustain collaboration 'together with the state': a federal system of government with powers relevant to urban planning, services and infrastructure distributed between three (rather than two) levels. In these cases, there tend to be state actors initiating or sustaining collaboration at one level when interest wanes or is redirected to new projects at another level. For example, local government in Montréal and Melbourne sustained collaboration on urban policy while involvement on policy and projects was withdrawn at the provincial level.

Collaboration at the local level was sustained because of multiple factors, including established working relations with organized non-state actors to deliver urban policy goals. Also, these municipalities were used to fluctuating policy agendas set above and prepared to respond opportunely when needed. Not only were they used to change, but they were also accustomed to austerity given the predilections of higher levels of government. This scalar condition means, on the one hand, local government necessarily relies on collaboration despite conflicting ideological beliefs with other levels of government (and others), but on the other hand, is practised in developing and managing relational dynamics to favour local development outcomes.

For example, former mayor Denis Coderre's administration in Montréal between 2013–2017 adopted an opportunistic approach: rather than overtly opposing austerity, the municipality worked quietly with and supported those organizations resisting austerity, including trade unions and the community sector. Similarly, some representatives from the City of Greater Dandenong collaborated with social organizations, education bodies and business representatives to maintain a focus on urban revitalization efforts while interest by the Victorian State Government waned between 2010 and 2014. In this case, the Victorian Government redirected the focus of the State's development authority, cutback resources for the revitalization effort (for example a team of more than 20 reduced to one person) and did not invest in any new local infrastructure projects. Conversely, the local government doubled down and escalated investment in renewal projects, for example in redeveloping the local produce market or building a new library and town square, so that together with local stakeholders, projects could be implemented to preserve the revitalization process instigated by the Victorian Government in 2006.

Such local capacity stands in contrast to other cities in this study, typically in highly centralized two-tier systems like Leicester in the UK, where national-level cuts have weakened the capacity of local governments to the extent that only basic statutory services could soon be left and where municipalities have a more limited conception of their role. In Leicester, the municipality also tried to mitigate the worst effects and compensate for austerity with counteractions, for example by investing in city centre revitalization to attract investors – the 'shop window' perspective described earlier.

Two characteristics sustaining collaborative initiatives 'together with the state' are, favourable leadership in government and past collaborations between sectors. For example, the chief executive officer (CEO) at the city of Greater Dandenong in Melbourne started in his role in 2006, the same year the urban renewal initiative commenced. Relationships built over time between the city and non-state actors benefited from consistent and committed managerial leadership for collaboration at the local level. Many of these relationships preceded the GEC, such as links established with the local interfaith network (1989) or the establishment of the South East Melbourne Manufacturers Alliance (2003). In this case, actors from different sectors were accustomed to working together and acknowledged their mutual dependency, which meant that the joint work involved in the revitalization process built on a firm foundation of collaboration. Here, collaboration is not new, but it is re-framed as new policy agendas emerge. The different experiences of collaboration over time not only contribute to urban policy definition but at the same time strengthen community organizations as they become practised in articulating their goals and informed about local services and policy procedures along with opportunities for funding and organizational development that serve their goals.

In a more pronounced case, discussed in greater depth in Chapter 3, Nantes Mayor Jean-Marc Ayrault came to power in 1989. His and his successor's continued political project has been centred on collaboration. The commitment to participatory governance and a 'culture of proximity' became 'recognized Nantes know-how' (Senior Officer cited in Griggs, Howarth and Feandeiro, 2020: 96).

While state actors were found to lead in generating and sustaining collaboration through increasing opportunities for participation, our research also demonstrates how the state can curtail the agency of non-state actors. In particular, and as referenced previously particularly in the cases of Athens, Baltimore, Dublin and Leicester, collaboration is in practice a supporting measure to a model of governance that increasingly seeks to reduce the role of the public-sector in service delivery and occurs with large CSOs and private business as a form of marketized or contractual governance. In this regard, governance models rest on private sector or large non-profits, sometimes operating locally (Baltimore), sometimes transnationally (Athens), and less on state leadership. The ties between the state and major non-profits significantly shape governance. According to a government official in Baltimore (cited in Pill, 2016):

Some organisations have an extreme amount of influence on where the resources go … some of them are very influential, powerful players here in the community. … There's a lot of interaction between philanthropy in government and non-profit and the universities. I mean, we all sort of run in the same circles. The more high up you are, you know, you run in the same circles and it does become very much of a kind of a cosy club.

The engagement of civil society groups with the state is thus constrained by funding parameters and dominated by larger, professionalized service providers with special interests. Many of these organizations operate with corporatized models of governance, their services are required to generate revenue and their reach is limited regarding the needs of the most disadvantaged. The emergence of regimes dominated by local and extra-local elites is repeated across contexts, demonstrating a shared trend of dependency between government and fewer, larger policy partners. Furthermore, the progressive reduction of the baseline funding for social services delivered by CSOs has led them to search out new sources of funding, from charities and private foundations in many cases. For example, in Athens the city government endorsed an 'enabling' role, facilitating CSOs to pursue funding opportunities through the design of social policy on an ad hoc basis, 'subject to funding availability' (City of Athens cited in Chorianopoulos and Tselepi, 2019: 91). This scenario creates insecurity and can lead to instability in service delivery, but also reduced the autonomy of these organizations in collaboration.

Another hazard of the state designing and sustaining collaborative institutions for participation by non-state actors is the risk of co-optation. Rather than effectively mediate and negotiate, some institutions placate civil society to try and ensure that no real resistance movements emerge to contest the undoing of welfare and fiscal conservatism. For example, in Dublin a range of collaborative partnerships were created through the 1990s through EU structural funds which were considered by some commentators to afford local communities a voice in local policy, while others argued that they co-opted local communities and neutralized resistance and dissent (Gaynor, 2020a). In some extreme cases, institutionalized collaborative processes operated in parallel with coercive state processes, like racial targeting in Baltimore, which created distrust and limited scope for collaboration 'together with the state'. In some instances, this kind of coercion leads to collective action against the state.

Against the state

Socio-economic crises and austerity affect the ways people interact with each other and the state. As described previously, the scope of action by CSOs has in many cases been limited by funding cuts while others have found different avenues of operating through collectivism. In other cases, where socio-economic conditions following the GEC did not change significantly, collaborative modes have continued between state and non-state actors, in some cases showing greater experimentation and sophistication. Our research has found that where austerity bit hardest, active resistance against the state has often grown at times through traditional trade union movements but also new neighbourhood organizations or social movements. This occurred principally in Barcelona, Dublin and Montréal, as well as in Athens, though it has since dwindled there, and Baltimore predominantly through The Uprising of 2015, and indirectly related movements (for example Black Lives Matter). Resistance is carried out through single issue protests, broad-based boycotts, and in some cases through political transformations.

Activism in Baltimore has a long tradition of contesting authoritarian dimensions of neoliberalism which has been invigorated by new movements protesting inequity and police violence. For example, Baltimore United for Change stated that it is using community organizing tactics to 'deconstruct systems of oppression' by building up 'the grassroots to demand justice and police accountability' (cited in Pill, 2015). Their tactics include protest action in public spaces and support for members by informing them of their rights and conducting legal and activism trainings, such as in nonviolent civil disobedience, as well as offering bail support to those detained by the police. While these actions clearly position Baltimore United for Change as an agent operating against the state, they also undertake community development work despite the state, and marginalization from the state, for example by offering jail support and creating safe spaces for young people and families. Their work highlights the vital role of civil society in advancing social justice despite the state and against oppressive state-sanctioned actions.

Fiscal tightening and its associated governance processes have also produced a noticeable rise in resistance by non-state actors across several of the cases, particularly by social movements capable of bringing together disparate though equally disenfranchised groups. Some actors have disengaged from state-led collaborative institutions and their absence reflects their stance against austerity – Chapter 3 discusses these developments in more depth.

Overall, this section highlights diverse impacts of financial restraint on the capacities of state and non-state actors in collective work. While the GEC did not affect all cities equally and some went against trends to eschew austerity politics in the aftermath, all of them reduced discretionary spending on public investment and simultaneously have seen greater involvement of stakeholders on policy issues over the study period. Greater demand for participation by civil society, the need to find ways to manage spending cuts and neoliberal notions of efficiency have led to increasing calls for collaboration, predominantly as state-led initiatives. Local nuances pick up on important factors for facilitating and sustaining state-led collaboration, such as leadership and mutual dependency. These experiences also highlight the importance of the situated agency of those in a position to effect meaningful collaboration, for example the role of key figures in local government (for example mayor in Nantes, CEO in Melbourne case).

However, as the cases hit hardest by austerity showed, collaboration becomes difficult to sustain by underfunded state and smaller non-state actors in contexts of growing demands for services and support, as well as the rise of political scepticism towards the state as such. In some cases, this has led to new ways of organizing and addressing demands through new collectives (Chapter 3). In other cases, the landscape of social organizations has diminished, together with a narrowing public service remit. Often joint working is realized through 'purchaser-provider' models between governments and large, corporatized organizations (CSOs, foundations) to the exclusion of smaller social organizations and other entities. The ideal of collaboration as joint working between interdependent actors with complementary strengths comes somewhat undone when the pool of actors involved loses diversity and collaboration is limited to elites. The growing reliance on large non-profits was common in those cities worse affected by austerity regimes, particularly Athens and Baltimore, but also Dublin and Leicester. Together, the many ways collaboration occurs between state and non-state actors shows that neoliberal policy is not rolled out uniformly and is negotiated by the local state, as well as other local sector leaders.

Finally, non-state actors can blur the lines of distinction between acting 'together with the state, despite the state or against the state' as they craft and execute multifaceted plans of action focused on social change. This is unsurprising in Western contexts where even in the worst experiences of austerity politics, including state repression, most actors seek change by bettering the existing system of governance, compared to some Global South contexts where social movements seek autonomy from oppressive regimes. For example, one experience of informal settlement or shack dwellers' movements, like Abahlali baseMjondolo in Durban, highlights the historical agency of oppressed people not only to address needs like housing despite the state but to powerfully reject the inadequate conceptions of democracy in place and to create autonomous politics and governance practices (Pithouse, 2008). In contrast, the eight cities demonstrate a vital role for strong civil society organizations, though their actions are overwhelmingly directed in ways that address and seek to change state apparatuses.

The spaces of collaboration

The preceding analysis of collaborative governance discourses and the agency of actors involved pointed to the different kinds of spaces utilized to build alliances and effect joint action. This section looks in more detail at these spaces. It considers traditional spaces such as those created by governments in pursuing collaboration, as well as those created by trade unions which have played historic and contemporary roles in organizing collective action. It then examines the growing space occupied by large CSOs, including philanthro-capitalist multinationals operating across cities, in aiding governments to deliver public policy ends and in influencing urban policy definition. Finally, this section explores the new collaborative spaces created by social movements in influencing urban governance. It considers the territorialization of social movements (such as the importance of the neighbourhood) and new capacities of linking up disparate groups to partake in resistance.

In relation to the collaborative spaces created by governments, the research highlighted a wide gamut of structures in place. There are regionalized models, such as the Québec model, whereby Montréal has different mechanisms of tripartite consultation between trade unions, employers and government (Laroche and Barré, 2012). There are also spaces that share many common attributes between the cases, such as formal advisory boards providing strategic advice to state departments on policy matters, spaces of coordination between different tiers of government or different municipalities in metropolitan regions (for example Nantes), and ad hoc modes of consultation to partnerships that posit the public sector as a 'purchaser' of services. The formal spaces of collaboration uncovered in the cases received detailed attention in separate publications, along with many informal practices shown as vital to the workings of collaborative decision-making (issue 42(1) of *Journal of Urban Affairs*). The experience of Barcelona remains the most unique in relation to the extent of governance transformation led by the local state, reflected in discourse and materialized in new spaces. In this model, a qualitative transformation has occurred in urban governance with the development of spaces for the 'co-production' of local policy:

> One thing is the CMBS, which has made an excellent job with specific thematic working groups, with reports on what should be done, on what orientation should policies take. ... A different thing is, for example, the myriad of open centres that work jointly as a network, with civic associations and the representatives of the Social Welfare Department, to decide how they align their strategies ... which are the existing shortcomings and how they work. ... For me, this is the leap. This is not a space of participation, but of co-production. (Elected politician cited in Blanco, 2017)[1]

Trade unions also have institutionalized spaces for use by members, for example offices in which representatives and members host meetings, connect with other interested organizations and conduct work with government. Some even own member facilities such as gyms and community centres. While trade unions suffered debilitating setbacks in several cities, our research suggests that that they continued to play a role in organized movements against austerity. This is because they were concerned with and affected by high unemployment, but also because they have a long history of experience in negotiating with governments, in linking up with traditional solidarity organizations and in striking. In Athens, unions organized many general strikes over the study period, but also contributed knowledge and skills in supporting new social movements to resist austerity. The connections built between solidarity organizations and trade unions and their heritage of advocacy activities provided a strong foundation for new social movements in Dublin, Nantes and Baltimore (together with churches in the latter). One of the notable features of many of the social movements is that their anti-austerity position is linked in a secondary way to primary concerns around other issues like racism (Baltimore and Barcelona) and climate change (Nantes). In other places, like Athens, Leicester and Montréal, governments continued to extend their control over union activities, reducing their space for action and diminishing their capacity to advocate and organize strikes against austerity. While the unions played a prominent part in Athens and Montréal, there were aspects of state-led reform that restricted union activity, together with neo-corporatist approaches signifying what Hamel and Autin (2017: 181) called the 'iron cage' of state bureaucracy.

A major trend found in this study was the growing role of large CSOs in institutional arrangements for service delivery as well as in defining the scope of policy in cities. In Athens, local government endured severe budget cutbacks and in adapting to these conditions, has cultivated entrepreneurial rationalities, and in doing so, a new type of collaboration based on an alliance between the municipality and CSOs, supported financially by transnational organizations, such as the EU, and third-sector philanthro-capitalist multinationals. This reflects the emergence of what Chorianopoulos and Tselepi (2020) called an 'elite pluralist' governing regime, like the longstanding example of Baltimore. In such a regime, the spaces of state-civil society collaboration become restricted to a few policy players, with non-profits playing a larger role, and becoming enlarged as governments concentrate contract funding in bigger NGOs (for example Leicester).

Conversely, Melbourne and Montréal demonstrate the advocacy potential of networked CSOs to influence social justice debates and policy definition. In Montréal, unlike Baltimore, prominent foundations came together to denounce and contest austerity measures proposed by the Québec government. In Melbourne, large not-for-profit organizations have traditionally been organized to make representations to government, for example by the Australian Council of Social Service.

Finally, the comparative study of the eight cities highlights new and expanded capacities of social movements in resisting neoliberal reforms. The new trend relates to the territorialization of social movements. For example, in Dublin, organized community resistance to state policy occurred often in the past (for example, the tenant and housing movements of the 1970s; the 'tax marches' of the 1980s, the anti-drugs movement of the 1980 and 1990s), however a unique feature of the Irish anti-austerity movement was its genesis in early 2014 within communities and neighbourhoods themselves rather than among CSOs, unions, or political representatives (these became involved later as the movement developed). In Barcelona, grassroots movements were very active at the neighbourhood level in resisting gentrification and privatization of local public spaces and services. New local spaces also emerged to resist and mitigate public sector cuts and privatizations, for example of nurseries in Barcelona. Longstanding neighbourhood associations continued to play a vital, somewhat revitalized role in collaborative governance with the city and in linking up with new grassroots neighbourhood movements.

The other significant feature of the social movements that influenced change in policy and politics was their ability to unite atomized groups by aligning interests as well as attracting new actors, often individuals without a history of involvement in resistance. A clear case was the unrest as a response to police violence and racism in Baltimore, from the 2015 Uprising to renewed Black Lives Matter mobilizations in 2020. A community activist explained that that the unrest had provided opportunities to get key city government actors to come and listen to residents, later reflecting that 'our best relationships with the public officials have come typically after a big fight or tension' (Pill, 2015). The anti-austerity movement in Spain, discussed in Chapter 3, can also be characterized as encompassing multiple groups and individuals not previously engaged in actions against the state. The experience of Dublin also highlighted the augmented potential of social movements to engage a broader public: 'One of the most important things about this movement, and what made it extremely different to the other boycott campaigns, was that it wasn't led by the traditional left or any organization. It was genuinely driven, in terms of the perspective and the political understanding of what the implications are, it was by ordinary people' (activist cited in Gaynor, 2017).

Conclusion

This chapter sheds light on trends in post-GEC collaborative governance across eight diverse cities. While some discursive realignments were uncovered, the crisis did not lead to a major deviation from neoliberal approaches to governance, though with some exceptions. Most notably, the shift to co-production between state and civil society actors in Barcelona represents a redefinition of collaboration that emphasizes the transformative power of organized social movements, the strategic role of local government and the potential for joint working. Otherwise, our research suggests that usual practices continued with some deepening or disruptions associated with austerity politics.

Overall, the research provides evidence that urban policy can be committed to collective work with deep involvement by non-state actors, including citizen and civil society organizations. It also shows, however, that urban policy can also be used as a tool to co-opt the initiatives of communities and facilitate the devolution of service responsibility from the state to often inadequately supported non-state organizations. In this regard, an array of possible motivations and forms of collaboration were described, from empowering to coercive state-led practices as well as influential citizen-led movements, across the areas of discourse, agency and space.

Regarding agency and space, the state can play an active role in leading collaboration, which is an obvious but important tenet of democratic governance. The post-GEC transformation in Barcelona is a case in point. These experiences highlight an awareness of the mutual dependency between actors and build on important traditions of negotiation between them, for example between trade unions and governments. They also show how continued joint working can support more complex and sophisticated approaches to engagement by non-state actors, exhibited in the creation of formal networks between business or community sector representatives. These cases also brought to the fore the unique benefit of a three-tiered system of government which acts as a safeguard against abrupt changes in governance approaches administered by one level. Overall, the research outcomes attest to the potential of strong and robust public institutions to deepen democratic participation through collaborative governance.

One feature that stood out in the comparative analysis was the role of local political leadership in sustaining commitments to collaborative governance. Despite the French context of austerity or the Québec government's *rigueur* and political centralization, leaders in both Nantes and Montréal mediated the influence of structural conditions by maintaining commitment to and strengthening local collaborative institutions. Similarly, in the Melbourne case, executive leaders within local government showed prowess in cultivating links with partners in their communities, across community, business and education sectors, to sustain urban revitalization when fiscal constraint and policy redirection was pursued by the provincial level government. Leadership, particularly in managing external relational dynamics, is a fundamental attribute of collaborative governance.

While the chapter confirms that states still led urban governance practices in a post-GEC context, it also reinforces the fact that they do not govern alone and operate with a plurality of non-state actors. However, the plurality of actors has become more limited in places because of fiscal tightening, and the interdependency generated between some elite public, private and community sector institutions has been augmented and harbours regressive tendencies. In particular, the deepening reliance on ever larger non-profits and foundations noted in Athens, Baltimore, Dublin and Leicester cultivates dependencies that exclude other actors and reproduce urban policies that disadvantage the interests of those excluded.

Nonetheless, the dispossessed and disadvantaged are not passive agents. On the contrary, experiences in some cities signified the transformative potential of organized social movements in urban policy and governance. These examples are discussed further in Chapter 3. One case highlighted how agency can be stifled: in Leicester the ever-present potential of coercive discipline from the centre towards local government, the culture and (non-insurgent) traditions of British social democracy and the power of austerity discourse actively discouraged the contestation of ideas about resisting change or the notion of collaboration beyond the partnerships necessitated in its outsourced model of service delivery. Overall, however, our research highlights that transformative practices of collaboration can be created by different agents even when austerity grips, often precisely because it is questioned and shown to be unnecessary by social movements. The work of movements makes clear that 'collaborative' institutions that rely on exclusions can be overturned or changed and there is no one 'meta-narrative' (Blanco, 2015a: 129) of collaborative governance given the agency of different actors and the micro-politics between them.

Overall, the preparedness of civil society to act despite the impact of austerity on people's lives and declining trust in government in many places reveals an important source of hope in the still common, though by no means universal belief in our cities that government will respond or can be transformed to recognize and respond to demands. This belief in democracy is put into action through multiple collaborative strategies to pursue social justice from outside government. When governments fail to deliver public benefit, particularly because of austerity policies, civil society can rapidly organize and effect change. Our research demonstrates that where governments pursue public benefit outcomes, civil society does engage and has an important role in defining and delivering public policy. Overall, we found that while there are multiple pathways for collaboration, the goal of broadening genuine involvement requires the existence of a strongly organized, multi-faceted civil society.

3

Austerity Governance, Political Resistance and Urban Transformation

Our book details and documents the impact of austerity governance on a selection of cities. Yet for some commentators, cities and urban spaces remain the 'new theatres of struggle' in our contemporary condition (Hamel, 2014). This chapter critically assesses the forms of social and political resistance that emerged across the eight cities in our study. Building on themes introduced in Chapters 1 and 2, it argues that cities serve as crucibles for a diverse set of political contestations, responses and initiatives, but they exhibit differential capacities to shape their environments. Indeed, it demonstrates the complex 'mix' of political traditions, institutions, socio-economic structures, practices and ideological systems that come together to constitute the city as a political engine. In so doing, we draw particular attention to the shifting locus of resistance to austerity across communities and neighbourhoods. Our analysis and evaluation suggest that the future projection of cities as 'spaces of hope' rests on the twin challenges of 'scaling up' neighbourhood protests into broad and anti-systemic political projects, while reinvesting in the construction of progressive relations with the local state that open local spaces of manoeuvre to challenge national regimes of austerity.

Against this background, we turn first to our initial presentation and discussion of the eight cities, focusing on Melbourne, Barcelona and Nantes, whose distinctive characteristics provide the parameters for the analysis of all the cases. We then examine and describe the cases of Athens, Baltimore, Dublin, Leicester and Montréal, analysed here as in Chapter 1 through the lens of austerity realism. Finally, we focus on the cities of Barcelona and Nantes, which we deem to be exemplary cases of cities that have most contributed to social and political change, both in terms of the development of creative governance arrangements, and with respect to the social movements and political groups that have emerged within and beyond the official spaces of politics. Our characterization and evaluation establish the potentials, limits and contingency of new urban struggles and politics, whose forms are shaped by a concatenation of variables at multiple levels of analysis, and we conclude by setting out the challenges faced by these incipient and in many cases fleeting forms.

Establishing parameters: Melbourne, Barcelona and Nantes compared

As was explained in Chapter 1, Greater Dandenong (Melbourne) is best viewed as something of an outlier amongst our cities, as it bucked the trend of fiscal tightening and followed a more Keynesian pathway of stimulus following the GEC. The language of 'austerity' is not typically used in Australia's urban policy discourse to characterize public fiscal cutbacks, constraints or institutional change (for example corporatization, privatization). Instead, our research disclosed that post-GEC a more episodic rhetoric of 'crisis' was used by politicians to frame and rationalize specific cases for policy reform involving spending reductions (Henderson, Sullivan and Gleeson, 2020). The city was therefore not marked by active political movements or sustained citizen engagement from below in relation to austerity politics. Furthermore, in Australia's federal political system, state governments and their agencies are dominant forces in the allocation of resources which tends to limit the capacity of municipalities to act as assertive collaborative entities in contexts that invite or demand the 'joining up' of policy settings. In fact, Australian local governments are accustomed to this dependency and have also experienced tightening fiscal conservativism due to falling funding allocations since the 1970s (Dollery, Crase and Byrnes, 2006).

Both state and local tiers of government often undertake joint work on complex urban problems in Melbourne, in part reflecting the limits faced at the municipal level and reliance on the Victorian Government to fund and manage large-scale projects. There were many significant collaborative activities in relation to the revitalization effort in Central Dandenong, manifested across multiple policy areas and between different sectoral actors, as discussed in Chapter 2. Regeneration initiatives in the city, were often depicted in collaborative terms, where the discourse was laced with terms like 'relationship-building', 'community-building', 'formal 'cross-government' 'structures and processes', 'partnerships' with non-government entities', and 'informal strategies for effecting change in a multi-actor context', though the defining feature of these relationships was their informality. Indeed, in the views of many of our respondents, while formal structural relations between agencies and institutions were often weak or non-existent, the role of actors and their practices were extolled as effective elements of governing and policy making.

Of overriding importance in the Dandenong case, then, was the fact that the idea of 'fiscal conservatism' functions as the dominant political and ideological trope for both major national (and state) political blocs. As evident in expenditure cutbacks in specific areas, coupled with reductions of institutional effort and capacity, this trend towards the restraint of public revenue and expenditure over the last 15 years (and earlier) was a persistent theme. Nonetheless, these goals and ambitions have not been thoroughly achieved in practice, as public expenditure and revenue remained at historically high levels for all branches of government during the research period post GEC (Henderson, Sullivan and Gleeson, 2020).

Even at the municipal level where transfers have been reduced since the 1970s, many local governments like the City of Greater Dandenong have utilized their powers, from rates and charges like carparking fees to development contributions or taxes, to compensate revenue streams and develop locally led projects. Over the last decade in Dandenong, most of these projects have been designed to revitalize the centre area, for example with a new library, council offices, open space projects, landscaping improvements and upgrading the local theatre and fresh produce market. At the end of this research, the state government capped the level of rates collected by local governments and this generated significant concern among local actors that revitalization efforts, among other initiatives, would be curtailed. Early research on the impact of rate capping suggests 'that while total spending did not fall, budgets for "invisible" services, like aged care and disabled services, did decline' (Yarram, Dollery and Tran, 2020: 1).

Our investigation thus suggests that internationalized notions of 'austerity' had little traction in the Australian context, and for this reason activism associated with austerity was not a prominent feature in the city's politics and government. Yet different forms and logics of partnership were evident in the dominant visions of urban governance. Moreover, Melbourne is also a useful point of contrast with Barcelona, which in respect to organized protest is its opposite. In Melbourne, while organized movements take protest action from time to time, this typically is in reaction to specific, contested issues like industrial relations legislation reform or the treatment of asylum seekers, and has not coalesced in the formation of new radical political parties or coalitions since the GEC. Some of these movements, together with other NGOs and CSOs find spaces of negotiation with government or form alliances with opposition parties in efforts to move policy or policy platforms towards accommodating their concerns. These spaces of dialogue can contain and co-opt alternative movements, while also providing opportunities for negotiation and reform.

In Barcelona, especially since the mid-1980s, we find various forms of active collaboration and a vibrant set of protests and political agency. Indeed, despite facing a stringent dose of austerity following the GEC, such tendencies have continued to flourish and embed themselves in governing institutions and practices. In many respects, then, Barcelona constitutes something of a paradigm case of a city that can act and function as a political engine of social change, as it exhibits a series of collaborative forms of governance, together with a vibrant and formative set of organizations and practices in civil society. For this reason, we provide a more detailed characterization and discussion of this case in the following section, when we bring it into a comparative conversation with Nantes and Montréal.

Nantes finds its position closer to the case of Barcelona than to that of Dandenong. As the regional capital of the West of France, Nantes has vigorously sought to reconstruct itself as an attractive and environmentally conscious city of culture following the deindustrialization of the 1970s and 1980s. An integral aspect of this new urban imaginary is the way Nantes has extolled itself as a 'collaborative city', in which it has sought to engage and stimulate active citizen participation in its governance structures. Indeed, it is striking that the current Mayor, Johanna Rolland, following illustrious predecessors like Jean-Marc Ayrault (Chapter 2), made the practices of co-construction and citizen dialogue one of the priorities for her first term in office. The city council has thus committed itself to renewing participatory governance, in which there is a 'constant dialogue' between local councillors and citizens. Framed in political terms, the commitments of the city council to co-production are best viewed in terms of a response to the multiple crises facing Nantes and other cities in France, Europe and beyond. On the one hand, citizen dialogue is viewed as a means of countering the broader crisis of politics and social exclusion within communities. On the other hand, it is claimed that participation offers a better way of capturing the expertise of citizens as service-users, thus offsetting the deficiencies of traditional models of public service delivery. We now turn to exploring discourses of 'austerity realism', prominent in several of the cities (a term coined by Davies and Thompson, 2016).

Governance through austerity realism

As Chapter 1 argued, the five remaining cases under consideration fit relatively well into the category of 'austerity realism', and sometimes 'austerity idealism', though each is marked significantly by the issues, circumstances and concerns of their context. We here focus on how austerity realism influences practices of collaboration, as much as it does fiscal and economic policy. In material terms, Athens was clearly the most impacted by the global financial crisis and the subsequent logics of austerity. As Chapters 1 and 4 explain in more detail, fiscal policy preoccupations shifted the attention of the national authorities to the local level, seen as a tier capable of absorbing a share of cuts to public spending. The steep rise in municipal unemployment and poverty figures, and the clearly defined population decline trend, suggests that it is in the city that 'austerity bites' (Peck, 2012).

In a context of economic crisis and political dislocation, set alongside a spiral of protest and social struggles, significant sections of the Greek and Athenian populations started to construct the policies of austerity in a more explicitly political fashion, while beginning to resist the dominant channels and devices that sought to legitimize and rationalize the logic of austerity as the only way to overcome crisis. As Roussos put it (2019: 6), 'the economic grievances were transformed, rearticulated and mobilized in a wider political process, which was mainly targeted at the functioning of the neoliberal order: democratic deficits, social inequality and injustice, labour precariousness, technocratization of governance as well as citizens' exclusion from decision making and democratic control'. Following the occupation of the squares in Athens (and elsewhere) during 2011 and 2012, the dissemination of the new repertoires and discourses of self-organization and solidarity, which had been forged within the squares' everyday general assemblies, fostered the creation of neighbourhood assemblies and local social solidarity projects (Arampatzi, 2017). Such experiments and initiatives emerged outside the mainstream left-wing organizations and institutions, while seeking to invent alternative infrastructures and networks that are concerned with the self-organization of labour and other everyday needs.

In short, then, after widespread popular protests and political resistance, which partly inspired a radical change of government in January 2015, when the left-wing Syriza won national elections, overt citizen protests and resistance declined, and a period of governmental 'realism' began to predominate. Nonetheless, despite the perceived deradicalization of Syriza, which eventually accepted the terms of the EU's austerity packages to manage Greece's debt in July 2015, as well as the diminution of mass popular struggles and protests, grassroots campaigns and alternative social visions continued to persist and emerge in Athens and the country more generally. But these emergent campaigns did not translate into a broad anti-systemic movement or challenge. Our evidence suggests that over time trade unions were worn down by the demands of the struggle against austerity, as well as the impact of high unemployment on membership and resources. Equally, grassroots campaigns, which centred on self-organizing and solidarity networks, operated between everyday support for communities and resistance to austerity, exhibiting little collaboration with local government. Indeed, in the aftermath of the political retreat of Syriza in 2015, the challenge for these grassroots solidarity campaigns was to become transformative and widen their appeal and effectiveness. Hence, while opposition to austerity remained widespread in Athens, austerity realism and some idealism had become hegemonic within the local state.

Similarly, Leicester and Dublin were also subordinated to the hegemony of 'austerity realism', thus exhibiting little evidence of being agents of urban change and social transformation, at least until the 'water wars' in Dublin discussed later. In Leicester, for example, political resistance or popular protest was either absorbed or displaced, and the dominant system perpetuated. The local council experienced 39.9 per cent cuts to its budget in real terms, with the ensuing reductions to local public services causing a rise in urban poverty, alongside the imposition on welfare claimants of a national authoritarian workfare regime. Implementation of these drastic cuts to funding produced a politics of austerity realism across the council that served to contain and fragment resistance. The discourse of austerity realism foregrounded in part the futility of opposition experienced among local state and some civil society actors and framed it as an opportunity to deliver service reorganizations and efficiency gains, which masked efforts to re-compose state-civil society relations in the city. The council retreated from frontline community engagement mechanisms, while increasingly awarding voluntary sector contracts to larger providers, hollowing out in the process the local community sector, including removing funding from many of the black, Asian and minority ethnic groups that made up the informal community governance coalition established across the city in the 1980s (Davies et al, 2020).

Equally, the local state created multi-service hubs across neighbourhoods, a process which served to further fragment opposition to cuts across the city. This austerity realist regime thus muted potential city-wide resistance against austerity, aided and abetted by the 'shadow' of the failure of previous campaigns to prevent cuts and restructurings in the 1980s. The consequence was that, apart from small scale and issue-specific campaigns, there was little evidence of successful resistance to austerity as such. Indeed, the case of Leicester exemplifies the capacity of the local state to mute opposition, reproducing as it did the fragmentation of community opposition and distancing between the local state and civil society.

Since the 1990s, the collaborative governance regime in Dublin is best described as a form of 'urban entrepreneurialism', which has brought the creation of various partnership structures and networks designed to address unemployment and social exclusion in deprived neighbourhoods. The period of austerity was accompanied with the rhetoric of renewing local accountability and democracy through local government reforms, even though policy practices and decision-making have become increasingly centralized. Indeed, as normative commitments to collaboration decline, so these arrangements have been regarded as mere 'talking shops'. Although various collaborative and deliberative ventures continue to seek to incorporate actors and agencies in policy discussions, concrete policy is still formed within central government departments, leaving some discretion to the council CEO (formerly City Manager – an official appointee) to develop some initiatives (Gaynor, 2020a).

Not unlike the case of Montréal, then, collaborative mechanisms and the discourse of partnership in Dublin resulted in the incorporation of trade unions into regimes of austerity governance, negating opposition to cuts to public spending. However, logics of corporatist incorporation were unable to contain community struggles and non-formal civil society resistance against austerity. In 2014, government plans to introduce new charges for domestic water supply triggered mass demonstrations, ultimately forcing concessions from central government. The protest, although ostensibly over the demand for 'the right to water', linked the new charges to general discontent with austerity, with many campaigners expressing fears that cuts to public services had 'gone too far' (Gaynor, 2020a). A key aspect of resistance in Dublin was that it did not come from the formal civil society sector (state funded CSOs) but arose organically from local neighbourhood community groups on the ground (Gaynor, 2020a). As such, the movement mobilized a population of campaigners best characterized as 'new activists', who had not previously been involved in political protests, as well as drawing its membership from across social classes and neighbourhoods. Although supported by trade unions and political parties, it was in practice an organic bottom-up movement, led by women, and adopting multiple strategies including water meter installation protests and civil disobedience. In opposition to the dominant collaborative discourse of 'partnership', it thus called for new forms of political dialogue and participation.

Baltimore also displays many features of 'austerity realism', though refracted through its distinctive history and traditions. As explained earlier, the city's perennial 'culture of scarcity' is connected more to the de facto devolution of Reaganomics than the 2008 crisis, which is not regarded as a significant turning point. Instead, the signifier of a 'fiscal squeeze', referring to falling revenues and increasing need, appears more regularly in official discourses, where it is employed to bolster a narrative of 'harsh realities', which frames the aims and objectives of urban governance. The idea of collaboration is more framed in terms of public–private partnerships in economic development and the collaborative relationships between philanthropic (private) actors, anchor institutions and the city.

A key over-determining aspect of the Baltimore case is the thorny issue of race, which has strongly marked the city's spatial organization and politics for at least a century. Indeed, after the death of Freddie Gray, the subsequent Uprising represented a key moment of political resistance and renaissance in the city, though it was not directed against austerity per se, but the criminal justice system and carceral governance more generally. As Chapter 2 recounts, young African American activists have risen to prominence, protesting these inequities, while seeking policy reform particularly in the realm of policing and criminal justice (at the Maryland State as well as city scales). Further resistance has grown, which mixes outsider strategies such as street protests and vigils with insider strategies of partnership. However, there were ideological differences among protesters about whether the groups and movements involved were locally embedded; questions about their willingness to collaborate; as well as about the strategies and tactics that were adopted. Despite new groups being formed, on a neighbourhood and/or issue-basis (leading to tensions of competition and overlap), those able to provide a longer-term perspective emphasized the lack of state and philanthropic funding support for general operating costs, and particularly for community organizing and 'training neighbourhood leaders'. This was linked to the emphasis on outcomes and thus programmes and capital projects; and to the 'lack of listening' on the part of city elites. Some organizations prioritized by city resource flows did stress the importance of community organizing, but their approach can be critiqued as instrumental and co-optative. In short, while forms of resistance across the city have reinvigorated community grassroots organizing, the governing regime has remained relatively insulated from demands for reform (Pill, 2020).

Not unlike Melbourne, Montréal was relatively protected from the full force of the GEC and the age of austerity. Instead, echoing Baltimore and Nantes discussed below, austerity was more often represented in terms of *rigueur* and is part of a deeper and more profound restructuring of the welfare state and economy in Canada and the Québec Model, originating in successive and ongoing crises the 1970s. So, the policies and programmes of austerity were not just solutions to an immediate economic or financial crisis but rooted in a neoliberal and conservative vision of the state in Canada and its role regarding social solidarity. Austerity was not, therefore, constructed by key actors as a necessary policy in times of crisis, but more a policy and politics of state restructuring, which was part of 'neoliberal ideology' (Hamel and Keil, 2020: 110). Many interviewees thus distinguished between

> a supposedly necessary austerity in countries undergoing economic crises such as Greece or Spain, for example, and austerity measures rooted in a conservative ideology such as the ones implemented by the federal government under former Conservative Canadian Prime Minister Harper (2006–2015) and by Québec Premier Philippe Couillard's Liberal provincial government. (Autin, 2016)

As Chapter 2 explained, a further element in Montréal was the articulation and condensation of the different levels of government and decision-making at the local level and its scale of operations. In Montréal, a longer history of collaboration is evident amongst these different levels of government, which have always coordinated their activities in key governance and policy areas. At the same time, the three tiers of government – federal, provincial and municipal – can diverge with respect to their ideological and political orientations:

> Thus, when the provincial administration undergoes serious austerity measures and cuts different programmes, the municipal administration has to choose between increasing their participation in those programmes (for example in public transportation), in order to supplement what has been cut at the provincial level or maintain their financial participation and ask the other tiers of government to maintain commitments. (Autin, 2016)

This implies that the municipal government's importance, at the local level, as a financing and regulating power, increases with the relative withdrawal of the provincial and federal governments.

Importantly, and in equal fashion, collaboration is not only a feature of the relationships between the three tiers of government but is also evident in the relationships between the actors of civil society, community organizations, the business sectors, and trade unions. Such interactions between these actors have existed for a long time, though this may, as in the case of Dublin, place such groups and networks in an uncomfortable position, as they are often imbricated in the complicated process of both managing and contesting austerity measures. The dilemma of providing a service, while also becoming a substitute for the state, must thus be mediated and negotiated by the different actors engaged in collaborative practices, which is symptomatic of the deeper tensions of state restructuring in Montréal, Québec, and Canada in general. While previous urban regimes – from the 1950s to the 1970s and from the 1980s to 2010 – have failed, Montréal is still in search of a new regime (Hamel and Keil, 2015). The questions that arise, should a new urban regime emerge, are how the existing mechanisms of collaboration within the new context of austerity measures will be reconfigured, and what sorts of impacts and constraints this context will impose on actors and agents.

In fact, alternative demands that challenged embedded tripartite relations did emerge across Montréal as our research began. Building in part on the 2012 'Maple Spring' revolt against tuition fees, students took to the streets again in 2015, but after the so-called 'narrow demands' of 2012, their 2015 protest demanded action against austerity and cuts to public services, particularly in health and education. These demands reinforced, albeit fragile, alliances with community groups and workers' struggles. For example, in early November 2015, 1,300 community groups went on strike against cuts to funding. This protest movement, supported by the anti-privatization coalition 'Main Rouge', established in 2009, remained a vector for collaboration between trade unions and community groups. Such demands arguably resonated with the appeals to gender equality and diversity, urban renewal, public transport and citizens' needs in the campaign of Valérie Plante who became the first woman Mayor in Montréal in 2017 on a progressive platform, 'Projet Montréal'. However, as we stated previously, these emergent alliances remained fragile, while the model of social partnership risked incorporating trade union demands into the governance of austerity (the 'iron cage' mentioned in Chapter 2). In addition, the election of Plante demonstrated the limits on the local state, and its capacity in Canada to be controlled by the regional or state tier of government.

The exemplary case of Barcelona

As we have noted, the global financial crisis had a major impact on the socio-economic structure of Barcelona, causing a spike in levels of poverty and social exclusion, while exacerbating social and spatial inequalities. At the same time, austerity measures, the growing effects of mass tourism, and the speculative dynamics of the local housing market, accelerated the logics of socio-spatial polarization, while excluding and marginalizing social groups who cannot afford to live in the city because of the sharp increase in living costs and growing job precarity. In this context, respondents highlighted the increased inequalities between different urban areas and the disproportionate impact of austerity on historically disadvantaged urban areas.

The high social costs of this urban development regime, together with the long tradition of grassroots mobilization in the city, stimulated powerful political responses via new social movements like the '15-M' (the 'Indignados' movement) and the Plataforma de Afectados por la Hipoteca (PAH) (which can be translated as the Platform of Mortgage Victims) in response to the housing crisis. Such forces built political coalitions and discourses that placed responsibility for the crisis on the political and economic elites, and they used a diverse array of non-conventional forms of communication and mobilization to voice their grievances and demands, including lengthy sit-ins in public squares, public demonstrations and media campaigns using digital social networks. The crisis of 2008 led to a major expansion of solidarity practices and movements.

At the same time, the governance of austerity in Barcelona and Spain entailed a deep recentralization of power in the hands of national government, which in turn was opposed both by the independence movement in Catalunya and the progressive municipalist movement, which arose from prolonged anti-austerity mobilizations. Such forces have intermingled and struggled with the national independence movement in Catalunya, which has grown considerably since 2010, partly in response to the intensification of austerity and its territorial effects in a relatively prosperous region.

Such trends and logics have moulded new forms of urban governance. Stretching back to the mid-1980s, as previous chapters have made clear, the governance and political dynamics of Barcelona have long exhibited a tradition of intensive collaboration among public authorities, private interests, and community associations and groups. Indeed, collaborations in the form of public-private partnerships, intergovernmental consortia, metropolitan-wide arrangements for inter-municipal strategic planning and service provision, and various mechanisms of citizen participation at the neighbourhood, district and city level, continue to constitute a vital strategic mechanism for the mobilization of resources and the creation of consensus and cohesion among different groups and interests.

Of course, such collaborations can exhibit different forms and ideological hues. The two austerity coalition governments that governed from 2007 until 2015 (2007–2011: Jordi Hereu, PSC, the Catalan social democratic party and 2011–2015: Xavier Trias, CiU, a conservative-nationalist coalition) brought about an accelerated and intensified logic of nonlinearization. This trend was manifested in enhanced public-private partnerships and the contracting-out of public services to both Third Sector and private organizations, as well as the adoption of an emergency and charitable approach to social policy and the outsourcing of social services to private firms. However, in May 2015 the continuity of this regime of austerity governance was interrupted by the election of Barcelona en Comú (BeC), whose approach sought to rebalance urban political power by strengthening the role of social and community organizations, while also constructing alternatives to neoliberal austerity and growth (Blanco et al, 2020).

The strategy of the new government stressed the limitation and regulation of the most negative effects of tourism; overturning privatizations and programmes that run counter to what is constructed as the 'common good'; building the endogenous economic resources (like industry) of the city; the role of the local and social economy; the creation of decent jobs; and the feminization of politics. A commitment to the co-production of policy formulation and implementation underpins the core political principle of the new government. Under the conceptual umbrella of notions such as the 'urban commons', the social economy, community action and collaborative economies and social innovation, the platform focuses on fostering an active and autonomous society capable of acting beyond the state sphere. Such ideas and principles form part of the strong co-operativist tradition in the city. Nonetheless, the Barcelona en Comú platform remains a minority government, now consisting of 10 out of 41 councillors, and is compelled to strike agreements and build coalitions with like-minded groups and opposition parties. It has thus faced difficulties in building political and cultural hegemony, partly because of the strengthening of an alternative radical project, the independence movement, which sees Barcelona en Comú as an impediment (Blanco et al, 2020).

In many ways, Barcelona en Comú is an exemplary instance of a radical left citizen platform, which has drawn together several social movements and political organizations. Yet it offered a distinct conception of the municipal state, which was constructed around new ideas of autonomy. Efforts were also made to free municipal politics from the economic relations and institutions to which they are usually beholden, while deconstructing and rethinking the liberal notion of the state–society relationship as a binary opposition. Barcelona en Comú thus endeavoured to change the way the dominant institutions operate by 'enhancing the channels of public control, citizen participation, and public community co-production of public policies' (Blanco et al, 2020: 28). In other words, this form of resistance worked in and with the differentiated characteristics of urban governance, while seeking to take the struggle between political coalitions into the workings of the local state itself.

In short, then, political resistance to austerity can be characterized as highly successful and the democratic legacy of grassroots resistance is evident in the emergence of Barcelona en Comú. More precisely, the political agenda of the new municipalism combines the traditional agenda of socio-spatial redistribution, with that of direct democracy, the 'urban commons', and radical forms of co-production and social innovation. At the core of this agenda was the feminization of politics, symbolized by Ada Colau and other women leading her cabinet, and beyond in the leadership of community solidarity groups. Importantly for our analysis the case of Barcelona thus demonstrates how anti-austerity resistance can morph into a movement-party (della Porta et al, 2017) that gains at least a degree of political control of the local state. Such 'constructive' relations with local government distinguished the case of Barcelona from Athens. However, the experience of Barcelona en Comú also foregrounds the potential limits of the local state as a vehicle for progressive transformation, operating as it does within the confines of market economies, in and against dominant central states, local administrative inertia and the dynamics of electoral competition. Equally, relationships with community groups and social movement organizations waxed and waned over time while trade unions or the organized working class remained at the margins of the struggle, caught up in the corporatist politics of partnerships and collaboration as well as attrition through job losses.

An official discourse of collaborative governance: the logics and limits of Nantes

Collaborative governance in Nantes was widely touted as a model of 'good practice' in the building of a more democratic, efficient and 'green' city. Claims were made that it offers alternative forms of dialogue, resource coordination and innovation to overcome 'wicked problems' associated with demands for sustainable development in sectors such as urban transport, energy and housing. Indeed, the public discourse of Nantes city council was articulated around the myth of the 'jeu à la Nantaise', 'the Nantes game' or Nantes Model, which functions as a 'surface of inscription' for registering the multiple demands and dislocations affecting the city. Originating in the passing game of the famous Nantes football team of the 1970s and 1980s, 'the Nantes game' was first injected into public political discourse by Jean-Joseph Régent, who was centre-right chair of the local chamber of commerce in the late 1970s and early 1980s. This functioned, we argue, to facilitate the construction of a particular discourse of place, while embodying a distinctive ethos of public collaboration across the city, which frames its visions and policy objectives. Not only does it help to account for the resilience of these practices, but it also attributes distinct forms of agency to the 'people' of Nantes and its political leadership. Indeed, at its heart, the myth crystallizes the norms of interactive collaboration, as well as the aspirational values of collective and participatory decision-making. Framed as such, 'citizen dialogue' is seen as a way of dealing with the limits of the French model of public service delivery and the crisis of politics, while drawing upon the expertise of local people to lead co-produced projects and services that are responsive to clients.

However, the same practices of collaboration have also been charged with introducing new forms of hierarchy and advancing novel modes of urban governmentality. Indeed, collaboration was often seen to facilitate post-political 'consensual' patterns of decision-making and greenwashing that excludes and coerces certain groups and citizens. Demands for further engagement were directed at the very definition of the Nantes model. For example, one trade unionist argued that 'we cannot highlight a participatory democracy which does not exist and for the moment ... it does not exist despite the statements [that are made]' (interview with trade unionist). In fact, neighbourhood forums were characterized as an 'inconsistent [form of] democracy', which 'do not change fundamental decisions', or which 'too often ... put [communities] in front of things' that have already been decided (Interview with Community Campaigner) (citations from Griggs, Howarth and Feandeiro, 2020).

Perhaps more importantly, it was argued that such forums did not engage with those people most in need, a view which challenged the stated desire of officials and policymakers to combat social exclusion. Community campaigners outside the council's participatory arenas commonly posed questions about the legitimacy of those civil society actors who were involved in participatory forums, as well as their capacity to represent communities across Nantes. In the words of one community campaigner, 'people who are truly in vulnerable positions are not in the know, or do not keep themselves in the know, or are not free, for these types of things ... they do not go to these meetings' (Community Campaigner cited in Griggs, Howarth and Feandeiro, 2020: 102).

Criticisms focused on the perceived democratic and legitimacy deficits of the Nantes model are intertwined with the highly technocratic method of engagement that has been rolled out across the city. Citizen dialogue in the neighbourhoods was often flagged up to be 'top-down', while participation was often depicted as 'highly managed'. For example, when referring to neighbourhood councils and meetings, one neighbourhood officer described it as a 'system, well-supervised for 20 years and integrated into general public action' (interview with neighbourhood officer). Another officer alluded to the heavy, technocratic participatory machinery, which was described as 'very standardized, very precise, quite intelligent', but one that 'stifles' and runs the risk 'of a drying up of the [participatory] dynamic' (interview with neighbourhood officer). Developing this theme, a senior officer thus spoke of the installation of 'a big engineering [system] so that citizens can, collectively, produce a point of view and recommendations in terms of the questioning that we propose to them or which they propose to us'. In keeping with its design principles, the so-called Nantes method therefore maintains political dominance over decision making, thus ensuring at the deliberative and legislative levels that it is 'the elected politician who has the final decision' (quotations from senior officer in Griggs, Howarth and Feandeiro, 2020: 102).

It is also clear that those civil society actors who were advancing anti-austerity projects of a counter-hegemonic kind, focusing for example on social housing, chose not to engage in the formal structures of citizen dialogue across the city. Actors in this domain saw little strategic value in investing in such arenas, because 'they (the city council) do not want to hear certain things. So [the dialogue] becomes completely stuck in these meetings' (community activist). More militant citizens thus questioned the legitimacy of participating in neighbourhood meetings, both because of their own potential complicity and because of the nature of the structures themselves. Or, as one city councillor put it, those who resist are often seen to reflect 'a political party or a political opinion or ideologies' (councillor). Indeed, one official admitted that conflict is frequently squeezed out of such participatory arenas 'exactly because these spaces are spaces of dialogue' (senior officer) (citations in this paragraph from Griggs, Howarth and Feandeiro (2020: 103). In short, then, it is argued that at least in particular forums practices of urban regeneration in Nantes do not come up against 'counter-powers' (Devisme et al, 2013).

Against this background, it is difficult to ignore that much of the resistance and opposition to socio-economic crisis and austerity within civil society existed outside the formal participatory apparatus of urban governance. Parallel forms of 'dialogue' appear to be one of the defining contradictions of the Nantes model of participation and these idiosyncrasies of urban governance 'the Nantes way'. Consider, for example, the plan to build an international airport at NDDL to the north-west of Nantes. Indeed, radical activists from across France and Europe increasingly began to occupy land earmarked for development from 2009. Activists occupying the land sought to work alongside local farmers and citizens, determined to 'make use of abandoned spaces to learn to live together, to cultivate the land and to be more autonomous from the capitalist system.' In the process, they transformed the land from its planning definition as a 'zone to be developed' into a 'zone to be defended', the '*zone à defendre*' or 'ZAD', as it is more commonly known (Mauvaise Troupe Collective and Ross, 2018). Indeed, the struggles at NDDL began to prefigure alternative models of living, organization, and sustainable urban development, whose new ideals and patterns of social life run counter to the vision of the Nantes metropolitan authorities.

In many ways, before the abandonment of the airport project in January 2018, it had already become a nodal issue for linking together several demands against both national and local policies, so that protesters against the airport also contested the dominant narrative of urban boosterism, which has underpinned the official public discourses of the Nantes regime. The displacement of the ZAD's opposition to the airport into a questioning of the dominant narrative of metropolitanization was spearheaded by Nantes Nécropole and the Collectif Nantais Contre l'Aéroport (CNCA). CNCA – the Nantes collective against the airport – was formed in 2010, with the aim of bringing the struggle against NDDL into the heart of the practices of urban governance across Nantes (Mauvaise Troupe Collective and Ross, 2018: 24–25). The CNCA broadened its struggle in 2016 to challenge what it deemed to be the logic of metropolitanization or 'the planning of the city and the discourse that drives it forward, as well as the planning of the rest of our lives.' The CNCA accepted that 'you cannot fight against this airport without fighting against the world that goes with it'. The politically charged naming of its mobilizing campaign forum, Nantes Nécropole, a deliberate play on Nantes Métropole, the collaborative vehicle of Nantes and surrounding municipalities, denigrated the aspirations of metropolitanization (Griggs and Howarth, 2020). In short, in the act of naming its style and practices those of 'co-governance' in 2015, and in the definition and development of its specific methodology of citizen participation, the Rolland administration and its predecessors created the very conditions for the articulation of rival understandings and challenges to its mode of collaborative governance.

Conclusion

Albeit unevenly and set against a buffeting and cascading series of social and natural forces, there is little doubt that cities continue to be integral sites for the interaction and clash of the dominant logics of our time. Not only do they serve as the crucibles for a diverse set of political contestations, responses and initiatives, but they also exhibit differential capacities to shape their environments. Some cities felt the full brunt of the GEC and the ensuing austerity, whereas others were relatively immunized; some were complicit in the advance of the dominant economic and social logics, whereas others developed innovative and creative responses. Indeed, this chapter has demonstrated the complex 'mix' of political traditions, institutions, socio-economic structures, practices and ideological systems that come together to constitute the city as a political engine. It has foregrounded the difficult and 'messy' task of drawing critical assessments of any urban regime and how it might prefigure alternative strategies that challenge regimes of austerity governance. For even if Barcelona functions as something of a paradigm case of an inspiring city, from which many draw hope and in which bottom-up forces in civil society combined with institutional weight, its experience is not without its constraints and fragilities, particularly following electoral setbacks for municipalists across Spain in 2019. Nor can it be explained without reference to its historical legacy and political traditions.

In fact, stepping back from the analysis of the individual cities themselves, our evidence suggests that, although the differential impacts of austerity partly shaped the different social and political responses to the crisis, they did not determine their form and character. Such political responses can take, as we have shown, the form of more institutionalized, top-down forms of governance, whether collaborative, participatory, or otherwise, or they may express more bottom-up social movements and popular initiatives. Put differently, the direction or vector of urban agency is not unidirectional and uniform. In some cases, popular forces and governance forms can coalesce to challenge relations of power and domination, such as neoliberalism, austerity, racial and national exclusion, gender oppression, and so on. But new forms of governance can also serve to enhance dominant logics or lead to subtle logics of collusion and complicity between powerholders and those ostensibly opposed to them. Ultimately, what direction such struggles took was mediated and shaped by pre-existing political institutions and traditions that characterized the different urban regimes investigated, as well as the national political traditions and institutional configurations within which the urban regimes were themselves embedded. At the same time, resistance and challenge also depended on the innovations and strategies that were articulated and developed by both governors and citizens alike and the configuration of issues and circumstances confronting each of the cities.

Yet, equally, it is possible to identify across the eight cities a set of common trends and challenges. For one thing, we have observed in all eight cities the continued reconfiguration of urban struggles from the traditional and formal arena of the workplace to alternative and informal spaces of community and neighbourhoods. In general, trade unions were not at the forefront of the resistance to austerity, particularly where established social partnership models arguably locked them into the governance of austerity. Rather, community-led struggles, bringing together multiple groups across civil society, and often led by women, came to serve as the locus of opposition to austerity. These community and neighbourhood movements entered complex oppositional and ambiguous relations with the local state, even when they made the transition from movement to party in office. In fact, we suggest that the future projection of community and neighbourhood resistance to austerity faces two primary challenges. A first challenge is how to scale up neighbourhood protests into an anti-systemic project against austerity that can be maintained over time. Indeed, our evidence suggests that community networks can become 'locked into' the everyday provision of support and solidarity to communities, with little space or time for building broader political coalitions for change. The second challenge is how to redefine the often-ambiguous relationship between new social movements and community activism, and the resources and capabilities of the local state. While we have identified the capacity of the local state to recompose and disorganize civil society, we have also demonstrated how the electoral capture of the municipality can advance progressive outcomes, even if it does not overcome the obstructions of local bureaucracy and national austerity regimes. How progressive movements and activists seek to answer and rework these challenges will determine in part the future of the cities as incubators of a new, more hopeful politics.

4

Rescaling through
Austerity Governance

Introduction

The reality of austerity in our eight case study cities and elsewhere has been strongly shaped by a phenomenon, long studied by geographers and recognized across the social sciences as well as by practitioners in policy making, politics and activism: social, political and institutional spaces are structured through a hierarchy of spatial scales that is not pregiven but socially constructed. Emphasizing scale in this manner confirms an intuitive assumption we make on a daily basis – when we go to work from our home, or when we go on vacation – that 'spaces across the world differ from one another' (Brenner, 2009: 27). What might sound trivial, is an important marker in the way we understand the world around us. How, then, does scale matter specifically? We all know the concept of scale from the ways we use a map or a measuring tape. In this colloquial usage, we presuppose that there is a natural quality to the concept: we rely on its truth as given. If you use a map for a cycling trip, and its scale tells you that one centimetre on the map represents ten kilometres, you assume that if you plan a trip represented by five centimetres on the map, it means that the distance you will travel is, in fact, 50 kilometres in reality (never mind the hills and valleys).

While this 'natural' understanding of scale underlies its use in this chapter, we add to it the notion that scale in social life is, for the most part, not a given but socially constructed. Being part of the general vocabulary with which we seek to understand the uneven spatial development of modern society, scale reveals its true explanatory power when we realize that it is a plastic concept that is subject to interpretation and negotiation. When we use scale in this manner, we refer to 'the vertical differentiation of social relations among, for instance, global, supranational, national, regional, urban and/or local levels' (Brenner, 2009: 31). We say: scale is socially constructed and use participles such as 'scaling' or 'rescaling' to refer to the more or less intentional activity to shape this 'vertical differentiation.' Political decision makers and activists refer to the scale of government at which they want their action to count: the nation state, the region, the county, the municipality. When we describe the outcome of those activities, we refer to them with the adjective 'scalar'. If we look at scale this way, it is just as easy to understand that the idea of a 'continental scale' for example includes vastly different spaces such as Europe and Asia, as it is that 'at the scale of the city' involves highly differentiated notions of how we define a city. These ideas are immediately clear to the tourist who goes on vacation (America is bigger than Europe; Leicester operates at a different scale than Los Angeles). But the fact that the notion of the 'scale of the city' or the 'scale of the neighbourhood' is dependent on that reality of specific places, is fundamental to the ways in which politicians and policy makers across our urban world make decisions on a daily basis. It is also clear that what happens at one scale is not separated neatly from what happens at other scales. In fact, most political outcomes are achieved through an interplay of activities across spatial and institutional scales, as Kian Goh (2021) has recently shown with an intricate analysis of multi-scalar and interscalar interdependencies of 'local' politics of water and flood protection across New York, Rotterdam and Jakarta. This is perhaps nowhere as clear as in the European context, where a related concept has taken hold that aims at explaining this interplay: 'multi-level governance.' As one of its chief proponents has put it: 'It evokes the idea of increasingly complex arrangements for arriving at authoritative decisions in increasingly dense networks of public and private, individual and collective actors' (Piattoni, 2010: 1). It is often the ingenuity of political actors to cut through the maze of these 'complex arrangements' through 'scale-jumping' tactics that both disrupt the momentarily given spatial and institutional hierarchy of power and create new opportunities for actors that are usually denied influence.

In this chapter, we show how the study of scale is enlightening when trying to understand how austerity has functioned in our eight case study cities. In order to put forth a clear definition of how we use the concept, we also propose a definition of scale and promote a synthetic and multi-faceted definition such as the one suggested by Byron Miller (2009: 62): 'a set of territorially nested, malleable relationships among territorially embedded or constituted agents and institutions, shaping their responsibilities, capacities, opportunities, and constraints through territory-specific rule regimes, resources, and identities'. The chapter explores several different dimensions of scale, as it pertains to neoliberalism, austerity and the struggle for social justice – which also takes the form of struggles over the definition and classification of scale and territory.

Austerity and scale

The production of scale(s) has been tied, in recent memory, to processes of neoliberalization and to the establishment of austerity as a principle of governing through which those scales become weaponized in cities and communities around the world. In the USA, for example, a discourse that has vilified the wastefulness of 'big' (federal) government and has called for devolution and austerity at lower levels of state and local government has characterized politics since the presidency of Ronald Reagan. The federal systems in Australia and Canada have three levels of government/politics but there is also an important fourth level/scale of sublocal politics which, for all intents and purposes is equivalent with civil society organizations and the neighbourhood scale. In addition, of course, Indigenous institutions and territories of governance don't fit neatly into the constructed scales of those settler societies but, in fact, provide alternative examples of political ontologies and spatial scaling (Magnusson, 2015). For the Dandenong case in metropolitan Melbourne, it is found that 'some issues raised at the local level have not yet found an adequate resolution at the community level (for example car parking and traffic planning)' (Henderson, Sullivan and Gleeson, 2020: 138). At the other end of the spectrum is the less clearly defined 'global' scale which inserts itself into our case study cities through the general (post) crisis situation. The global includes the supra-national crisis regimes that impose austerity on countries like Greece, global investment streams and, in immigration cities such as Leicester, Montréal and Melbourne and other cities taking on border functions such as Athens that become home to refugees, diverse populations.

Austerity comes to the fore of concerns in the urban context precisely at the time when cities are in the spotlight of the crisis of global social development and when they are paradoxically called upon as arenas and theatres from which this crisis is to be addressed (Blanco, Salazar and Bianchi, 2020). In fact, a focus on scale accentuates the role of the urban in larger contexts of change (Ruddick et al, 2018: 390):

the downloading, dismantling, and restriction of institutional supports for social reproduction—from nation to city, from city to household, and from global north to global south—enacted through the monetization and withdrawal of the basic infrastructures of survival. Coupled with resurgent right-wing nationalisms, the ensuing precaritization of employment, and indeed of all life, precipitates national and transnational migration and forced displacement, and is metastasized as slow (and fast) structural violence. If this is the planetary urbanization that is characteristic of our time, even on its own terms, it is one that forecloses the right to the city.

Experienced universally but in diverse and variegated fashion, austerity impacts have been felt as 'sharp, deep, and uneven' (Gaynor, 2020a: 78). It is not only because of devolution of cost cutting measures from upper-level governments to lower-level administrations that austerity has been strongly linked to the municipality as an arena of action. In fact, it has been noted that cities are often put into the situation of having to do the 'dirty work' of neoliberalization and austerity regime building on the ground (Keil, 2002). As other chapters in the volume show, this means that municipalities have often been forced to make tough decisions on funding for social programmes, housing or public health while they have little influence on the circumstances that produce economic or financial hardship in their jurisdictions. Jamie Peck notes that 'there was something distinctly urban about the political economy of austerity' (2018: xiv), an observation that was confirmed in our research that showed that austerity has 'bitten hardest' at the scale of the city.

The uneven and multi-scalar geographies of austerity interest us in this chapter especially as they revolve around local and municipal politics and the question of collaboration. As noted, these geographies are constantly changing. The idea of devolution being 'a process and not an event' can also be applied to austerity. Viewing it as a process means that austerity in cities is the outcome of a layering of decisions, often not at the municipal level, that leads to frequently self-propelling processes of steadily increasing fiscal frugality. While sometimes initiated by an event-like 'shock', austerity plays itself out through a grinding dynamic of attrition in which previously established social and community rights (to the city; to the welfare state; to services) are whittled away gradually. This also entails that any notion of multi-level governance (so relevant, especially in the European context as we will see below) must be imagined as a malleable set of 'tangled hierarchies' (Cerny, 2006). In addition to scales, we also see 'tiers' which are 'distinguished in terms of the types of actors whose activities predominate – elites, the middle, and the marginal – who have different resource capacities or power to' (Pill, 2020: 144).

This concept of 'power to' alongside 'power over' is of great significance in the realm of municipal politics as the outcome of political processes that depend more than in most national politics on the collaboration of non-sovereign actors. As a constructive concept, 'power to' means essentially that getting stuff done requires knowing how to work with other interests in the municipality and align their resources. These tiers add an important moment of explanation when we talk about collaborative governance, the relationship of rescaling and the radius of action of civil society institutions in our cities. They also correspond spatially to the scale at which actors linked to specific tiers try to intervene, such as small-scale neighbourhood intervention at the local scale versus large-scale urbanism. In addition, for the Montréal case, Hamel and Keil (2020) distinguished four different types of relationships of community actors among each other and with the state at various scales: antagonistic, institutional, activist and philanthropic.

While geographies of austerity matter and must be analysed comparatively in order to understand the complete picture, we also need to remind ourselves that what we encounter today in terms of austerity policies and effects are the product not just of a recent crisis (in most cases a reaction to the financial crisis of 2008 and the Great Recession of the recent period) but of a 'long arc of three decades or more of state rescaling, punctuated by localized crises' during which 'new rules of the game have been established' (Peck, 2018: xxv). At the outset, we therefore acknowledge with Mark Davidson and Kevin Ward (2018: 7), 'the complicated, contested, and long history to austerity.' In fact, austerity has its national, regional and local histories and geographies, many of which are on display in the analysis that follows in this chapter and in the book more generally. Of particular significance has been the relationship of the roll-out of neoliberalism and the role austerity regimes played in this process both as outcomes and eventually enablers of further neoliberalization and the establishment of what we earlier called 'austerity realism' (see also Lammert and Vormann, 2017; Petzold, 2018). In addition, we are keenly aware of and factor into our analysis the many ways in which austerity, especially at the local level, has been cause for widespread 'urban rage' (Dikeç, 2017) as well as powerful anti-austerity protest, especially in the nodal points of globalizing urbanism (Schipper et al, 2018). As earlier chapters document, the rebellion of the poor remains always a threat at the one end of democratic process and an impediment to regime stabilization.

Calls for the conjoining of struggles against austerity across scales always include demands for the connection of diverse politics that lay bare the root processes of austerity as a neoliberal strategy. Such calls mistrust the 'naturalness' of the world in which we live. While normally, citizens and politicians alike might, for example, view 'collaboration between local and state governments' as 'innate' (Henderson et al, 2020: 136), resistance and opposition might probe the naturalness of such collaboration and ask what the disruption of its status quo might yield for disadvantaged and disenfranchised groups. In the Canadian context, for example, the issue of who is responsible for responding to the housing needs of refugees and immigrants to the country became a key 'wedge issue', as local, provincial and federal governments positioned themselves for elections, and austerity was provocatively (and potentially dangerously) linked to discourses of citizenship, rights and responsibilities. The chief question here is whether municipalities are to 'pick up the tab' of the consequences of government action at higher scales.

Just as much as 'rage', 'resistance' and 'revolt' have been inscribed in opposition to austerity everywhere, the perplexing sustainability and longevity of governance based on austerity has rested predominantly on making it 'governable' (Davies, 2021) and producing 'co-governance' arrangements that allow for temporarily stable governance. This does not always mean 'selling out' but it might mean making progress in a context of adversity. As much as there is compliance and resistance in co-governance arrangements, they ultimately rely on a degree of collaboration. Over the years covered in our study, there has been a tentative, but recognizable international trend towards progressive municipalism against all odds, both in thought and practice (Hatherley, 2020). The courageous mayoralty of Ada Colau in Barcelona was called by one commentator a 'flame of municipalism that showed a way forward for cities' (Godrej, 2019). In the same spirit, Godrej wrote about Cooperation Jackson, an initiative in that Mississippi city, that they promote 'building democracy through people's assemblies; building a solidarity economy through a network of co-operatives; and getting progressive political candidates elected at city level.' This is impressive in the context of the former federal administration in Washington under President Trump, which showed open animosity against grassroots politics, especially when put forward by people of colour, and in a State that has historically disenfranchised its black population (Godrej, 2019). The outcry, in July 2019, of local Baltimore communities, long victimized and abandoned by federal and state institutions, against the racist insinuation by Trump that they were 'infested' demonstrated a scalar rift in the USA that cuts across race, class and geography. Furthermore, during the COVID-19 crisis and in the wake of the massive Black Lives Matter demonstrations following the murder of George Floyd, many municipalities in the US and around the world showed solidarities with those in their population that were marginalized by systemic racism and socio-economic exploitation.

Lastly, then, we reiterate the significance of collaboration as a central theme in this book and in the governance of austerity more generally. What we are specifically interested in, especially in this chapter and Chapter 5, is 'collaboration as a vehicle for austerity management', often in the sense of mobilizing the local state 'to create 'action spaces', assuming a key responsibility for local social and developmental prospects in collaboration with 'civil society' (Chorianopoulos and Tselepi, 2020: 40). The contribution of this chapter is to imagine collaboration as 'multi-scalar', operating variously at the neighbourhood, city and sub-regional levels. It is continually re-scaling – generally and in response to national and international trends (Davies, 2021; see also Chorianopoulos and Tselepi, 2020). Hollowing out of community services (a case made very strongly in Dublin and Leicester for example) goes along with the insertion of collaborative practices across horizontal planes in most of our case study cities. The latter may, then, be considered a type of downscaling, or even dumping. In fact, in a downward spiral, we see processes of rescaling that lead to austerity, and we see austerity that triggers rescaling.

There are four modalities of collaboration that feature in this context:

- There is intergovernmental collaboration (at the same scale or between scales).
- There is – and this is the main area of our attention here – collaboration of state and civil society actors. Such collaboration can have long histories and is actualized through existing structures of inequality, as is the case in Baltimore where 'collaboration between the local state and civil society has made use of the neighbourhood as a key scale ever since the creation of neighbourhood associations in the early twentieth century to undertake exclusionary practices' (Pill, 2015).
- There is also collaboration between the public and the private sector, and among groups critical of or in opposition to austerity measures, as in the examples of bottom-up solidarities in Athens or Barcelona as well as in Montréal. This latter modality of collaboration has also been linked to longer standing instances of cooperation and solidarity among urban popular groups, communities and territorial units (neighbourhoods, quartiers) (Hamel and Keil, 2020).
- Above all this, although visible to varying degrees, are higher-level institutions and networked relationships that condition the ways in which local actors manage austerity. In the next section, we turn our attention to those higher scales.

Supranational rescaling levers

The EU is a particularly illustrative case of the new types and contours of supranational authority that arise on account of globalization. The speeding up of the European integration process since the mid-1980s has been predominantly cast as a response by neoliberal member states to global economic integration; an attempt by the national authorities to compensate for their diminished capacity to influence the economy politically, by constructing new and market prone scales of intervention at levels higher than the national one (Wissel and Wolff, 2017). The emergence of novel policy arenas at the EU level was anything but smooth, marked by dissimilar underpinning principles and intense power games. The European Monetary Union, or the transfer of monetary regulation from the national to the EU terrain, is a key example of such contentious institutional remodelling.

The prevailing idea behind the Eurozone is that of the Optimum Currency Area, accentuating the transactional benefits of a shared currency and downplaying the relevance of a corresponding fiscal authority and federal socio-political institutions (Koehler and König, 2015). This is essentially a 'monetarist' arrangement, arguing that governments should focus on price stability, as the amount of money in circulation should correspond to economic growth (De la Porte, 2017). In this light, the regulation of the single currency is based on a multilateral surveillance mechanism that scrutinizes member countries' budgetary accomplishments, triggering in a quasi-automatic way the sanctioning of the ones which do not meet the Eurozone's strict fiscal performance standards. Accordingly, in case of a significant downturn in economic activity, member states are compelled to instantaneously instigate restrictive and pro-cyclical fiscal policies. As noted in the latest economic crisis in the EU, however, the prescribed adoption of austerity does not spark economic growth (Chorianopoulos and Tselepi, 2019). Instead, it reinforces a feedback loop of lower demand and cumulative production losses, followed by a drop in government revenues and an increase in the public debt/GDP ratio. Lacking federalized structures of economic governance, the Euro in times of crisis is primarily regulated by the national authorities, which must follow a pre-defined 'recovery' path obstinately connected to austerity (Matthijs and McNamara, 2015).

As also noted in Chapter 5, the imposition of fiscal retrenchment in a slowing down or contracting economy is accompanied by a notable 'scalar dumping' trend (Peck, 2012), meaning that higher authorities 'devolve' responsibilities to lower-level ones, but without commensurate resourcing. Eurozone-stipulated austerity is channelled from the national authorities to cities, shaped by the transfer of new duties and obligations amid shrunken grants and reduced local authority revenue. While recognizing the relevance of national and local settings in shaping rescaling trajectories, the EU is also influencing urban responses to austerity. Reference is made here to the prevalent narrative and practices of EU spatial policies, framing policy goals and regulating access to funding.

The set of standards and rules that define access to EU Structural Funds, for instance, together with smoother modes of power that foster specific priorities, against others, delimit policy objectives at member state level and encourage the re-composition of policy networks (Giannakourou, 2012). From the EU viewpoint, cities and urban regions are apprehended as key nodes in the processes that fashion the global economy. They have, therefore, to be entrusted with the competences required to place themselves confidently within the flows of the global economy (Pelkonen, 2013).

In this light, the EU has devotedly promoted for almost three decades now, a localized development agenda that revolves around the goals of enhanced responsibility in a context of local financial self-sufficiency. Structural funds are increasingly channelled in support of entrepreneurial initiatives that hinge upon locally constructed collaborative governance networks. Local collaboration, in fact, is a precondition for the release of funds, aptly outlined in a series of regulations and guidelines that define the 'European Code of Conduct on Partnership' (CEC, 1993: 9; CEC, 2014). Such scale-sensitive strategies also address territorial issues in member states. Regional authorities, for instance, are portrayed in EU documents as governance platforms, capable of coordinating and directing broader local development efforts. Attempting to impel and frame change along these lines, participation in the EU Committee of the Regions is reserved solely for directly elected regional authorities at Nomenclature of Territorial Units for Statistics (NUTS) 2 level, referring to a typology used for dividing up and classifying territories in the EU (CoR, 2009). Similarly, the eligibility of local municipal authorities to administer the National Strategic Reference Framework or other EU-funded projects rests upon specific administrative, financial and operational capacities, certified by the structural funds, allowing limited room for atypical and non-conforming scalar settings (OJEU, 2013: 400).

Beyond the EU, however, the direct leverage of which is exerted on a limited number of states, there are other overriding forces constraining local political choices across national borders. Credit Rating Agencies (CRAs), by surveying, monitoring and assessing cities' fiscal and policy profiles, tacitly impose austerity preoccupations in local agendas, swaying rescaling paths in an indirect fashion (Peck and Whiteside, 2016). To reiterate earlier points, local choices are often defined by the context of ever-reducing budget allocations from higher to lower tiers of government.

Credit rating agencies

CRAs are private sector companies which evaluate and grade the creditworthiness of a debtor, whether a company, a state or a local government. Their enhanced presence and influence in the global financial markets since the 1990s reflects the limited role of states or supranational authorities in the provision of such information. The pace and traits of global economic integration were shaped by the willingness of nation states to resile from key economic governance functions, acknowledging the role of market forces in regulating the global economy (Perrons, 2004). The very purpose of CRAs, in other words, enhances the neoliberal traits of globalization.

CRAs' rule over cities has grown recently, following the increased complexities of municipal financialization, involving among other instruments, loans, bonds and derivatives, with overlapping sets of legal rights. CRAs simplify the picture and provide a sum of perceived local authority creditworthiness via a three-letter rating system. The seemingly neutral and impartial quality of CRAs' reports, based on solid figures and technical commentary on the fiscal impact of local policy choices, conceals their role as powerful constructs that promote specific discourses of fiscal responsibility and crisis handling (Hinkley, 2015). In the case of cities, for instance, a potential downgrade of a local authority's creditworthiness instantly raises the cost of borrowing. CRA reports, therefore, have overt financial consequences and carry the capacity to shape indirectly the set of actions of those seeking their positive response (Sinclair, 2005: 18). Regarding our case studies and centring on Moody's, one of the major CRAs that evaluate cities, the framing of local policy choices was readily visible in the respective reports.

In Moody's reports, our cities are approached as isolated political entities, urged to adopt and follow particularly stringent fiscal routes at their own initiative, irrespective of developments at the national level. Moody's monitors activities at the municipal level, commenting on the impact of specific local policies on budgetary trends setting up fiscal limits, which are not to be surpassed if positive rating is to be renewed. The example of Athens is apposite. As stated in the 2018 report, '[t]he City of Athens' self-imposed fiscal discipline and controlled spending was key for the city to achieve the positive performance over the past six years, despite the challenging economic environment in Greece. ... However, the city's debt-to-operating ratio should not exceed 32 per cent, a level which Moody's considers as moderate and manageable for the city' (Moody's Public Sector Europe, 2018a).

The monitoring of cities' finances is particularly meticulous and assumes the form of explicit policy cautions and concrete reminders. In the case of Montréal, for instance, Moody's highlights the 'positive announcement' made by the city that 'it would look to find savings in pension and labor costs'. In turn, rating reports focus on specific policy details, holding Montréal accountable for their implementation. On the labour costs issue, for example, Moody's underscores that 'the administration has targeted a reduction of 2,200 positions, roughly 10% of the current level, over the course of the next five years', transforming the role of a rating company into an audit one (Moody's Investor Service, 2014).

In Barcelona, municipal finances are rated positively by Moody's, reflecting 'the city's good budgetary management and solid financial fundamentals'. Reports on the city, however, broaden the scope of inquiry into the traits of central-local relations: they forthrightly point at Barcelona's tight 'operational and financial linkages' with the national government, to stress that 'the city does not have sufficient financial flexibility to justify a rating above that of the sovereign'. What is unreservedly noted as problematic here is that '[t]he central government retains control of Spanish municipalities via legislation, the level of transfers, and the management of pay-raise packages for civil servants'. Attention is directed, therefore, to the scalar articulation of power in the country, putting forward a preferred arrangement of greater local self-sufficiency; one that the local authority should strive for. Otherwise, as stated, 'should Spain be downgraded, Moody's believes this would likely have rating implications for Barcelona's rating' (Moody's Investor Service, 2012; Moody's Public Sector Europe, 2018b).

Calls for local self-sufficiency are also addressed to higher tiers of administration, building reform pressures up. Moody's ratings on the US state of Maryland, for example, although overall positive regarding the shape of state finances, feature an explicit warning against the continuation of fiscal support to local authorities, in our case, the city of Baltimore. As stated, Moody's 'acknowledges the state's economic exposure to … above-average debt and pension burdens stemming from the state's practice of issuing debt and absorbing certain pension costs on behalf of local governments', considering the respective policies as one of the main 'factors that could lead to a downgrade' (Moody's Investor Service, 2018).

CRAs, in short, operate in a similar vein to the EU, yet in more subtle ways. They do not finance local initiatives, as the EU does, circumscribing local choices and policy directions. Nevertheless, they set the tone for local authority borrowing costs and business investment decisions, rendering some policy directions more feasible than others. More importantly, as noted in our case studies, pressure for reform following financial self-sufficiency and pro-austerity budgetary logics is exercised in multiple tiers of administration at the nation state level, permeating political discussion and influencing perceptions of alternative political choices.

These top-down pressures, from the EU level and from credit ratings agencies, highlight the coercive characteristics of vertical scalar relations and the hierarchical face of 'collaboration' as mandatory, and through which urban governance is managed from above. In the following section we explore novel rescaling initiatives in our eight cities, and their implications for driving neoliberal agendas. The most obvious attempt of this type is the reorganization of state space, offering a tangible opportunity to rearticulate the meaning of local policy spaces.

The rescaling experiences of our cities

Rescaling is approached in the literature as a fluid and goal-seeking process, aiming at changing policy objectives and ways of governing, albeit often contested by a variety of actors. In this light, the redrawing of municipal boundaries and the devolution of formal state powers to local authorities seems too rigid and schematic an attempt to alter local policy views and ways of working. Territorial reorganization as a way of promoting rescaling, however, has been noted in most of our cities. There are two prominent and interrelated reasons accounting for this trend. The first one echoes the widespread perception of a municipality or a region as a coherent unit, acquired through a sustained approach of treating such areas as integral entities. Social and economic indicators, for instance, are clustered and collected in these levels, fostering an essentialist view of territory as a solid socioeconomic 'container' (Brenner, 2009). As substance is projected to form, therefore, there's a reflective belief that by altering the structure and devolving pro market duties to cities, the traits of governance will follow suit.

The second reason behind the adoption of the territorial restructuring path lies in the opportunities that this trajectory creates for imposing a particular mixture of policies, decided singlehandedly by the political tiers that define the reform, compelling change. Dublin and Athens fall into this category.

Forced rescaling in bailout countries

The particularity of Dublin and Athens lies in the shattering impact of the 2008 global financial crisis on the two national economies, the Irish and the Greek one respectively (see Chapter 1). Evidently, the grounds vary. In the case of Ireland, for instance, the banks were affected first, as they were excessively exposed to the global bond markets. The government response, an unlimited guarantee to meet liabilities proved very hard on the national economy. By the end of 2010, the state's bank guarantee continued to escalate, and the government was forced to seek and accept a new arrangement from the European Commission, the European Central Bank (ECB) and the International Monetary Fund (IMF), widely referred to as the 'Troika'. The bailout agreement of €85bn, however, came with austerity strings attached, as explained in Chapter 1, and in Gaynor (2020a). It is the structural reforms, however, that put the rescaling wheels in motion.

Amidst the sovereign debt crisis, the Minister for Environment, Community and Local Government in Ireland, issued an 'Action Programme for Effective Local Government', involving a fundamental set of changes for the sub-national tiers of government (DECLG, 2012). Many of the reforms suggested in this document came into effect in the following two years, primarily under the 'Local Government Reform Act' (DECLG, 2014). In short, the main reorganizing aspects of this initiative were the following:

- Local authorities were amalgamated and reduced from 114 to 31 units, decreasing the number of elected councillors from 1,627 to 942.
- The ten regional authorities that existed at that time were dissolved and replaced by three regional assemblies, reducing participating members from 290 to 83.
- A new tax on residential property was introduced in 2013 aiming to fund local authority services. The property tax is levied and collected by the local authorities, diversifying the overall tax base.
- Local authorities' role in economic development was revised and expanded through the establishment of Local Enterprise Offices (LEOs) in cities. LEOs are development-oriented platforms that pursue a locally defined plan that is funded by the national authorities and is in line with the respective national strategy.

Ireland comes across as a particular case, one in which the government decided to socialize private sector banking debts, paid for through cuts in state spending. The national authorities, in fact, strived to present the banks' bailout decision and impact as an isolated incident, thereby distancing the Irish example from other crisis hit countries in the Eurozone. The phrase 'Ireland is not Greece', was uttered repeatedly by the finance minister attempting to reassure investors about the soundness of the country's fiscal indicators (Gaynor, 2020a: 75). As we shall shortly note, there were key differences in the economic settings of Ireland and Greece, accounting for the diverse impact of the global financial crisis on the national economies and public finances (see also, Parker and Tsarouhas, 2018). Such differentiating factors, however, were not reflected in the economic adjustment programmes or the rescaling trajectories the two countries followed.

Centring on Greece, the impact of the global financial crisis on the national economy preceded the Irish one by a few months and was primarily indirect. The already troublesome fiscal performance indicators in Greece were severely affected by the crisis inflicted recession. Fast falling revenues were further aggravated by successive speculative waves, leading in early 2010 to the demotion of government bonds by credit rating agencies to below investment rankings. As the national authorities lost access to the international financial markets, and to sidestep a solvency deadlock, the government settled urgently in a series of loans with the same 'troika' of institutions that appeared in Ireland six months later. The loans agreed with the European Commission, the ECB and the IMF in May 2010 were also conditional upon Greece adopting an adjustment programme in the form of a Memorandum of Economic and Financial Policies. Despite the different crisis contexts, however, the recipe for economic recovery had the same austerity prone and labour market deregulation ingredients. What is equally noticeable is the similarity of the state spatial reorganization routes the two countries pursued. In the case of Greece, the respective reform was launched in 2010, featuring the following points of attention:

- Local authorities were amalgamated and reduced from 1,034 to 325 units, abolishing, simultaneously, 4,000 (out of 6,000) local authority legal entities, enterprises and corporations.
- Prefectures were abolished and regional authorities were transformed from an administrative arm of the state into political authorities, with a directly elected head and council.
- A new property tax was introduced (2013), imposed on all real estate properties in the country. The tax is levied by national authorities and is distributed subsequently to municipalities as part of their annual central government funding.

• An enhanced local authority role in economic development was also introduced through the establishment of localized 'Stability and Growth Pacts'; written agreements aiming to ensure that regional and local plans are in line with the national plans (Chorianopoulos, 2012).

Both Ireland and Greece are approached in the literature as centralized states, and the reforms were presented by the national authorities as a long-awaited response to calls for an enhanced local authority role in local socio-economic affairs. Local authority amalgamations, for instance, were portrayed as generating the necessary economies of scale for the cost-efficient provision of services, also capable of supporting stronger synergies for locally defined development paths (DECLG, 2012). The reorganization of state space during austerity, in other words, was supplemented by the rhetoric of an overdue rationalization of structures, brought forward by extraordinary economic circumstances (Gaynor, 2020a). Interviewees from Athens and Dublin city councils, however, had a different view of the effects of the new governance arrangements. Instead of empowerment, or collaboration, they stressed the cutbacks in local budgets and the reductions in their staffing numbers, exceeding 20 per cent in both cities in the 2010–2015 period (see Callanan, 2020; Chorianopoulos and Tselepi, 2019).

At the same time, the transfer of power and funding from national to local government, and the simultaneous withdrawal of national authorities from key social and developmental duties, rendered the two cities as institutions of last resort. In the realm of social policy, for instance, the severe social repercussions of austerity called for welfare intervention initiatives the cities were entrusted to deliver but did not have the means to perform (Chorianopoulos and Tselepi, 2019). As eloquently stated by a Dublin City Council respondent, 'I think their [Dublin's local authority] approach has been to try and do the impossible with less resources. I mean, the central funding was slashed. And the demands, particularly in the area of housing, have increased exponentially. So, with less resources they have had to deal with more problems' (Gaynor, 2017). By the same token, as we were told by a local politician in Athens, 'clearly, the crisis offered a window of opportunity to the national authorities to transfer responsibilities to lower government tiers. It's a ... now YOU take it 'cause I can't do it any more, kind of logic, as the resources weren't there anymore'. It is from this viewpoint that local respondents perceived rescaling as an attempt to devolve the axe in an era of budget cuts, rather than foster local socio-economic dynamics in cities that had instead been stripped of the very resources required to fulfil local aspirations.

The high degree of similarity in the rescaling traits noted in Athens and Dublin, echoes the coercive quality of institutional dismantling prescribed in Greece and Ireland by the troika creditors. The respective interventions were based on a monolithic and predetermined diagnosis of the reasons behind the fiscal crisis, and on an unvarying neoliberal plan for economic recovery – quite the reverse of the collaborative and empowerment rhetoric through which these measures were imposed. For that matter, the very act of placing matching policies in diverse national settings illustrates the condescending traits of neoliberal ideology. The way rescaling unfolds in the two countries, however, is not likely to be similar, or evolve in a straightforward fashion, as envisaged by its initiators. Previous power structures and policy choices, and the institutionalized commitments that grew out of them, condition the direction of current restructuring efforts (Pierson and Skocpol, 2002). Common assumptions about typologies of European welfare regimes may have to be re-evaluated in this emerging comparative context. Moreover, as shown by other cities in our research, opposing and contradictory understandings of what is effective and ineffective, even within the dominant frame of austerity politics, perceptions of linear transition are put to the test, unleashing episodes of experimentation and flux (Pike et al, 2018). Dandenong in Melbourne and Leicester are examples of this. Dandenong speaks to the ways in which a municipality can compensate or adapt to decentralization pressures, while Leicester underscores the asymmetrical and haphazard trail of state spatial restructuring in the UK, a country that, unlike Ireland or Greece, did not experience a bailout mandate.

Centrally controlled decentralization

The Australian experience has many similarities to varied yet discernible EU local governance trends. In both cases, local governments have faced significant constraints, inducements and commands since the 1990s, 'including increased networked governance for policy-making, decentralization, increased democratic accountability pressures, and governance changes characterized by increasingly competitive intergovernmental multilevel relations for influence and resources' (Brunet-Jailly and Martín, 2010: 240). Additionally, local authorities in Australia have also suffered from diminishing national transfers since the late 1970s and experienced four decades of adapting to fiscal conservatism. In this regard, the Melbourne case study of Dandenong showed how local financial management and planning skills were brought to bear in dealing with fluctuating commitments by the Victorian Government to the revitalization project. This is illustrated by undertaking targeted, area-based investment in the centre area, in renovating the fresh produce market or the theatre, and in building new council offices, library and open spaces. More broadly, the local government's capacity to compensate declining transfers is illustrated by increasing revenue through rates, charges, fees and taxes from 76 per cent of the local budget in the 1998/99 financial year to 79.5 per cent in the 2016/17 financial year. The strong financial administration and ability to sustain and grow some services is further illustrated in growing equivalent full-time employees from 400 in the 1998/99 financial year to 700 in 2016/17 financial year. Our research also highlighted the role of advocacy by local government, often together with local business leaders and non-profit organizations, to lobby for infrastructure and service investments to be made in the local area. While these changing roles and capacities do not replace the need for reliable and workable allocations to be made, it is evident in some cases, like the City of Greater Dandenong, operating in a context of fiscal conservatism has become the norm and they creatively adapt to move out of their spheres of competence to achieve certain policy aims (Henderson, Sullivan and Gleeson, 2020).

The increasing need for financial self-reliance has been compounded in Victoria since rate-capping was introduced by the Victorian Government in 2016. Research indicates that this new measure of fiscal conservatism has not affected total spending, however it indicates that services for the most vulnerable like the aged and disabled have declined in many places as a result (Yarram, Dollery and Tran, 2020: 1). The effects of fiscal conservatism and spending reductions that affect the most vulnerable was a theme in our research in general and specifically in Dandenong, where for example services for former refugees and asylum seekers living in the community had been reduced in 2014. Such pressures were also noted in Leicester, yet they surfaced in a more turbulent way.

There are several key episodes in this process, involving first the formation in 1994 of the Government Offices of the Regions (GORs) by the Conservative administration, representing Whitehall departments in nine English regions. Soon after, the establishment of Regional Development Agencies (RDA) was announced by the newly elected Labour government in 1998; setting up nine non-departmental bodies that were funded by the state and operated at arm's length from ministers. The two structures worked alongside for more than a decade, with RDAs' tasks centering on the administration of the EU structural funds, and gradually encompassing broader socio-economic development duties (Sandford, 2006).

In the first two years after the 2008 global financial crisis, the role and future of RDAs was intensely discussed. The Labour government in office assigned yet more responsibilities to RDAs, viewing their role as key in the country's plan for recovery. Conversely, the Conservative party in opposition argued for cuts in public spending via a sturdy rescaling programme, arguing for the devolution of RDA tasks to politically accountable local authorities (Roodbol-Mekkes and den Brink, 2015).

After the 2010 general election, the austerity state project put forward by the Conservative-led coalition government in the UK pursued a deficit reduction imperative. Amidst crisis rhetoric calling for irrevocable state contraction, the abolition of all regional tier institutions (GORs and RDAs), was announced in the 'emergency budget' of 2010 (Pike et al, 2018). In their place, the government invited local areas to create Local Enterprise Partnerships (LEPs) in 2011, voluntary platforms of collaboration between the local state and the private sector, supported by scanty public funding allocated through competitive bidding processes. There are now 38 such partnerships in operation, usually at the metropolitan scale, offering yet another change of direction in the scaling of economic development in the UK. Alongside LEPs, the government also encouraged the establishment of 'combined authorities' metropolitan governance structures with further powers over local economic development, infrastructure and transport. In this frame, the Leicester example illustrates the variability with which rescaling is translated and articulated locally.

In Leicester, the Leicester and Leicestershire Economic Partnership (LLEP), covers the commuting and urbanized areas immediately beyond the administrative city boundaries. Its purpose is to aggregate sub-regional economic activity, enhance business investment and draw down funds. While the LLEP functions at the metropolitan level, the process of establishing a 'combined authority', with substantial devolution prospects for Leicester and Leicestershire, was derailed. In 2016, the UK Treasury made the agreement conditional on creating a 'metropolitan' Mayoralty. If this happened, it would strip the existing city mayor of powers for economic development and upscale them to the sub-regional level, a higher tier authority with potentially different political priorities. All local authorities involved in the metropolitan structure rejected this option. One senior official commented of the process: 'we were told if you don't go for a mayor, you won't get the full fat option ... I said, 'this is a really friendly, joined up bid so we will take the semi-skimmed' (Davies, Bua and Cortina-Oriol, 2017).

Overall, it appears that in the UK, the nebulous rescaling process that has been unfolding is hardly devolutionary in terms of allowing for democratic participation from below, or indeed giving local authorities a real say in their future without threats (Berry and Giovannini, 2018). The agenda has been set by central government, which controls the purse strings, decides what sort of institutions should be established and what the rules of the game ought to be. As commented by a local authority official: 'unfortunately we are in one of the areas that is not wanting to have a directly elected mayor, so our allocation of money is much less I think than it otherwise would have been' (Davies, 2021: 85). More importantly, from a governance point of view, rescaling seems to erode democratic accountability. The LLEP is a non-governmental body with no direct democratic oversight and little community or voluntary sector representation. It operates at a distance from constituent municipalities, muddling and thus disempowering local democratic processes. As one official commented in a different yet relevant context, 'the public don't really know which services are provided by councils and which by hospitals ... and I think that's got more and more deliberately obscured by privatizing public services, and by things being centralized to government'. The implications of rescaling for public knowhow and democratic accountability is understood here as contributing to an aspect of de-politicization, linked in the literature to rolling nonlinearization of economic development and its official collaborative mechanisms (Moini, 2011; Swyngedouw, 2018).

While in the case of Leicester, the pace of city-regionalization is held up by the unwillingness of local authorities to endorse it, the following case study offers the opposite example. The city of Nantes engaged proactively in territorial reorganization, prompting the pace and providing substance to the competitiveness-oriented urban policy shift noted in France. Seen from the angle of both cities, the local state emerges as a key rescaling actor.

Re-territorializing policy-making from below

France is a paradigmatic case in the rescaling literature, approached as a unitary state that attempted concertedly throughout the post-war period to simultaneously manage developmental and redistribution-related goals. The 'métropole d'équilibre' notion, in particular, that guided spatial planning interventions from 1964 to 1974, aimed at moderating the pace of development in fast growing urban regions, and accelerating it in 'lagging' areas. According to this framework, a network of eleven urban regions was defined across the country, informing the actions necessary to attain balanced development across the national socio-economic space (Levy, 2017). To try and regulate the concentration of growth in the Parisian region (Île-de-France), for instance, perceived as taking place at the expense of other areas in the country, particular development restraints were put in place, including the issuing of central government permission for firms wishing to invest in the area (Lefèvre, 2003). Accordingly, efforts to spread growth to lagging urban areas involved, among other measures, industry (re)location incentives, as well as major investment in housing, public utilities and transportation. This objective of territorial equalization has been ruptured since the early 1980s, as neoliberal forms of state-economy relations were projected and took progressively hold at the local scale.

Arguably, local authorities in France started to gradually experiment with local economic initiatives in the mid-1970s, hesitantly disentangling their fate from diminishing national subsidies and grants (Dikeç, 2006). The wave of institutional reform that took place in the following two decades, however, consolidated a self-serving stance to local development, breaching the comprehensive view of the national economy that informed redistributive targets (Brenner, 2004). Nodal points in this rescaling route include, among others, the Decentralisation Acts of 1982 and 1983, which established the regional tier of administration and transferred extensive state responsibilities to all subnational governance levels. Subsequently, the steady shift in national spatial planning priorities towards urban competitiveness is noted, underscored by the backing of Paris's role as a global city, and the marked support of twelve French cities in their effort to position themselves competitively in the European economic space (Newman and Thornley, 2002). Ever since, urban problems have been increasingly approached by the national authorities in a piecemeal and fragmented way. Throughout the 1990s, for instance, a series of socio-economic intervention programmes focused on specific urban neighbourhoods, defined by the local authorities and funded by the national authorities on an ad hoc basis. More importantly, two acts introduced at the turn of the century, reframed the way urban areas are governed. The 'Chevènement Act' (1999), at first, provided a formal framework for intermunicipal cooperation, establishing joint local authority types with tax raising capacities and statutory policy making duties. The 'Voynet Act' (2000), in turn, institutionalized the role of civil society and the private sector in the new structures. In fact, area-wide policy goals are discussed and have to bear the approval of the 'development council', a participatory platform that reserves a decision-making role to non-state actors (Lefèvre, 2007). In this briefly sketched storyboard of rescaling events in France, the city of Nantes in the country's Northwest is always present, actively engaged and shaping each episode.

Nantes was one of the urban regions that participated in the '*métropole d'équilibre*' framework of post-war spatial planning. It has also managed to address de-industrialization and diversify its economic base, currently exhibiting socio-economic indicators that outstrip the national average. The socio-economic transformation entailed, is attributed by and large to an urban growth coalition, present in the city since the late 1970s, but particularly prominent under the leadership of Jean-Marc Ayrault, Mayor of Nantes from 1989 to 2012. Although somewhat derided by opponents as a clientelistic party machine, the 'system Ayrault' pursued an economic boosterism strategy with a clear rescaling dimension (Griggs, Howarth and Feandeiro, 2020).

Ayrault's economic development agenda was based on large scale urban regeneration projects in the city's neighbourhoods and industrial heritage sites. Branding Nantes as a 'sustainable' and 'creative' place, was part of an internationalization attempt, looking at enhancing local prospects within the Single European Market. Promoting the internationalization of a medium sized city, however, fared better if more forces were drawn into it. Following the broad rescaling trajectories already prevalent at the national level, therefore, an ad hoc 'district authority' was set up in the area in 1992, establishing an intermunicipal cooperation platform chaired by the Mayor of Nantes (Pinson and le Galès, 2005). The advent of collaborative policy making in the region drew from the dominant narrative of local competitiveness and was shaped by the gradual withdrawal of the national authorities from the urban policy field. In this light, it should be approached as an emergent territorial arrangement with a nascent identity, exercising a certain degree of influence at both the local and the national level. Its very presence, in other words, together with other similar examples in the country, called for and justified the Chevènement Act (1999), rendering cross-authority collaborative ventures a formal dimension of state spatial contours (Galimberti and Pinson, 2017). Soon after the launch of the Act, the district authority developed into the 'Communauté urbaine de Nantes' (2002) and, two years later, morphed into Nantes Métropole, with shared planning schemas for Nantes and the adjacent harbor of Saint-Nazaire. In 2014, the French state reinforced Nantes Métropole's tax raising powers and capacities in leading economic growth and competitiveness, research and innovation, urban development, transport and roads, and sustainability. The metropolitan authority brought together 24 different communes with a combined population of approximately 590,000, placing Nantes at the head of the new urban region (Griggs et al, 2020). Nantes looked beyond its municipal jurisdiction, therefore, in attempting to reconstruct its economic development strategies at the city-regional scale. In addition, the corresponding authority also reterritorialized policy making in the city of Nantes, seeking political legitimacy via participatory social policy initiatives (see Chapter 3).

The impact of deindustrialization in Nantes spread well into the 1980s, manifest in the loss of industrial jobs, social unrest and one of the highest rates of industrial striking days in the country (Pinson and Le Galès, 2005). The local authority, trying to respond exhaustively to the proliferating national programmes of integrated urban intervention of the time, divided the city into 11 neighbourhoods, while participatory councils were created in each of the new districts (Lefèvre, 2007). Commitment to participation and proximity governance has been a trademark of the local administration ever since. The mayor at the time of writing, for instance, Johanna Rolland, publicly declared the project of community engagement to be a central plank of her political programme. In fact, in 2015, the local authority put out a position paper detailing the method of civic engagement in policy making. The traits and degree of democratic involvement in Nantes's participatory governance example are discussed more closely in Chapter 3, in view of the engineered and orchestrated quest for consent that the respective processes entail. For the purposes of this chapter, the example of Nantes is illustrative of the interplay between state spatial reorganization initiated at the national level, and the surfacing of new political and territorial actors locally. In this frame, local actors emerge as key reform agents, actualizing rescaling in novel and locally specific 'sites of regulation and arenas of social negotiation' (Nelles and Durand, 2012: 106).

The city of Barcelona reinforces the point that local actors are key agents of rescaling by bringing to the surface differences in the neoliberal model of urban development (Brenner, Peck and Theodore, 2010). Barcelona and Spain illustrate the processes via which EU austerity constraints and global pro-market forces moulded a restructuring route, which was gradually influenced, however, by the path dependent traits of the national and local socio-economic context. In the process, the local level was claimed and asserted by a new social movement, reinventing the role of the local political tier as a contested terrain and revitalizing neighbourhood politics – a form of rescaling through grassroots mobilization discussed particularly in Chapter 3. To unravel the interplay between external pressures and concrete domestic dynamics and legacies, the discussion will now zoom out from the city to remark on the turbulent marks of Spanish urbanization.

Financialization and contested rescaling

Cities in Spain experienced a persistent wave of expansion throughout the post-war era, with average urban population growth rates exceeding 3 per cent per year in the 1950–1970 period (CEC, 1992). Urbanization was part of a wider process of modernization characterized by a shift in economic orientation from a dominant and underdeveloped agrarian sector towards urban–industrial economies. This course of socio-economic restructuring, however, differs substantially from the ideal-typical northern European example. Beyond its belated occurrence, it attests to the particularity of the political and economic features of Spain, but also of Portugal and Greece, framing an urbanization paradigm that has been termed 'Mediterranean' (Leontidou, 1990).

Drawing from the post-war experiences of these three countries, all under authoritarian rule, the Mediterranean city thesis argues that industrialization was not the main pull factor behind the urban concentration trend. Instead, the post-war growth of cities in these countries was driven by the low standards of living in rural areas, backed by a quest to escape political persecution and control, more easily avoided in larger areas. Both reasons, in turn, triggered an informal migratory process, marked by the unpreparedness of cities to accommodate the population influx (Chorianopoulos, 2002). In the case of Spain, the absence of the planning apparatus in regulating urban growth pressures in the post-war era was manifest in housing shortages, reaching one million dwellings in 1961 (Gaspar, 1984: 226–227). Responses to the acute housing issue include the proliferation of illegal self-built constructions in the urban outskirts, seconded by a turn to owner occupation, and the surfacing of the private sector as the prime housing provider. In fact, investment in housebuilding during these years constituted a vital part of the Spanish economy, supported by the state through a relaxation of planning regulations, elevating the role of the construction sector as a key lever for economic development. At the same time, urban social movements emerged in Spanish cities, celebrated in the literature through the work of Manuel Castells (1983). The issue of housing and collective consumption framed popular mobilization, and the goal for political self-determination acquired a distinct urban meaning, rendering the local state as a key policy-change terrain in the struggle for democratic transition (Martí-Costa and Tomàs, 2017). Regional identities notwithstanding, it is also against this background that Spain's new democratic constitution in 1978 earmarked and assigned key social welfare responsibilities to subnational government tiers (Blanco, Salazar and Bianchi, 2020).

In the following decades, the country's economic trajectories were influenced by accession to the EU (1986), and the onset of neoliberalism. Despite the fundamental transformation entailed by aforementioned processes, economic liberalization adjusted soundly around the central role of real estate in the national economy. Two key developments since the late 1990s elucidate the place-specific unfolding of this course. The first, the introduction of the 'Land Regulation and Valuations Act' (1998), eased spatial planning controls in urban areas and increased the supply of land available for residential usage, thereby lowering land values (Cladera and Burns, 2000). The second was the inflated liquidity of the global financial markets, exploited further by Spanish banks via the launch of mortgage securitization policies. The resulting concentration of funds, in turn, was directed by Spanish banks to land developers, pursuing the opportunity for urban investment. The accelerated construction of new homes led steadily to a real estate boom, increasing the country's housing stock by one third in the 1998–2007 period (García, 2010).

What is readily noticeable in the foregoing sketch, is the key role of deregulated global finance in facilitating access to surplus investment sources in Spain. The channelling of these funds to construction activities, however, reflects the specific traits of Spanish urbanization. Financialization trickled down to the urban level following the strong position of the real estate industry in the Spanish economy, and the prevalent social norm of owner-occupation, constructed step by step in the post-war era. Therewith, the introduction of facilitative land-use reforms increased the supply of developable land and mitigated local authorities' capacity to intervene and guide urban growth. Financialization, in other words, operated at different territorial levels, retuning relations between statehood and private capital, as well as among the regulatory scales of the state apparatus (Coq-Huelva, 2013). Likewise, it triggered the redefinition of the housing problem at the local level.

The sudden drop in liquidity that followed the 2008 GEC, led to a banking crisis and, eventually, a sovereign debt crisis, as the state attempted to bail out ailing financial institutions. Soon after, the Spanish government negotiated and agreed upon a financial assistance programme for bank recapitalization with the Eurozone, based on the imposition of austerity measures and structural reforms, like those already noted in other crisis hit EU Member States (CEC, 2012). Austerity in the ensuing recession exposed further the fragility and the deep social inequities associated with the housing market configuration. As unemployment peaked and mortgages couldn't be paid, a wave of home repossessions forced more than 377,000 families out of their houses, while more than three million properties were lying vacant in the country (Blanco and León, 2017: 2177). It is also worth noting that in Spain, repossession does not end the liability of the mortgage holder. At this critical conjuncture, the introduction of stringent fiscal reforms and overriding austerity rules, narrowed down the scope of policy intervention. The 2011 Amendment of the Constitution, aiming to appease Credit Rating Agencies by cementing a commitment to balanced budgets, put into law the concept of 'fiscal stability' for all public administration tiers (Martí-Costa and Tomàs, 2017). The normalization of austerity in Spain was projected downwards from the national to the local level, stunning local authorities and disempowering them in the face of enhanced socio-economic challenges. It is at this moment that a new social movement burst into the political scene.

On 15 May 2011, massive demonstrations in more than 57 Spanish cities sent a signal to Spain and in the EU that austerity and its social repercussions were not to be put up with. The 15-M movement, as it turned out to be known, comprised a great variety of autonomous groups, activists, neighbourhood associations and trade unions, with an unclear stance, at that time, towards entering state institutions (Mayer, 2016). One notable strand of this movement, however, La PAH, created the local electoral platform Barcelona en Comú, leading to the election of 2015 discussed in earlier chapters.

The assembly-type mode of civic engagement of La PAH, centred on the struggle against foreclosures, generating combative responses that reflect the underlying 'footprint' of Spanish urbanization. The social movement that originated from the new housing crisis, however, is more diverse and plural than the one noted in the post-war era. It also responds to global processes, redefining the role of the local level in defending and rethinking social services and welfare institutions against neoliberalism. As the example of Barcelona illustrates, alongside Nantes, rescaling is not a unidirectional process. It creates opportunities for social movements to affirm their local political presence and confront insistent neoliberal narratives and seemingly unavoidable policy choices (Blanco and León, 2017).

Conclusion

In this chapter, eight very different cities are brought into conversation with each other, showcasing the realignment of political–territorial entities toward new policy roles and priorities. Despite the wide spectrum of backgrounds and settings, the chapter brings to light several common rescaling attributes. In all our cities, rescaling was notably influenced by multiple entities, actors and institutions, operating in different regulatory tiers and realms. Key examples include the national and regional authorities, the EU and credit rating agencies, using an array of levers for driving and, if necessary, coercing the reconstitution of policy spaces. Rescaling is intractably linked to fiscal retrenchment and a shift in local governance towards financial self-reliance. Amidst a tidal wave of budget cuts of varying intensity, ostensibly linked to prudent administration, local societies are urged and increasingly compelled to fend for themselves, raising their own revenue and addressing their own problems. In this frame, collaboration is wrapped up in a rhetoric of enhanced local political accountability, and straightforwardly promoted by funding clauses that render support conditional upon the creation of local partnership arrangements. While the collaborative governance shift is purportedly linked to calls for the promotion of a localist agenda, austerity, financial co-dependence and the blurring of the local authorities' role in decision-making, have alarming political consequences.

Regardless of the contingent or even disordered ways with which local political re-orientation is promoted in some cases, the uncompromising qualities of the rescaling message are particularly clear, sent almost concertedly by the governance shapers discussed earlier. From this perspective, neoliberal rescaling advances a paradigm shift in the political positioning of the local level. In parallel, local level efforts to challenge or contest the new urban governance, are also directed outwards, addressing the multiplicity of actors that guide the rescaling course. The emergence of new urban social movements in our case study cities is conditioning and conditioned by the dynamics of scale, rendering cities visible as sites of struggle; incipient yet tangible spaces and places of hope in the abstract and unaccountable global space of twenty-first century capitalism.

5

The Local State in
Austerity Governance

This chapter seeks to better understand how austerity governance has been experienced in the eight cities, from the perspective of the local state. As earlier chapters demonstrate, austerity governance is a real challenge for cities and local states, which can often have competing priorities and imperatives. This is because traditionally, local managers and elected politicians are more inclined than those of the upper tiers of the state to listen to and be responsive to the residents of their local constituencies, because they are closer to them. Consequently, the principles and rules in municipalities for managing public budgets are usually more responsive to social demands. However, if the democratic local state is a political unit, with at least some autonomy to enact its values and citizen preferences, it is also subject to a range of structural and contextual constraints. These include cultures and practices of neoliberal marketization and the level of resources available through transfers and taxation. In that respect, local state managers and elected representatives are caught in a difficult situation. On the one hand, they seek to respond to the needs and priorities of their constituents while, on the other, they operate within the constraints set by national priorities of neoliberal marketization and cuts to resources. This leaves them looking two ways, trying to overcome continuous contradictions, conflicts and uncertainties that arise from this difficult positioning.

In addition to these immediate and contradictory demands on local officials, questions of local state power are strongly connected with urban culture. This idea can be captured, at least in part, through the concept of '*mémoire du lieu*' (memory of place), as defined by Todd (2017: 468). This '*mémoire du lieu*' frames the way local actors perform and build collaboration, and is an important component of local culture which, in turn, informs popular preferences. Thus, local culture, local preferences and pressures arising from the national and international sources discussed in the previous chapter all combine to set conditions in which local states operate in juxtaposition with market and civil society forces. The compromises reached are therefore partly the result of different strategies of civil society resistance that have proven more or less effective in promoting local autonomy and social solidarity.

This chapter is divided into three parts. First, we consider literature on the local state and governance to frame contemporary changes in structure and function. In so doing we pay particular attention to issues of legitimacy and democratization. As Pinson (2015) highlighted, governance – including all the efforts made by researchers to contribute to its understanding – converges with a theory of the state that is still in development. We do not agree with versions of governance theory that suggest a weakened state. On the contrary, from a political standpoint, governance means restructuring and reorientation, rather than retreat. In this context, collaborative governance can be particularly useful in highlighting how the relations between state and civil society are negotiated and restructured, while growing social polarization, redeployment of class divisions, and the future of democracy are on the line.

Second, returning to the economic crisis of 2008 and the concerns about social solidarity and welfare measures arising from it, we consider local state responses and adaptations. How is it possible for local states to address the choices made by national political elites who are focused on the ideology and practice of 'austerity realism' or 'austerity idealism' discussed in earlier chapters? This also draws attention to the need to contextualize the relationship between collaborative governance and local state power.

Third, drawing from our case studies, we consider how local states adapt to and manage demands linked to austerity struggles. As local states experiment in diverse ways with austerity governance, territorial differences become very important. The way actors in civil society – including social movements – challenge austerity policies in practical terms raises the question of how local state hegemonies are defined and involved in building sustained collective action.

Local power, governance and state restructuring

The introductory chapter touches on how the rise of 'governance' as a theory of governing is tied up with the decline and crises in the so-called Fordist mode of labour organization and mass production from the end of 1960s and significantly accelerated by the oil crisis of 1973. Even though the crisis of Fordism and post-Fordist restructuring were geographically diverse, some general features can be associated with it. According to Clarke (1990: 75), the limits of Fordism were numerous, with technical, economic and social aspects:

> The technical limits are defined by the exhaustion of the possibility of raising productivity by achieving economies of scale, by de-skilling

workers and by intensifying labour. The economic limits are defined by the falling rate of profit which results variously from the rising organic composition of capital, rising wages in the face of declining productivity growth, or the limited market for homogeneous consumer goods as incomes rises. The social limits are defined by the growing pressure on profitability, on managerial prerogative and on public finances imposed by the growing demands of the mass worker.

The consequences of those limits were reinforced by the promotion of neoliberal values emphasizing individual responsibility in relation to social concerns, social welfare and the conduct of private life (Beck and Beck-Gernsheim, 2001). Keynesianism, defined as a dominant approach for elaborating public national strategy, was also declining in favour of the promotion of globalized markets. The resultant social and political fragmentation then replaced what used to be considered a stable situation for the majority.

In the face of these restructuring processes, intellectuals and political classes began looking to the idea of governance to revitalize governing, changing the institutional conditions in play and looking for new forms of social and political regulation, given that actors of state, market and civil society were becoming implicated in new relationships. As the pioneering British public administration scholar Rod Rhodes put it, 'So, like Humpty-Dumpty, I have to assert that "when I use a word it means what I choose to mean – neither more nor less" … and wearing my public administration and public policy spectacles, I use governance to refer to the changing boundaries between public, private, and voluntary sectors, and to the changing role of the state' (Rhodes, 2012: 33).

The crises of Fordism and the rise of governance as a new governing model had a significant influence on how people came to understand the role and agency of the local state (Cockburn, 1977). Situated in the space between broader national (and international) systems and structures while also being concerned by social divisions, including class conflicts, their choice of local policies and priorities reflected a negotiation of both these broader structures and local agency. Even if the local state was recognized as being responsive to social demands, it was clear that it was above all an economic and political actor within a larger system, and an inherent part of the nation state. In other words, its destiny could not be imagined without considering the main trends in the development of the nation state, in this context, the crises of Fordism and the turn to neoliberalism. Finally, the role of the local state in supporting economic growth, but also in promoting and managing welfare cannot be understood without considering what was occurring within the institutions of the nation state as a whole.

In the 1980s and 1990s, changes in the role of local governments were related to several factors both internal and external. It became clear that local policy frameworks emanated above all from the nation state, even if local authorities played a leading role. The historic account by Eric H. Monkkonen (1998) of the growth of US cities, for example, underlines the difficulty of understanding who is responsible ultimately for guiding urban policies. Therefore, the configuration of actors and forces is part of an endless process of reassessment, revisiting alliances and modalities of collaboration. Despite its limitations, the theory of governance has been very influential across the international public sector, in suggesting that governing has shifted from hierarchical and state-centred approaches to more plural and inclusive mechanisms involving business and civil society actors beyond state boundaries (Piattoni, 2010).

The most optimistic commentators argued that the theory of governance heralded a new model of collaboration, where class conflicts could be overcome through participation and deliberation. Accordingly, the way it was implemented through policy represented an effort in addressing, on the one hand, the institutional crisis of the state and on the other, citizen demands for democratizing social and political life. The big challenge facing governance thinkers on the left is how in highly marketized global economies, new social-democratic or progressive compromises compatible with egalitarian, multicultural and inter-cultural cities can be built.

This challenge for governance in a globalized, neoliberal age has been the focus of discussion and debate among a many researchers, commentators and activists in the urban field. For example, Le Galès (1995) suggests that the concept of urban governance, as distinct from government, allows us to understand more clearly how local actors are involved in collective action around urban issues, because the state is no longer in a position, on its own, to steer or direct public action. The state remains important, but it has been diminished. It has become just one actor among many others. In that respect, new attention is accorded to sub-national politics and to the different segments of the state involved in guiding or implementing policies.

The redefinition of relations between state, business and civil society tends to transform understandings of the state and more broadly of 'the political'. Above all, the role of civil society comes to the fore. Despite major differences among countries and cities, the ubiquitous move towards governance means that more attention is now focused on institutional and social fragmentation. As Borraz and Le Galès (2010: 146) emphasize: 'The city is proving more elusive, populations more diverse, governments are being rescaled and new modes of governance are being structured'. Local governments and local states are seeking new sources of legitimacy as national sovereignty comes under attack. Globalizing trends combined with growing social demands due to increased social inequalities and polarization have forced local authorities

94

to adjust, even though they are not monolithic and include multiple interests (McGuirk, 2000).

Though governance discourse is largely accepted, promoted and widely disseminated, it has not necessarily lived up to its promises of greater democratization and participation. Network and/or participatory governance do not automatically transform the way policies are implemented, with experts and technocrats still in control. As Hajer and Versteeg (2008: 168) contend, the new practices defined under the governance umbrella 'whether they were labelled as communicative, collaborative or deliberative, might have been vehicles to create more intelligent solutions, but were weak in linking up to the well institutionalized logic of the nested institutions of representative government'. In addition, one can also recall situations when government authorities refer, on the one hand, to the ideology of governance and, on the other, continue to implement reforms with a technocratic approach or through a top-down model of public action (Hamel, 2006; Davies, 2007).

Without getting too deeply into what Hajer and Versteeg call the 'dramaturgical dimension of politics', the reason why proponents of governance have difficulty in establishing its legitimacy is quite simple. Despite the prevalence of governance discourse and/or governance networks in public space, it is the traditional image of representative democracy which still best conveys the best symbol of democracy (Hajer and Versteeg, 2008). This is particularly reflected through the importance given by the media to modern political institutions, with the parliament being the first and foremost place to legitimize political decisions: 'Hence, despite the overwhelming evidence that much politics takes place elsewhere, the media continue to portray the staged moments of collective decision making in parliament as the very essence of politics' (Hajer and Versteeg, 2008: 176). This media bias reflects an important failure of networks and collaborative governance processes. It is as if deliberative democracy and/or participatory democracy, often promoted through governance networks, has been relegated to mini-publics or marginal experiences while mass democracy remains rooted in traditional forms of representation where dramaturgical dimensions of politics come to the fore. According to Hajer and Versteeg, the omission of dramaturgy as an attribute of political legitimacy is one explanatory factor for shedding light on the precedence that the media and the public – mass democracy – continue to give to classical-modernist institutions. So too are continuing class and power conflicts and inequalities. But the lack of public legitimacy of governance is also of prime importance: Why would citizens accept being part of processes that are not recognized as valid, or that they have never heard of? What would motivate them to take part in procedures that are difficult to control? The dramaturgy proposed to them seems to reproduce the power relationships currently in place. Moreover, the most common instruments of governance – such as public hearings – offer few guarantees of results. Finally, most of the time, the impacts are predictable and do little to change pre-existing hierarchical decision-making processes.

In many ways, new governance arrangements are connected to institutional changes in the upper tier of the national state. However, the observations on which they are based also derive from claims made by citizens at the local state level, which then fall on the wider state apparatus. In other words, social claims made by citizens around local issues percolate through other tiers of the state, challenging the traditional hierarchical model of state decision making. At the same time, as we saw in earlier chapters, new social movements are challenging the traditional representation of the political as promoted by political elites. Highlighting the limits of the old political paradigm, these actors who call for diversified forms of engagement and mobilization (Castells, 2012), have contributed directly and indirectly to democratizing politics. According to Cohen and Arato (1992: 562):

> The success of social movements on the level of civil society should be conceived not in terms of the achievement of certain substantive goals or the perpetuation of the movement, but rather in terms of the democratization of values, norms, and institutions that are rooted ultimately in a political culture. Such a development cannot make a given organization or movement permanent, but it can secure the movement form as a normal component of self-democratizing civil societies.

These new values have also been transferred to the institutional mechanisms of the state, interpreted by political authorities in terms of governance, understood as a response to the legitimacy crisis of the state and of liberal democracy (Bauman and Bordoni, 2014).

However, the expectations raised by social actors since the 1960s onwards regarding the democratization of the state and civil society remain a work in progress, to say the least. But what does governance have to do with this? If collective action and claims initiated by the new social movements challenged, to quote Offe (1985), the 'boundaries of institutional politics', the impact of their actions proved difficult to assess, especially when considering the social, cultural and political consequences involved.

Collaborative governance and local state power

The usual understanding of local governmental sovereignty, even though authorities in different national contexts do not share the same view about who ultimately bears legitimacy, is contested by the active role local states are increasingly playing on the global as well as national scenes. This situation has been experienced through our case studies in a variety of ways. The local responses to austerity resulting from the economic crisis of 2008 were expressed accordingly. Christian Lefèvre (1998) draws attention to how the adaptation of metropolitan governments in western countries to globalizing transformations always involves a compromise between, on the one hand, local responses to international competition, and on the other hand, the defense of local values specific to a given territory. In that respect, the problems of legitimacy for local states are not less sensitive or less important in comparison with experiences at the scale of city-regions. 'Politico-institutional' fragmentation also exists within local states. And collaborative governance is never a fool-proof normative model of decision making and action.

It is at the local state level that social demands for democracy were historically most significant. This demand for democratic behaviours and the forms of urban agency connected to them have continued into the contemporary era. As Clive Barnett (2014) highlighted, the literature on urban politics has had difficulty up until now in connecting two distinct strands: one defined around the right to the city and spatial justice, and the other considering neoliberalism from a critical juncture and seeing democracy as an antidote to injustice. Consequently, this is why until now urban studies did not offer an appropriate theory of democratization.

In this respect, we suggest that a more nuanced picture of how urban culture forms part of democracy in action is required. As exemplified in our case studies, collaborative governance – often converging with participatory governance – relies on a 'mémoire du lieu'. Though this notion is usually invoked in relation to nations, to show how specific national values can last over time, our cases show how this also applies at a more local, urban level. In the analysis Todd provides, it is the presence of values passed on by individuals residing in a particular place and through daily interactions that this 'mémoire du lieu' is perpetuated. 'Mimetic behaviours' also play a role in diffusing local values inherited from history and forged in relation to contextual and geographical conditions.

Hamel and Keil (2020: 113) explain that the 'mémoire du lieu' leads us 'to consider what was passed down by previous generations in terms of past experiences and struggles'. But one should recall not only the more visible aspects of this memory but also the intangible ones involved in the cultural dimensions of the social fabric. In that respect, as we know, collective action elaborated by social actors and social movements does not always succeed. The representations and values introduced by these actors feed nonetheless the 'mémoire du lieu' and consequently contribute to framing the general cognitive world within which it is possible to act. In that sense, relations between local actors are entrenched in a web of interactions constantly revisited through narratives, representations and strategies, as alliances are in a constant process of revision and re-definition. Collaborative governance, employed by actors as a template for action, is then affected by multiple influences and tensions. From here, conflicting interpretations are present, often with implicit understanding of democracy.

This situation has been examined at length by political scientists who have both brought to light the difficulties originating from increasingly plural societies and mentioned the incapacity of political authorities to overcome the crisis of the liberal democratic model (Welsh, 2016). This last conclusion is worrying but it is not a surprise. The current problems with democracy, and local democracy, include not only discriminations, exclusions and social inequalities produced by neoliberal capitalism with all its contradictions, they are also impacted by the social and political conflicts of the past that have not been solved. In addition, new controversies have appeared in relation to the environmental, gendered and racial dimensions, making the outcome of political experiments difficult to predict.

In this regard, the example of hybrid forums is instructive. These forums are intended to enlarge the way democratic deliberation can be experimented with in a practical way when considering controversial issues from multiple standpoints, including scientific knowledge, the role played by experts in public forums as well as the presence of information produced by science concerning non-human species. Their specificity is outlined by Farias and Blok (2016), who insists on the importance of the democratization of knowledge production in relation to multiple components ranging from science, technology and the environment to government action on specific issues.

Citizen participation and the willingness to getting involved in these forums raises the question of how such constrained spaces of deliberation can be related to a larger dynamic pertaining to democracy at the national scale. Deliberation is then necessarily confronted with the limits of rhetoric or its bias through demagogy. This problem is endemic to democracy particularly when hybrid forums or mini publics are transferred to a larger scale. But even at the scale of the local state, if not at a smaller scale like the neighbourhood, it remains difficult to connect collaborative governance to broader processes of democratization. Several reasons are given by Farias and Blok (2016) to explain this. The imbalance of resources between social actors is one significant reason. But it also includes the 'design' of these forums, as well as the fact that the focus is mainly on citizen participation, leaving aside other experts or those who do not share the same definition of the context and/or the issues at stake. Therefore, when trying to better understand the content of collaborative governance and its overlap with experiments in deliberative governance, we emphasize that the social and political experiments underway are collective endeavours, where local contexts, including collective 'mémoire du lieu' play a major role.

Local state strategies in an era of urban governance

Our discussion so far has revealed several complex and, at times, contradictory developments in governing contemporary local states. There can be significant asymmetries in power and influence between local and national arenas. While the local state is closest to residents, the challenges and problems these residents face can often be the consequences of policies and decisions taken at higher levels, both nationally and, with the advent of neoliberal, entrepreneurial cities, globally. The many contradictions between the much vaunted 'hollowed out' state of the contemporary collaborative governance era and the persistence of technocratic norms and practices of more traditional, top down bureaucratic and authoritarian practices within local states are also clear. And yet, all this is occurring at a time when there are demands for increased voice and participation in city affairs among residents, together with resistance to the severity of austerity cuts and retrenchments. How these demands are managed, be they ignored, silenced, disciplined, mediated and/or facilitated, tells us much about the continued and continuous restructuring of local states as important sites of local voice, democracy and hope.

Revisiting Borraz and Le Galès' observation that 'the city is proving more elusive, populations more diverse, governments are being rescaled and new modes of governance are being structured' (2010: 146), our final section draws on our eight case studies to explore the rescaling and restructuring of local states within the context of austerity. Specifically, in an era of shifting strategies and scales of urban governance, we are interested in identifying and unpacking the different strategies employed by local states in managing the multiple and often conflicting social demands and practices linked to austerity struggles. In addition, recalling the importance of Todd's 'mémoire du lieu', we draw attention to local cultural practices and governing norms.

Looking across our eight diverse cases, we identify five distinct strategies, presenting these in what follows as somewhat ideal types. However, it is important to stress that the rapidly shifting terrain of urban governance is far messier and more complex than ideal types suggest. As will hopefully become apparent, local states in all our contexts have adopted one or more of these strategies in somewhat different ways, drawing on local practices and norms, and resulting in significantly different political, social and democratic outcomes.

Local state restructuring

Possibly the most radical strategy within our cases comes from Barcelona in the form of the restructuring of the local state through the success in the local elections of Barcelona en Comú (Blanco, Salazar and Bianchi, 2020). As earlier chapters explain, the strength of this movement is partly linked to the intensity of the country's austerity crisis linked with increasing centralization within the national state, but it is also a reflection of the strong tradition, or indeed, in Todd's terms 'mémoire du lieu' of municipal grassroots activism in Barcelona. The movement's political agenda combines a traditional agenda of socio-spatial redistribution and radical forms of co-production and social innovation in both policy and processes of policy making, opening up spaces for deliberation and innovation at neighbourhood levels. In recent years, grassroots mobilizations in Barcelona have incorporated new social groups and benefited from the expansion of digital social networks – notably the Decidem digital participatory platform.

Although the local electoral successes of left-wing activists in Dublin's 2014 local elections marked a similar structural change, unlike Barcelona, this did not herald a 'new municipalism' (Gaynor, 2020a). Despite much talk of 'reform' and decentring of power, traditional top-down cultures and norms prevail with city councillors and officials remaining highly constrained in what they can and appear willing to achieve. Reflecting a strong centralizing tradition within Irish politics from the founding of the state onwards, in Dublin the local council functions primarily as a stepping stone towards the national parliament. Thus, while engagement in local formal political institutions can certainly offer opportunities to unlock the hope for more just and equitable policy alternatives, these are by no means a given. The effectiveness of local state restructuring remains dependent on the effective power of the local state vis à vis other levels. And this is a result of existing 'mémoire du lieu' – of local state and civic activism.

Myth and narrative construction

A second strategy which appears across several our cities is one whereby the construction and reproduction of particular narratives or stories across multiple networks and spaces within the city forge shared understandings and practices. Drawing on very particular local contexts and cultures, this is most evident in the Nantes case where the 'Nantes game' or 'jeu à la Nantaise' explained in Chapter 3, and as outlined by Griggs, Howarth and Feandeiro (2020), is built on a shared narrative of pragmatic municipalism advancing a mode of collaborative governance which has resulted in the fostering of various forms of citizen engagement. However, the political effectiveness of this narrative is increasingly questioned as more recent modes of collaborative governance come face to face with traditional top-down norms and practices. The old classical-modernist order as depicted by (Hajer and Versteeg, 2008: 176) and discussed earlier, with its 'staged moments of collective decision making in parliament as the very essence of politics' appear to prevail in this case, despite local state efforts and successes at myth construction.

Common narratives are also apparent in Leicester, Dublin, Montréal and Melbourne. To varying degrees and reflecting different local cultures, these draw on narratives of rationalization, hardworking entrepreneurialism and shared sacrifice and solidarity. As Davies et al (2020: 65) outline in Leicester, 'city branding [of Leicester's multiculturalism] is reinforced by mythologies surrounding the entrepreneurialism of Ugandan Asian refugees and their successors. It represents Asian entrepreneurialism as an exemplary, even performative model of urban citizenship'. The entrepreneurs migrating to Leicester were credited with underpinning the economic resilience of the city after the crash, especially thousands of Indian businesses in the city. This 'entrepreneurial resilience' narrative contributes to framing the city in ways that are not dominated by poverty and austerity and mapping a constructive sense of place as a way forward. Austerity measures in Dublin came with a new narrative about the origins of the country's crisis, which shifted the blame for the economic crisis from an elite coterie of property developers and senior banking executives to the public at large. Again, this narrative drew heavily on local cultural norms, in this case an ongoing (although changing) hangover of Catholic guilt and sacrifice translated into a strategy aimed at inventing and promulgating collective public blame (and indeed shame) for the crisis as a means of justifying the collective public sacrifice and pain to be endured (see Chapter 1, and Gaynor, 2020a).

In Montréal, Hamel and Keil (2020) argue that local practices of cooperation rooted in cultural norms of solidarity are key to local governance strategies in challenging the post-2008 context which has been imposed in a highly centralized, authoritarian way from the state level. The harshness of austerity policies has forced informal collaboration at local level, with some civil servants who disagree with austerity attempting to mitigate them and help local community organizations and social workers. Melbourne's ubiquitous 'economic rationalism' (a local variant of neoliberalism) as outlined by Henderson, Sullivan and Gleeson (2020) might also be understood as another example of narrative construction rooted in pragmatic fiscal conservatism, recognizing budgetary pressures without resorting to idealized forms of austerity. While these different narratives, appealing as they do to local histories and cultures, appear to have been successful to some degree in sustaining or conferring legitimacy on the local state – perhaps most notably in the Leicester case with its legacies of Thatcherism and the associated erosion of solidarity and resistance, and also perhaps in Montréal where resistance is now fragmented – they have met with resistance elsewhere, such as in Dublin where as we have seen, anti-austerity movements coalesced around the introduction of a new water tax and succeeded in overturning this policy in 2017.

Incorporating and factionalizing civil society

A third strategy apparent across several cases focuses on local state relations with civil society groups. Specifically, municipalities have attempted to both incorporate and factionalize civil society groups within city governance processes. In Montréal, a city with a strong collaborative tradition, Hamel and Keil (2020) argue that one of the main ways the local state controls dissent is through multiple separate or 'siloed' negotiations with the different sectors of the public services affected by austerity measures. This, the authors argue, has resulted in fragmenting resistance, as various sectors negotiate to preserve their own interests, thus dedicating less energy to the building of a unified strategy of resistance and intra-sectoral solidarity against austerity.

Incorporation is also evident in local state strategies for larger civil society groups in Athens, Dublin, Leicester and Baltimore. In Athens, Chorianopoulos and Tselepi (2020: 40) argue that austerity triggered a rescaling process that demarcated the local socio-political milieu with 'the selective incorporation of civil society perspectives and actors in the respective collaborative efforts, foreclosing alternative viewpoints'. Notably, global philanthro-capitalists have played a significant role in the city's governance, while local and smaller groups have been ignored. Philanthropic foundations also play an important role in Baltimore and are fully incorporated into the city's governance processes. As Pill (2020: 147) notes, 'Corporate developer and major 'ed and med' actors, particularly John Hopkins University and Johns Hopkins Health System, set the development agenda for specific sites and gain power to implement through resource alignment with other elites. ... Thus, major development overrides neighbourhood revitalisation'. In Dublin and Leicester, state supports to civil society groups has come to be increasingly focused on the compliant larger groups. Some factionalism is inevitable among the smaller struggling groups, as competition for resources tightens.

Dividing and weakening civil society

Accompanying this privileging of large civil society groups is the weakening of smaller civil society and community groups through cuts in funding and state supports. This was evident in the Athens, Dublin, Leicester and Montréal cases. In Athens, the selective incorporation of partners in the municipality's austerian collaborative shift sidestepped most anti-austerity challenges. It also bifurcated civil society into an elite sector partnering with the city, and a grassroots element that positions itself outside the austerity machine. This grassroots element takes the form of a wide range of solidarity networks that have grown during the crisis. Their goals and practices are particularly varied. They range from networks that gather and distribute basic goods, to solidarity structures that experiment with nonmonetary and collectivist initiatives (Chorianopoulos and Tselepi, 2020). In Dublin, although state moves to weaken and close more vocal community groups pre-dated austerity, efforts to keep them going were dealt a major blow over the austerity period, with cuts to these smaller, more politically active community groups of 35 per cent in the context of overall cuts in national government spending of just 2.82 per cent during the 2008–2012 period. Moreover, state supports to remaining groups became restricted to service provision alone, with research, policy and lobbying functions no longer funded (Gaynor, 2020a). As in Athens and Barcelona however, the crisis in Dublin also gave rise to a growing range of solidarity networks at community levels. With activities ranging from fundraising for local families, to soup kitchens for the homeless, these groups also position themselves outside the state, voicing a strong disillusionment with formal politics and, in some instances, experimenting with alternative more participative forms of collective organization (Gaynor, 2020b).

In Leicester, Davies et al (2020: 565) argue that, 'the local state accrued the governing resources to deliver austerity while disorganizing and containing resistance' through cuts meted out, in part, to the voluntary and community sectors. The same is true of Montréal, where significant cuts were made to both the budgets of local civil society groups and social services. However, in this case it was the state government of Québec which made these cuts, while bypassing the municipal authorities. This has put community organizations in a difficult and uncomfortable position where they need to resist and contest austerity and, at the same time, manage and deal with its effects. As Hamel and Keil (2020) note, civil society actors struggle to build a unified front to resist these measures, while some local state actors side with civil society groups in opposition to the provincial state's policies. While civil society groups in Dublin, Leicester and Montréal find themselves in a very difficult situation fighting for survival in the face of state cuts, new networks of solidarity, support and hope have grown in Athens, Barcelona and Dublin. Operating independently of local states and espousing alternative values and practices to those imposed through austerity, they have helped carve out tenuous new spaces of hope in some instances.

Marginalizing, ignoring and/or containing local demands and practices

The final strategy for managing local demands and practices which appears across several our cities is simply to marginalize, ignore and/or contain them. This is most clearly exemplified by the Baltimore case where, as Pill (2020: 143) notes, 'The elites governing Baltimore are corporate developers, major 'ed and med' anchor institutions, and nationally operating private philanthropies, with a mix of other non-profit organizations, anchor institutions, and philanthropies playing roles at the middle and lower tiers.

Citizens are excluded from these opaque governance arrangements'. Any citizen participation that does exist is characterized by Pill as 'marginal and tokenistic', with a schism existing between political leaders and institutions (including those of civil society) and the young African American activists who have risen to prominence in the city after The Uprising (discussed earlier) to protest its iniquity and carceral governance.

Athens shows similar characteristics. Although attempts at collaborative governance have been in place since the 1980s, with the most far-reaching of these attempts – so-called 'action spaces' responsible for local social and developmental prospects in collaboration with civil society – launched in 2010 (Chorianopoulos, 2012), the reality is that they have involved an elite sector of the increasingly bifurcated civil society sector. 'The views of grassroots networks regarding these collaborative governance policies launched by the city range from the guarded to the outright contentious.' (Chorianopoulos and Tselepi, 2020: 50) and the local state operates independently of these local solidarity networks.

In Dublin, although the state finally capitulated to the protests and demands of the so-called 'water movement', this only came following a concerted campaign to discredit, marginalize and contain this movement. All three of these cases demonstrate an extremely low level of legitimacy among marginalized groups and individuals in the eyes of municipal authorities, and vice-versa. Privileging the demands and interests of elite resource bases over those of their own residents, local authorities are engaged in a risky strategy given the strength of frustration and anger among increasingly marginalized communities.

Overall, our cases reveal a diverse range of strategies and tactics employed by local states in negotiating and managing the multiple and often conflicting demands of citizens struggling under the weight of austerity policies and retrenchments. A rescaling and restructuring of local states is apparent as local power constellations, combining norms of collaboration and participation echoing the earlier discussion of governance theory and with local cultural traditions and memories of place, vie with national and global political forces. As our cases demonstrate, the relative strength of each of these levels leads to very different outcomes – both for the structure and scale of local states themselves, and in terms of social justice and democracy more broadly. What is clear, however, is that the local state plays a very prominent role in setting the tactics and strategies that define the form of 'governance' in each city within constraints imposed by national policies of austerity and neoliberal restructuring.

Conclusion

The chapter explores how collaborative governance operates from the perspective of the local state, which we have defined in institutional, political and spatial terms. With that goal in mind, we explain the diverse paths taken by local states facing significant territorial and urban issues in the context of austerity and economic crisis. However, local choices and strategies are not elaborated in a vacuum. They rely and draw from local culture, including 'mémoire du lieu' as a meaningful element, whose role is embedded in the history of place. In addition, our cases demonstrate that local states are by no means completely autonomous social and political agents. Their abilities to guide local choices and to control urban policy and planning is the result of an interplay of internal and external factors, including global influences but also inputs from diverse components of the nation state. Due to this changing regulatory capacity, despite its inability to give a satisfactory account of state restructuring, the concept of governance proves to be useful in understanding the challenges facing contemporary local states. It highlights the institutional crisis of the state and helps us understand how the state's traditional model of regulation is contested and redefined in civil society. Collaborative governance in that respect may be characterized as going hand in hand with cooperation, even though social and political conflicts are inevitable.

But local state power is also at stake. The 'sovereignty' of the elected municipality is fragile and characterized by transitory arrangements. The notion of governance is also helpful in understanding this fragility. Local state strategies for negotiating and managing austerity vary considerably and involve a diverse range of actors. If their capacity to influence political choices and outcomes can be enhanced through collaborative governance, the strategies of these actors are often distinct and conflictual. However, given the importance of local culture which provides the substratum of democratizing processes, we reiterate the importance of the 'mémoire du lieu' in exploring the normative context within which local struggles emerge and are negotiated.

Our eight case studies have given us an opportunity to explore the nuances and complexities of how local states are responding to the multiple and opposing demands regarding austerity policies and measures. The five strategies identified in this chapter are not all equally effective in challenging institutionalized and dominant models of regulation. For example, when comparing Barcelona to Dublin, the new emergent left in Barcelona succeeded in creating new spaces for policy deliberation and innovation within local neighbourhoods, while in Dublin similar political changes at local council level did not materialize into a 'new municipalism'.

Local contexts also inform the narratives local actors employ either to mute resistance or build legitimacy for their own policy choices. This is observed in several cases, particularly Dublin, Leicester, Nantes and Melbourne. In addition, in countering resistance to their ideology, authorities have sometimes been successful in dividing and weakening civil society, although not always, and sometimes as the unintended outcome of austerity rather than deliberately. Resistance, in different forms, is still evident, where networks and groups are organizing independently of the state. In Athens, Dublin, Leicester and Montréal public authorities were able to adjust their discourses and policies according to sectorial issues (health, welfare, education and so on) for letting social actors believe that austerity measures were not identical for everyone. Finally, the last strategy exemplified by a number of cities in our study highlights the risks posed by elite, apolitical entrepreneurialism whereby local demands are simply ignored or contained. This is clearly the case, for example, in Baltimore where a strong corporate regime is in place. It is also seen in Athens and Dublin where local state legitimacy is extremely low.

These strategies illustrate myriad facets of austerity governance and why it is important to consider it from multiple perspectives, alongside the exigencies of global capital, the narratives of public authorities, and the multiple and, at times, competing discourses of social actors. As we have argued, the proximity of the local state to local priorities and demands makes it a key site of austerity and political conflict. This can translate into popular resistance as austerity is implemented. Politically and institutionally, the move from governing to governance discussed in the first section of this chapter provides an opportunity for local states to engage with and attempt to manage this conflict as well as the opportunity for residents to have a voice. Culturally, the local 'mémoire du lieu' plays an important role in influencing the dynamics of such governance interactions. While these local political and cultural dynamics provide some scope for increasing local democracy, this is necessarily constrained by broader national and global exigencies and ideologies. Local states, as critical actors within such governance arrangements, are caught between the competing exigencies of residents and those of austere, marketized nation state elites. The different strategies that local states employ to engage and/or fragment resistance within this broader context ultimately determines the democratic potential of local governance within different historical, political and cultural contexts.

6

Urban Cultural Diversity
and Economic Migration
in Austere Times

Introduction

Economic migration flows, accelerated by globalization, have substantially increased the cultural and ethnic diversity of Western societies with high GDP economies. As a large part of these migration flows are motivated by the aspirations of those living in the Global South, or the majority world, to improve their living conditions in more economically prosperous countries, the result in the host societies is not only a substantial increase in ethnic and cultural diversity, but also greater social challenges in accommodating difference as well as the policy challenges of addressing socio-spatial inequalities that already exist in cities. The rapid growth of inwards migration not only poses a formidable challenge from the point of view of intercultural relations, but also for the social and spatial cohesion of the destination societies. The resulting inequalities add to the racialized geographies of the early 21st century in many Western countries. The different kinds of migrants coming from the Global South – labour migrants, refugees, asylum seekers – and the places in which they concentrate, together with the local disadvantage created by histories of racism and colonialism of the last century, are amongst the most vulnerable to the dynamics of social marginalization and stigma. These dynamics have been exacerbated in many Western cities since the 2008 Global Economic Crisis (GEC) and the introduction of austerity policies discussed throughout the book.

This chapter discusses the way that (neoliberal) austerity has impacted social, racial and cultural inequalities and the ability of collaboration to support more inclusive democratic cities or resist exclusions. The basic premise is that cities play a fundamental role in the dynamics of social inclusion or exclusion of economic migrants and other racial and ethnic minorities, and in the way that societies cope with the challenge of recognizing and accommodating cultural diversity. This is due to at least three phenomena: first, cities are the places where the vast majority of the newcomers settle and where the greatest cultural and racial diversity can be found; second, cities concentrate a wide array of services and infrastructures and are the site of policy that creates or removes opportunity for the social inclusion of migrants and minorities – for example schools, social services, health and community centres, sport and cultural facilities, parks and squares, urban revitalization, public transport or migrant settlement services; third, cities are the places where most of the relations between different cultural and racial groups (i.e. migrants-hosts) develop, with the quality of such relations determining the social and political inclusion of minorities.

Starting from this premise, the chapter argues that the social impacts of neoliberalization and austerity have disproportionally injured cultural and racial minorities living in lower-income city areas. Moreover, in many of the cases analysed, the conditions of increasing economic hardship have triggered a sense of competition between the most vulnerable social groups, leading to xenophobia and the growth of the far right. In accelerating the dynamics of social and spatial segregation, austerity has also debilitated the spaces in which attitudes of recognition, respect and reciprocity between different cultural groups develop. Consequently, we suggest that neoliberal austerity threatens to intensify social disparities between different ethnic groups and seriously weaken the inclusive and democratic character of cities. The chapter, however, also reveals the existence of signals of hope – signals that are intimately related with the new collaborative dynamics that have emerged in urban areas as a reaction to austerity conditions in some cities. Socioeconomic hardship stimulates the development of myriad practices of solidarity and social activism in which ethnic minorities – frequently female cultural leaders – play a prominent role. Moreover, in many of the cities, horizontal practices of solidarity and mobilization have been complemented by new dynamics of public-community collaboration articulated around spatial and cultural issues, for example in urban revitalization efforts. If cities are the places where the dynamics of social, spatial and cultural exclusion can be most intense, they are also the sites where the pillars of political and social solidarity can be (re)built.

The chapter will compare the experiences of the cities in our study and consider the theoretical and normative lessons that can be drawn from the comparison for those concerned with racial equality and political solidarity. We developed a three-tiered analytical framework to explore the impacts of neoliberal austerity on political and social equality in cities and the role that collaboration can play as an intermediating arena. We developed this analytical framework from the analysis of evidence collected in the case study cities. These cities were not selected for their special characteristics with regards to cultural diversity. However, the heterogeneity of circumstances is illustrative of the different challenges and strategies that cities may adopt in relation to this question. We focus our attention on three cases (Dublin, Athens and Barcelona) that have gone through a rapid increase in economic migration in the last decades; three cases (Melbourne, Leicester and Montréal) with a more consolidated tradition of multiculturalism; and a singular case, Baltimore, in which the fundamental challenge stems from the long-term racially structured segregation of the urban population. The three pillars of the analytical framework rest on salient elements in literatures on cultural diversity in cities, including socioeconomic conditions, political orientation and institutional frameworks of cultural diversity and the quality of the public realm. Following the analysis of literature and the eight cases, we conclude the chapter by stressing theoretical and normative lessons and new lines of reflection for policy suggested by our study.

The impacts of austerity on cultural diversity and socio-political equality: an analytical framework

Cultural diversity in cities has been a central theme in the social sciences for a long time. Much of the literature has been concerned with the limits and possibilities of assimilation or pluralism as well as entrenched patterns of race relations. Since Simmel's pioneering analysis of strangerhood (1908) and Park's conceptualization of the 'marginal man' (1928), the experience of 'others' who do not belong to the dominant group has been studied and framed to show how social distance may persist or be dissolved over time. Urban sociologists from the Chicago School worked from the early to mid-twentieth century on a category of studies relating to cultural contact and conflict, defining much of the early work on diversity in cities through models of community succession (for example, Thomas and Znaniecki, 1918). More recently, social science and in particular urban studies has turned its attention towards the potential role cultural diversity can play in stimulating economic growth, enhancing vitality in neighbourhoods and supporting tolerance and equity (Fainstein, 2005).

After World War Two, the most common newcomers to Western cities with high income economies have been labour migrants and, while some are highly educated and from prosperous backgrounds, like many of Leicester's Ugandan Asian refugees in the early 1970s, most are ethnic minorities who locate in often downtrodden parts of cities to fulfil roles that are unappealing to locals (Alexander, 2017). These labour migrants are often on low wages and come from less developed regions 'which belongs to the world of "others" in opposition to which the hosts have elaborated their identity' (Zolberg, 2000: xvi). Many studies have tracked changes in racial and ethnic composition in Western cities since World War Two, for example in US and Canadian cities (Fong and Shibuya, 2005; Farrell and

Lee, 2011), in UK cities (Robinson, 2010) and Western European cities (Alexander, 2017; Arapoglou, 2012).

While some Western cities, like Melbourne, Leicester or Nantes have undergone multiple transformations since the end of World War Two in terms of ethnic makeup, for other cities like Athens, Barcelona and Dublin, labour migrants are a newer phenomenon and a small yet growing feature of the urban population. Racial divisions have a longer history and are much more consolidated in cities like Baltimore, that were planned on racist lines from the early twentieth century. The process of diversification is shared among many Western cities. However, there are significant differences in terms of patterns of residential segregation and integration, quality of the urban environment and housing and in the lived experiences of migrants and established communities. The affordability of the housing market for example is strongly determinate of residential living patterns. In Athens there are low levels of segregation and high levels of affordability (Kandylis, Maloutas and Sayas, 2012), while in Barcelona urban revitalization programmes and gentrification processes have produced the 'emergence of micro-pockets of marginalization of vulnerable populations (including) non-Western foreign groups' (Arbaci and Tapada-Berteli, 2012: 289). Discrimination in industrial employment offer and pull-or-push factors attached to existing ethnic or multi-ethnic neighbourhoods also can play a role in residential settlement patterns (Fong and Shibuya, 2005).

Realizing the benefits of diversity and achieving race equality in cities requires convivial interactions between groups, though the way racial and ethnic minorities are received within cities and their neighbourhoods varies from acceptance and indifference to fear and hostility (Alexander, 2017). A growing number of researchers have taken critical lenses to the city and neighbourhood levels as intricate sites, as 'micropublics' for negotiating social contact and reconciling cultural differences, despite occurring within the same national policy context (Amin, 2002; Lobo, 2010). Studies have shown that where existing residents feel threatened or invaded by migrants it is difficult to negotiate differences, residential segregation is stimulated, and often hostile reactions occur when exclusion persists. Conversely, when the host community reacts in a welcoming or even ambivalent way, many positive outcomes can emerge. For example, the presence and mixing of diverse cultures in one setting can help to 'dampen negative stereotyping' of minorities (Farrell and Lee, 2011: 1108) by minimizing mistrust or helping to revert processes of urban decay by reversing population decline or through entrepreneurship and creating a 'sense of vibrancy' by filling commercial vacancies or through street vending (Maly, 2005).

In considering the existing literature, we have identified three defining features of communities' receptiveness to culturally diverse 'others'. These features have a strong urban dimension and can determine the democratic and inclusive character of cities, and of the host society as a whole. First, there appears to be a highly synergistic relationship between pre-established well-being in a community and its capacity to empathize and relate to minorities. Second, a multicultural society will have a political structure that respects diversity and a set of policies directed towards supporting multiculturalism, typically with a focus on accommodating difference rather than an assimilation focus. With these baseline conditions in place, the third factor refers to the quality of public realm, which plays a fundamental role in supporting diversity (for example, in affordable and diverse housing typologies) as well as in providing a public sphere apt for lasting encounter and social mixing between culturally diverse groups. These categories seem the most important, though there are other reasons why a society may have differing attitudes to culturally diverse groups, for example past experiences of migration (an expression of memory of place) and certainly irresponsible media coverage.

The framework presented in Figure 6.1 helps highlight how neoliberal austerity can impact upon the democratic and inclusive character of cities, focusing on the capacity of the host societies to recognize and accommodate the cultural 'otherness' represented by migrants and ethnic minorities. The framework plays particular attention to the three aforementioned factors: the socioeconomic well-being of the host communities, the local institutional frameworks and the political orientation of local authorities, and the quality and character of the (urban) public realm.

We start from the assumption that these defining features of cities can be deeply (and negatively) affected by the social, economic and political conditions generated by neoliberal austerity. However, the final impacts of these trends can be filtered by collaborative practices that precede or

Figure 6.1: An analytical framework for the understanding of austerity impacts on cultural, political and social equality in cities

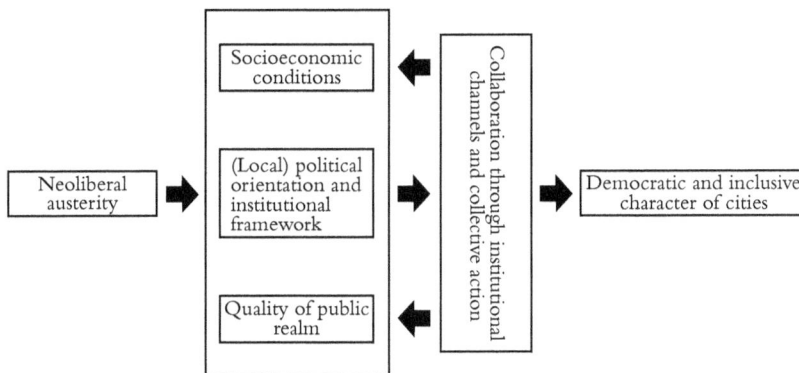

are stimulated by austerity itself, be it practices of horizontal collaboration between citizens or between (some segments) of the citizens and (local) public institutions. The dynamics of collaboration, in the context of austerity, might perform an ambivalent role. Practices of collaboration across different social and ethnic groups can contribute to the capacity of local communities to cope with socioeconomic deprivation and in more general terms to confront change. However, the kind of social ties that are generated through practices of social cooperation can also reinforce a kind of bonding social capital that contributes to the fragmentation of communities, usually along the lines of ethnic divisions, and generate new dynamics of exclusion. On the other hand, practices of solidarity can constitute new forms of bridging social capital that reinforce the dynamics of recognition, encounter and mutuality between different social and ethnic groups. The setting of institutional forms of collaboration and engagement such as advisory boards and other forms of public-community partnership exemplified in what follows can also perform a crucial role in the process of political recognition and empowerment of ethnic and racial minorities. The specific design and composition of collaborative and participative arrangements, however, may also respond to political patronage logics and reproduce pre-existing asymmetries between and within minorities.

In the following three sections we deepen this discussion of the meaning and the importance of the three defining features, both in theory and as we have discovered in practice from studying eight city contexts in the 'urban north'. Through our case studies, we consider how these aspects have been affected by austerity in different cities, and the role that collaboration has played in modulating these impacts. This analysis will result in a typology of different urban models of social and political integration among migrant populations, based on existing literature and expanded through the consideration of multi-case study findings on the intersection of economic migration, austerity and diversity.

Neoliberal austerity, socioeconomic distress and solidarity

The first overwhelmingly strong factor for supporting convivial relations between different cultural and racial groups in cities relates to the socio-economic conditions of the dominant communities as a precondition for supporting their capacities in confronting change. One particularly illuminating study on this topic was published in 2002 by Ash Amin, based on three English neighbourhoods where etihc cultural differences had been negotiated differently at the local level at a time of economic restructuring. He found that 'economic collapse removed the workplace as a central site of integration (and) ethnic resentment has been fuelled by socioeconomic deprivation and a sense of desperation' (Amin, 2002: 962). Since the study, socioeconomic deprivation has been compounded in the UK and many other countries by austerity policies and even more scarcity in welfare, community facilities and employment opportunities. Material privation or well-being is directly linked to capacity for empathy or likelihood of aggression in cultural relations.

Where there is a high sense of social worth, the presence of ethnic minorities becomes just one feature of diversity often recognized and sometimes celebrated. For example, Nyden, Maly and Lukehart (1997) found that in US cities where minority groups make up most of the population, their multi-ethnic character was often 'flaunted locally as one of the city's biggest assets in terms of the expanding array of ethnic restaurants and tourist dollars that these areas attract'. Where these conditions are absent and the sense of social worth low, the presence of new labour migrants of diverse backgrounds can be met with fear and rejection. 'Local residents, especially in poor neighbourhoods where labour migrants tend to settle, may feel their territory has been invaded ... feel 'trapped' (and) the reaction may be to 'defend the territory under siege' (Bauman, 1995: 10–11). This may express itself in local acts of violence or support for xenophobic parties' (Alexander, 2017: 32). Alternatively, households on relatively higher incomes may flee their neighbourhoods (for example white flight), producing patterns of ethnic and economic segregation where even fewer opportunities for ethnic mixing exist, for example in segregated local schools. As Fainstein argues 'without a national regime that is committed to equity, heightened competitiveness of a particular city will likely only produce polarization, and diversity may result in rivalry rather than tolerance' (Fainstein, 2005: 16).

The comparative analysis we undertook supports the argument that debilitated welfare systems, with pronounced social divisions, do not support an easy settlement transition for migrants, limiting possibilities for conviviality between existing residents and newcomers. International migrant flows started recently in Dublin, Athens and Barcelona (migrants make up only approximately 20 per cent of their populations, compared to 72 per cent in Greater Dandenong in 2016 or around 50 per cent in Leicester), in the context of intense economic growth since the second half of the 1990s until the GEC. In these cities, characterized by the weakness of their national welfare states, the dynamics of competition between the most vulnerable social groups was very strong already in the years of economic growth. Baltimore is a very different case, with a long history of socio-spatial segregation of the African American community, which accounts for 64 per cent of the local population and has been forced to live in ghetto conditions for a century or more (Rothstein, 2015; Pill, 2020). In some other Western cities, poverty is also concentrated in neighbourhoods, predominantly with people with colour as residents, as in Nantes. However, patterns of spatial segregation are most pronounced in the US case of Baltimore.

Conversely, we learn from cases like the City of Greater Dandenong in Melbourne, how lasting welfare has greatly enabled settlement and inclusion, particularly given access to public healthcare, transport, education at the primary and secondary levels, families benefits for unemployment and disability as well as the specific support provided to low-income migrants within the general welfare system, such as through translation for services as well as job-training in a buoyant metropolitan economy with relatively low unemployment (4.25 per cent in 2018). Here, we also discovered very strong inter-ethnic collaborative structures, such as the long-standing Inter-Faith Network of Greater Dandenong that brings together leaders across the highly diverse community to address common concerns, share in community celebrations and generally provide a supporting framework for local intercultural relations. Such collaborative structures have provided targeted access by governments to a linked-up community to gain insights about needs and preferences relating to policy change across issues ranging from domestic violence responses to urban revitalization.

While the intersection between social and racial or ethnic inequalities and the resulting dynamics of competition or collaboration between different social groups did not necessarily start with the most recent economic crisis, it certainly appears to have exacerbated divisions and created some new alliances. Echoing Amin's (2002) findings from the UK, our case studies reveal that economic recessions and austerity policies tend to stimulate the feeling of competition between the most vulnerable social groups, for scarce resources such as jobs and public services. For example, some respondents identified worrying signals of increasing racism in the poorest neighbourhoods of Barcelona, coinciding with the beginning of the economic crisis. According to a community activist, "This situation has been used to consolidate a very racist discourse, and to generate an atmosphere of competition: 'the priority must be the people from here', 'why should they give help to the migrants?' … This (discourse) has had a very important impact because it has been normalised" (cited in Blanco, 2017).

On the other hand, however, in some of the cities analysed, including Barcelona, conditions of scarcity have favoured the development of new dynamics of solidarity between different ethnic groups. Whereas Athens went through a significant increase in xenophobia and support for the far right, a significant expansion of solidarity with migrants and refugees articulated through NGOs and a wide range of informal networks has also taken place. In Barcelona, the anti-housing eviction movement – mainly represented by the PAH (Plataforma de Afectados por la Hipoteca) played a very important role in forging inter-ethnic bonds between natives and newcomers, highlighting common interests against economic and political elites. The slogan 'refugees welcome, tourists go home' captured this spirit. According to some respondents, these processes played an important role in counteracting the rise of xenophobic attitudes (in the sense of fearing otherness) that could otherwise have resulted from the escalation of the economic crisis.

In short, austerity may result in greater anomie and social fragmentation, but it can also favour the building of new bonds of solidarity. The kind of solidarity dynamics generated by economic hardship, however, can strengthen the ties between 'the equals' – i.e., the nationals – or facilitate new dynamics of cooperation between the 'the diverse'. Practices of 'solidarity' launched by the far right in Athens, for example, are restricted to the nationals and explicitly exclude non-Western foreigners. The only practices of horizontal cooperation that can promote the inclusive and democratic character of cities are those that build bridges between culturally diverse groups and join them in shared pursuits. We discovered such practices in those places affected by austerity, like Barcelona, as well as those less directly affected by this dramatic episode and with evidence of ongoing strong welfare to provide a basis for social and economic participation, as in Melbourne. Perhaps one difference here is that in places affected by austerity the joint struggles of diverse communities are on specific issues, such as housing, while in places with a strong foundation of welfare, the bonds of solidarity are not necessarily driven by crisis-related issues and form a regular collaborative practice of the community. The extent to which multiculturalism can help to articulate the working-class experiences collectively also depends on the political orientation of government administrations and institutional structures.

Local political orientation and institutional frameworks

Relations between culturally and racially diverse groups are profoundly marked by authorities' political orientation and institutional frameworks. The literature that stresses the importance of national responses to immigration through notions such as 'citizenship regimes' (Vink, 2017), has been recently complemented and enriched by other streams highlighting the significance of local-level policy variations and the impact of local politics and institutional frameworks in the integration of migrant communities. Michael Alexander (2017), for example, developed a comprehensive framework based on the comparative study of four Western European cities for identifying the various ways interactions occur between a host society and migrants based on local authority attitudes and policies (see Figure 6.2). The model presents four archetypes of relations and is based first on a temporal dimension: whether local authorities consider the migrants to be transient or permanent. In the first case, a transient attitude is evident in policy that tends to ignore the needs of migrants and any problems (for example spatial segregation) that emerge because it is considered they will pass. The next stage is when migrants are considered temporary. The final two categories occur when local authorities treat labour migrant presence as permanent. In this case, there are assimilationist-minded authorities assuming that migrants' Otherness will disappear over time or a 'pluralist' approach towards migrants whereby a local authority 'defines the city as a complex of minorities, subcultures and lifestyles, in which Otherness is a permanent feature' (Alexander, 2017: 36). Local authority actions reflect the wider host society's response to newcomers. At one extreme Alexander discovered xenophobia and ethnic tensions (for example, in Paris, Bradford) while at the other various forms of pluralism, for example in vibrant mixed neighbourhoods with interracial marriage. Mirroring these outcomes were, on the one hand, local policies directed at disregarding cultural minority needs or 'deliberately marginalizing ethnic-based political mobilization (such as Paris)' or on the other hand, policies directed at inclusion and the right to difference, such as specifically targeted support programmes in health and education or 'the establishment of ethnic 'advisory councils' (like Amsterdam)' (Alexander, 2017: 5).

In relation to this point, multiculturalism becomes a position maintained by politicians of different parties and coalitions and is reflected in strong institutions and backed by strong political and community leadership that offer local forums in which to negotiate differences, support mixing and build compromises. These values enshrined in institutional practices permeate down to the local level, where cultural communities find multiple ways to become involved and integrated, for example active participation in political roles by ethnic minorities.

The comparison between our case studies confirms the existence of significant differences between the local political and institutional responses to the challenge of cultural diversity, as well as significant differences in the resulting experience of migrant inclusion endeavours. As commented earlier, the most worrying political reaction to the economic crisis and austerity detected in our study was the rapid growth of the neo-Nazi party Golden Dawn in Athens, which gained four seats in the City Council (16.2 per cent of the votes) in the local elections of 2014 (it has since declined electorally and was designated a criminal organization in 2020). However, this belies some of the progress made in actual policy to support diversity at the city level. Foreign citizens accounted for 22 per cent of the city population in 2011 (not accounting for transit refugees), with most originating from outside Europe and from areas of political turmoil and war (north-east Africa, Iraq and Syria) (Chorianopoulos and Tselepi, 2020). Recognizing these trends, the 'Migrant Inclusion Council' (MIC) was set up at municipal level in 2011 seeking to influence local policy and achieve improved socioeconomic outcomes for migrants. Also, civil society has been particularly active on the refugee crisis, offering daily support at refugee camps and in public buildings

Figure 6.2: Alexander's model of host–stranger relations, expressed in local authority attitudes

	Modernist worldview — Stranger as temporary, spatially separable			Postmodernist — Stranger as permanent and pervasive
Host–stranger relations				
Local authority attitudes towards labour migrants	**Migrants as transient**	**Migrants as temporary**	**Migrants as permanent but their otherness is temporary**	**Migrants as permanent and their otherness will remain**
Assumptions re: temporal presence	Just passing through	Short–term stay (few years)	Permanent	Permanent
Attitudes re: otherness	Otherness ignored	Otherness tolerated	Otherness discouraged/ignored: assimilation or marginalization	Otherness accepted; genuine or exploitative 'embrace of strangers'. support for communal/ethnic–based difference
Attitudes re: spatial segregation	Segregation ignored	Segregation tolerated, perhaps formalized	Assimilation leads to spatial integration ('melting pot')	Some degree of segregation understandable/acceptable ('salad bowl')
Policy type/phase	*Non-policy*	*Guestworker*	*Assimilationist*	*Pluralist*

Source: *Cities and Labour Immigration: Comparing Policy Responses in Amsterdam, Paris, Rome and Tel Aviv*, Michael Alexander, © 2017, Routledge. Reproduced by permission of Taylor and Francis Group.

occupied by refugees, though this is not necessarily embraced by the city. On the contrary, as discussed in Chapter 3, tension between the informal social solidarity realm and the city was also noted here, manifest in the contrasting methods adopted to address the refugee crisis. During the timeframe of our research, in the city centre of Athens alone, 12 squatted buildings provided accommodation to approximately 2,000 refugees. As a local activist remarked:

> 'Now let's make it clear. We stated from the very beginning that we don't intend to take over or cover the state's responsibilities towards refugees. We're not 'good people' or philanthropists. But at the same time you don't exercise enough pressure towards this goal if you're not active in the field. So, we organized ourselves and we voiced our claim for a response to the refugee shelter issue.'

Athens, as a new migrant city therefore demonstrates both reactionary xenophobic responses as well as emerging, albeit divergent civil society and government responses to recognizing some of the needs of migrants and building solidarity.

In Spain, Ireland, Australia and Canada anti-immigration political parties have been weaker and the far right has not achieved prominence in national political institutions so far. The 'Spanish exception' though ended in the general elections of April 2019 with the election of Vox – a far right party born out of a split in the People's Party (PP) – to the national Parliament with 24 deputies. This party, however, did not win any seat in Barcelona City Council in the local elections of May 2019 and its presence in the region of Catalunya continues to be very marginal. This absence undoubtedly has much to do with the marked anti-Catalan character of Spanish fascism in general. While there has been some increase in far-right political movements in Australia and Canada, which mobilize xenophobic discourses, the traditional parties of the left and right sustained power at the national level. Though not escaping sustained attack, bi-partisan support for multiculturalism persists and is evidenced in public institutions. Multiculturalism is enshrined within bills of rights, such as the Victorian Charter of Human Rights and Responsibilities (Australia) or the Canadian Charter of Rights and Freedoms, with pluralist values upheld by the system of law (for example equal rights) and evident in multiple services and infrastructure bases, such as in the education curriculum, access to translation and culturally sensitive health and welfare services. However, there is a growing tendency in Australia – as well as in other places like many cities in Spain – for deal-brokering between the traditional and far right parties or independents, given minority government scenarios. While threatening, to date this has not deeply affected local institutional practices of multiculturalism and interculturalism.

For example, we observed how 'multiculturalism' with a focus on cultural pluralism rather than assimilation or integration was deployed in significant policy initiatives in Greater Dandenong. As a senior city official there commented, 'we want this council to celebrate and be a champion and leader of diversity. Diversity is not a threat; it's a great thing, and we want to praise it and celebrate it and remove any stigma of it'. Dandenong can be distinguished as 'a migration settlement city, a refugee welcome zone' (City CEO) and its multicultural character was identified as a point of difference and pride for many interviewees from government, businesses and the community, who highlighted parts of the city that represented specific cultural communities and practices (for example Little India, Afghan Bazaar, different faith facilities) and the ability of different cultural and faith communities to interact in a tolerant and harmonious way (for example, in daily shopping at the Dandenong Market or taking public transport). A business representative suggested that the local 'melting pot' was what 'enriched the area and the knowledge that is in the area: it creates a big hot pot of ideas and … new angles of doing things'. It was reflected on by many community sector representatives as well; the sentiment is epitomized in this excerpt:

'I think the Council has a lot to be responsible for with tolerance, it actually gives us a grant for helping refugees, asylum seekers, whenever I've had dealings with the Council, I've been really impressed with the fact that they emphasize the multiculturalism within this area, and they see it as a real positive, and I think they go out of their way to encourage it and to make people feel at home, even though they've only been here for a short space of time. I look at the celebrations that the Council put on for example, and the wonderful impact that has on the Muslim community within this area, and it's really saying that the Council recognises the involvement of these people.'

Similarly, in Leicester, the City Council and other key stakeholders embraced multiculturalism as a fundamental component of city-branding, emphasizing the economic benefits of cultural diversity and vindicating the entrepreneurial culture and practice of groups such as Ugandan Asian refugees, Poles and Somalis. This rhetoric was also present in the Melbourne case, where according to one senior City official, the revitalization process was 'obviously going to build off the success of cultural diversity'. Some authors suggest inauthentic practices of recognition are present in both Greater Dandenong (Fincher, Pardy and Shaw, 2016) and Leicester. Critics of Leicester's multiculturalism suggest that it is superficial, resting on cultural festivals and celebrations (Singh, 2003) that have diminishing resonance. Furthermore, in Leicester the hollowed-out welfare system and emerging patterns of geographically concentrated disadvantage, especially BAME groups, has not always engendered genuine processes of recognition of difference – meaning that despite its strongly multi-cultural identity, inter-cultural solidarity and residential mixing is more limited. There is a kind of entrepreneurial multiculturalism, though with residential segmentation and service depletion it is difficult to articulate a shared struggle among different cultural and ethnic groups. Lastly, in Leicester, austerity was perceived by some activists to have undermined the collaborative relationships between black and minority ethnic communities, and government. Specifically, grant expenditure cuts had significant impacts on the functioning of the voluntary sector and, in turn, its capacity for engagement with the city council, and representing different ethnic groupings. This included key cultural organizations the city previously relied on, as one senior official put it in 2013, to help 'us understand/engage with those communities of interest' (Davies et al, 2020: 67).

Attitudes and policies of segregation, as we have seen, have a long history in Baltimore, where the local policies of spatial segregation of the city's black population started with the enactment by the city government of a residential segregation ordinance in 1910 (Rothstein, 2015). In 1925, some of the city's neighbourhood associations banded together to urge property owners to sign restrictive covenants, prohibiting property sales to African Americans, a measure supported by city government. Policies of social segregation pursued in the city were assisted by 'redlining', the highly racialized practice of refusing mortgage finance, from the 1930s until the 1960s, and more recent (and subtle practices) of concentrating African American public housing residents in the most impoverished areas of the city. This tradition of segregation permeates contemporary policy making, for example with revitalization strategies 'to bring more white people back into the city' (interview with Anchor institution) or to relocate (poor, black) residents from stressed neighbourhoods subject to demolition, rather than continuing attempts to improve neighbourhoods perceived as beyond repair (Pill, 2020). A lack of recognition of the needs of Baltimore's long-marginalized black neighbourhoods creates divisions, reflected in governing institutions as well.

Devices of collaboration between the local institutions and the different racial and ethnic groups of the city can play an important role in the process of political recognition and inclusion. All the cities provide examples of this kind of formal collaborative mechanism, which in general terms can adopt two main forms: public-community partnerships for the development of specific projects, and more-or-less stable mechanisms of consultation around the adoption of public decisions. Amongst the first, we can highlight a sustained process of collaboration and engagement of different ethnic groups in the revitalization process of Greater Dandenong. In this case, multiculturalism has been deployed as a kind of brand, informing engagement strategies and supporting inter-cultural activities. With regards to mechanisms of consultation in Athens, for instance, the Migrant Inclusion Council sought to give voice to the different migrant groups in the making of policies concerning their socioeconomic conditions. In Barcelona, the Municipal Council of Immigration was set up in 1997 as a consultative and engagement body made up of migrant organizations, social agents and municipal political groups to formulate policies seeking to guarantee full citizenship rights for migrants.

In positive terms, these formal collaborations and engagement mechanisms contribute to the political empowerment and equality of migrant groups, allowing them to influence and take part in public initiatives oriented to the social and economic inclusion of ethnic minorities. In all cases, however, we also find examples of problems like the representational biases of those engaged in formal mechanisms and the co-optation of the organizations representing the ethnic groups. In Baltimore, for instance, some respondents observe a 'ton of unhappiness and dissatisfaction in the black community with the black leadership and the extent to which the black establishment has really been acting in the interest of black neighbourhoods' poor black residents' (Pill, 2020: 156). Our analysis in Melbourne also points to the possibility that governments may be reaching out to some community representatives and not others, sometimes arbitrarily selecting 'leaders' and creating tensions within and between groups. In Leicester, we observe signals of co-option and incorporation of community leadership, as well as a tendency to treat community groups as homogeneous, overlooking class, gender and age-related inequalities within communities. Jones (2014), for example, found that young people have virtually no presence in participatory governance mechanisms that draw in older community leaders. Finally, cuts in public grants to ethnic groups have been significant in cities like Leicester and Montréal, affecting the capacity of these groups to organize and keep an active profile in the public arena.

In short, whether austerity conditions result in more competition and exclusion or solidarity and inclusion amongst migrants and pre-existing populations largely depends on how socioeconomic conditions are politicized by local political actors and the extent to which local institutional frameworks and practices recognize and integrate cultural otherness in the governance of cities. Institutional forms of collaboration and engagement can play an important role in this latter sense. The examples of our study, however, show us how formal collaborative and engagement devices may reproduce inequalities within and between communities and limit their political autonomy.

The quality of public space

The third key factor in supportive migrant-host society relations is the quality and inclusive character of local public space. In this regard, the emphasis is on the 'everyday lived experiences and local negotiations of difference' (Amin, 2002: 967). Here, the public realm is made up of public spaces, such as parks and produce markets, where casual encounter and social mixing occur in ways that build understanding and tolerance. Local authorities may also organize events that promote mixing. Diversity or 'social differentiation without exclusion' is achieved through 'groups overlapping and intermingling across neighbourhood borders which are safe, 'open and undecidable" (Fincher and Iveson, 2008: 145). However, urban public places are not the only important feature of these communities as they alone may not support lasting multicultural contact. It is also important for what Amin has termed 'micropublics' (Amin, 2002) to exist, for example mixed workplaces, schools or libraries that offer spaces of lasting interaction. 'What goes on in them are not achievements of community or consensus, but openings for contact and dialogue with others as equals, so that mutual fear and misunderstanding may be overcome and so that new attitudes and identities can arise from engagement' (Amin, 2002: 972). Therefore, planning for the encounter is both enabling 'positive experiences of strangerhood' (Fincher and Iveson, 2008: 153) and a 'conviviality in urban life where diverse individuals can work together on shared activities, projects and concerns which don't totally reduce them to fixed identity categories either as 'citizen' or 'group member" (Fincher and Iveson, 2008: 154). For example, and building on Jane Jacobs' work, Nyden, Maly and Lukehart (1997) identified a central role for 'social seams' in their study of US cities. Grocery stores or retailing strips were particularly successful in 'sewing' interactions between different ethnic and racial groups, including ethnic minority restaurants. Schools, parks and festivals were also mentioned as important social infrastructure, as well as an important role for regular ecumenical religious services and multi-ethnic churches that created safe spaces for encounter between different congregations. Overall, while national and sub-national policy positions towards multiculturalism and pluralism, and the funding of basic services and infrastructure are vital to support convivial relations between newcomers and established residents, local neighbourhoods play an equally vital role in delivering forums of fleeting and lasting encounter.

The importance of a high-quality public realm in supporting migrant inclusion is exemplified again in the case of Greater Dandenong. As a city that was not exposed to austerity or recession, we identified increasing, though at times fragile public realm opportunities for social mixing in both superficial and lasting ways that build understanding and reduce intolerance. First, we found affordable and diverse housing typologies spread across the urban centre which provide a foundation for 'everyday multiculturalism' (Lobo, 2010), which has been important for building mutual understanding and a place identity based on cultural diversity. Second, the mix of different land uses attracts many people to the area and activates the central area, from the Dandenong Market, the library and train station to Harmony Square and cultural precincts, in a way that also supports safety, casual encounters and builds understanding across different groups. Public realm infrastructure and services also provide many opportunities for lasting connections between groups, for example in language courses run by churches and community centres. Finally, many migrants access education, training and employment opportunities as sites of lasting relationship-building among diverse people. The role of revitalization has been key in growing employment opportunities in areas such as construction and retail in the context of a contracting manufacturing sector locally.

The quality of the public realm can be severely affected by austerity, from the lack of maintenance of public spaces and the closure of services to flagging economic development and employment opportunities. Several studies have shown how austerity measures hit different social groups and different places in a very uneven manner, widening the gap between social classes and urban areas. In Leicester, for example, a city which experienced a 63 per cent decline in discretionary budgets, services for parks or the provision of libraries have been curtailed significantly and in a way that disproportionately affects poorer inhabitants. In terms of employment, respondents in Dublin stressed the very high 'incidence of low pay among migrant workers' and that many of the houses with severe overcrowding and unsuitable conditions are occupied by migrant families struggling with soaring rents. Labour migrants are also reported to be most adversely affected by austerity measures in Montréal and Barcelona, which has increased the economic disparities between the migrants and the host population and reduced the opportunities for social interaction. In Barcelona, school and residential segregation have significantly increased in the years of the economic crisis, reflecting not only a dramatic impoverishment of migrants, but also the desire of some local residents to live in socially and culturally homogeneous places. Though 'super-diverse', Leicester is residentially segmented to an extent, with predominantly white areas concentrated in the West, Asian heritage populations in the East and North East of the centre. Smaller African and African-Caribbean populations, however, are more distributed. In Montréal, new migrants are at the forefront of those most adversely affected by austerity measures, including reductions to welfare programmes, public services and to jobs, for example in tourism which is one of the few sectors accessible to new low-skilled migrants. If we consider the working conditions of immigrants, the situation in Montréal can be compared with what is going on in other Canadian cities, even though the general situation is probably less favourable. Immigrants, especially when they are racialized, are forced to accept low wage jobs, discrimination and insecurity. One of the activists interviewed for this research frequently gathers information on work conditions and tries to help immigrants struggling to win recognition of their rights. He contributed to creating a community group supporting progressive action in cooperation with other community organizations and, sometimes, with organizations of the labour movement: 'we're part of a fight for a $15.00 minimum wage. In this fight, we're developing alliances with various groups – such as the workers of Montréal's Old Port, for example – who are on strike, fighting for the same thing. We've adopted a collaborative strategy with trade unions' (cited in Hamel and Keil, 2020: 119).

Increasing social and spatial segregation debilitates the quality of the public realm, diminishing the spaces of social mixing and interaction. However, as we explained earlier, the new practices of social engagement and cooperation that the same socioeconomic conditions may generate – such as protest and solidarity activities – can facilitate the emergence of new spaces of social interaction between diverse (and unequal) social groups.

Conclusion

The chapter illustrates how the capacity of cities to accommodate cultural and racial diversity can be dramatically affected by economic crises and austerity. Ethnic and racial minorities and the urban areas they concentrate in, are among the most vulnerable to economic recession and public sector cuts. Austerity dramatically increases social, spatial and cultural inequalities and segregation. The same socioeconomic conditions exacerbate the dynamics of competition between different social groups. These dynamics of competition can be stimulated and reinforced through the rise of racist political discourses, formulated not only by far-right political parties, but also mainstream political forces that adapt uncritically to the xenophobic agenda. The risks of anomie and social fragmentation in this context are evident.

The chapter has also revealed the importance of cities in generating the conditions for building socially and culturally cohesive and solidaristic societies. Despite the seriousness of the challenges, the city studies point to a series of lessons that strengthen the message of hope in solidarity. The first lesson refers to the importance of the material living conditions of local populations and their access to basic social rights. The cities' capacity for accommodating cultural and racial diversity is very much related to the robustness of their welfare structures and the strength of their social policies. In the most positive cases, universal welfare policies are complemented with specific support programmes to low-income minorities such as language and translation services and job training. The main risk here is that public cuts are insensitive to the unevenness of their impacts upon different social and cultural groups, thus contributing to the exacerbation of social, spatial and cultural fragmentation.

The second lesson refers to the importance of multiculturalism as a political lens that recognizes and promotes cultural and racial diversity. The cities with more recent flows of migration have a lot to learn from some of those with a longer and deeper history of cultural diversity. In the most positive cases, like Greater Dandenong, local authorities have proactively recognized the right to difference and generated the local forums in which to negotiate differences, support mixing and build compromises between different cultural groups. Multiculturalism also permeates some critical city services like education and social and health services and is supported by national and state institutional frameworks – such as the Victorian Charter of Human Rights and Responsibilities. Beyond the national and the city level policies, our study highlights the vital role of neighbourhoods and of some critical spaces for day-to-day socialization among citizens like schools, libraries, squares and markets as forums in which to forge and sustain intercultural relationships. Mixed land uses and the existence of affordable and diverse housing typologies have also proved critical in the promotion of enriching and lasting encounters between different cultural groups. However, our cases also show that certain multiculturalist discourses can contribute to the trivialization of cultural differences and inequalities and the weakening of resistance to austerity.

The final lesson highlights the importance of collaboration and engagement as a fundamental strategy for the political recognition, empowerment and inclusion of migrants and ethnic minorities. In contrast with the tendencies of competition identified in some cases, economic hardship has also triggered new patterns of solidarity that often cut across ethnic and racial divisions. In Spain, the discourses of several social movements emphasizing the shared problems and pursuits of different cultural groups helped build bridges between them and counteract xenophobia that could have resulted from the economic recession. Our cities also reveal the importance of formal channels of citizen engagement and collaboration between local institutions and ethnic minorities. However, we have also detected the risk that these forums ignore the differences and inequalities between and within migrants and ethnic groups, missing the opportunity to give voice to women and young people.

Cities of the 'global north' are places where ethnic diversity has experienced a dramatic growth and where it is most evidently interlinked with social and spatial inequalities. The challenges this poses in a context of economic recession and austerity are formidable. Cities, however, are also spaces of hope, where it is possible to forge positive relations between the different cultural and racial groups, recognize multiculturalism and take advantage of diversity to promote vibrant, cohesive, equitable and democratic societies.

7

Conclusion

A central message emerging from the volume is that while austerity may sometimes be instrumentally rational for profit-seeking corporations and governments wanting to position their countries as low-regulation, low-cost capital havens, it is always a political choice and never a necessity. It is invariably a disaster from the standpoint of equality, solidarity and social justice, except when it runs into inventive and indomitable forces capable of subverting it. Such forces clearly do emerge. They come from the urban histories, traditions and memories of place, which catalyse new approaches throughout local states, economies and civil societies. The book shows on the one hand how damaging austerity has been in squeezing the capacity of local states to think and act outside the box of fiscal and legal constraint. On the other hand, however, it attests to the openness of the future, potentialities for change and, in certain conditions, for the privations of austerity to produce new demands, practices and solidarities. This is to suggest that the urban governance of austerity is 'ambivalent' (Enwright and Rossi, 2018), fraught with danger and opportunity. The coalitions, alliances and governing mechanisms created in cities make a significant difference.

As we explained in the introductory chapter and in Chapter 5, collaboration became a prominent idea in the global governance of cities, especially in the decade before the global economic crisis. States and groups of citizens and economic agents have always worked together in greater or lesser harmony, but the idea of collaborative governance gained currency as a virtue, a perceived strategy for resolving crises, mobilizing resources and potentially forging new expressions of solidarity through the crises of Fordism-Keynesianism and in response to the disorienting and fragmentary effects of neoliberalism. As a value-laden concept, it permeated academia, business and public policy in equal measure, while being greeted with scepticism among those who saw it as a flanking measure to neoliberalization (Davies, 2011). The research shows that in some ways, the age of austerity vindicated critiques of 'collaborative governance' as a medium of governmental control or 'responsibilization'. State-driven collaboration in the face of harsh austerity proved to be gestural, shallow and transient (Dublin and Leicester) or reinforced the power of elites (Athens).

However, in the wider sense of 'who does politics with whom', the concept of collaborative governance remains valuable for thinking about how to work against and build alternatives to austerity. In concluding, we therefore seek to draw positive messages about collaboration for those aiming to resist or otherwise overcome austerity. This endeavour is especially important in the context of COVID-19, and the iniquitous miseries it has inflicted and accelerated across class, race, generation, disability and gender. In many cases, underinvestment and over-marketization in health and social care services, or what might be called 'embedded austerity', has aggravated the damage to public health and economies, while also recreating elements of solidarity, community and public spirit. The remainder of the conclusion therefore reflects on the ambivalent experiences of collaborative governance in the eight cities, accentuating what might be useful messages for those opposing austerity and searching for just alternatives in, against or despite the state.

Discursive intelligence, agility and critique

The book shows that the language of austerity is associated with a multitude of political values. One such value, inculcated in different ways through several cities, was that of 'austerity realism', and the establishment of a common-sense view that no alternative to cuts and 'prudent' budgeting was feasible. This essentially managerial and anti-political view was buttressed by the very tangible hierarchies in which cities are embedded. In the context of COVID-19, it has become clear that the politics of 'austerity realism' are neither necessary nor sustainable. Passive compliance with austerity, and the de-politicized entrepreneurialism that often comes in tandem with it, has been extremely damaging, and is a recipe for failure if the objective set out by international organizations including the UN (2020), for cities to spearhead an inclusive and just global recovery, is to be fulfilled. Austerity realism impedes innovation, resistance and change, and undermines authentic collaborations. These depend on democratic local states taking cues from citizens engaged in the struggle for social justice and asserting autonomy from authorities upscale. This is undoubtedly difficult, where nominally progressive municipalities are situated in unsympathetic regions and nation states, and under regressive international rule regimes including the informal auditory powers exercised by investors and credit rating agencies. However, our research points to many smaller and more radical ways in which this can be done.

Moreover, since the research concluded, the ideology of austerity has lost its appeal for many national and international elites, particularly as governments mobilized resources to fight the pandemic. Widespread economic devastation today does not make austerity necessary tomorrow, and international organizations urge the contrary position and favour continued stimulus or sustained state-led investment. It is encouraging to see international actors reaffirming the role of cities in leading equitable, sustainable and inclusionary COVID-19 recoveries (UN, 2020). The rapidity with which 'austerity' was jettisoned holds a lesson for those who averred there was 'no alternative' in the 2010s. Political fashions can change very quickly, and what seems inevitable one year can become transient or passé the next. Permanence is as much an illusion as the impossibility of dramatic change.

Equally, there are many pitfalls in discourse shifts. The wordplay associated with the discourse of *rigueur* in Montréal reminds us that austerity can be smuggled in through other terminologies, particularly by governments of the right but also those of the centre-left, which signally failed to oppose austerity after the GEC and conceded mastery of the political narrative on debt and recovery to the right. *Rigueur* illustrates that governments might no longer admit their politics are aligned with austerity and seek to draw a veil of discretion over the fact. Actors committed to transformative COVID-19 recovery agendas, and to accelerating progress towards the 2030 UN Sustainable Development Goals, must therefore remain vigilant to the potential for subversion by forces seeking to restore austerity to political and ideological primacy. Many countries are still led by the individuals and parties that either proselytized austerity or followed it on 'pragmatic' grounds. This means that whatever language games are in play, a battle against austerity will continually have to be waged. The changing grounds of political discourse create some space in which such a battle can be productively fought. In highlighting geographical variations and fluidity in local understandings of 'austerity', our study demonstrates the potential not only for rejecting it as a principle of governing, but also subverting it and turning it against elites. This perspective calls for a very different orientation towards 'pragmatism' or 'realism' than that advocated by actors who made a remorseful peace with austerity; one committed to defining and shaping the contours of an open future. Amongst our cities, Barcelona showed most clearly the potential in future-oriented pragmatism, and also for turning austerity discourses against the excesses of the right. Moreover, beyond this most inspiring and resonant case, the global spread of 'new municipalisms' and 'community wealth building' programmes shows that strict compliance with the letter and spirit of austerity is unnecessary (Guinan and O'Neill, 2020; Thompson, 2020).

What is true of 'austerity' is also true of 'collaboration', or 'collaborative governance'. These vocabularies and practices are fruitfully contested and politicized. Chapter 2 highlights the importance of using language precisely and politically in discussing collaboration, or when trying to influence its form and practices in the state arena. The value-laden character and positivity invested in the term can make it difficult to question the virtues of 'collaboration'. In Nantes, for example, passive voice and positive language generated assumptions about working together in a process that was rather less inclusive and deliberative than implied by the city's vision. Most significantly, vague and affirmative discourses on collaboration can be used to co-opt non-state actors and diminish agency from the standpoint of socially just governing outcomes. The effects of 'social partnership' traditions on trade unions exemplify this, where longstanding incorporation to bargaining mechanisms muted their effectiveness and relevance when it came to resisting austerity.

The turbulent age we are in therefore raises important questions for opponents of austerity about the possibility and desirability of collaborative relations between local states and anti-austerity movements and struggles. For these reasons, it is important to be precise about the nature, ends and means of collaboration as a value, goal or strategy. The same can be said of related, and seemingly unobjectionable concepts like 'social inclusion', 'diversity', 'resilience' or 'wellbeing', liberally co-opted by actors with a very poor track record in delivering the goods conventionally associated with these terms. As Marcuse commented on the de-politicization of urban discourse (2015: 153), 'who "we" is, is perhaps the central political question in urban policy. It ought not to be ignored'. An important conclusion for anti-austerity activists, whether occupying positions within, against or at a distance from the state, is to be both sceptical of state discourses and adept at discourse framing, while pursuing the forms of political organization that can propel radical discourses into the public sphere and make them 'grip' (Grigg, Howarth and Feandeiro, 2020). The slogan 'tourists go home, refugees welcome' was a very good example of mainstream discourse inversion in Barcelona, coupled with the idea of turning 'austerity' against its authors. This framing contributed to the construction of an inclusive sense of 'us', clear grounds and principles for mobilization and squeezing the space for nativism gaining ground in other parts of Spain, Europe and the Americas (Blanco, 2017).

Ambivalent spaces of collaborative governance, subsistence and resistance

We now turn to a more detailed reflection on the experiences of collaboration discussed throughout the book, organized into four sub-sections. First, we discuss the ambivalent and contested characteristics of rescaling. The remaining sub-sections employ the headings developed in Chapter 2 in assessing the potentiality for collaborations together with the state, against the state and despite or without the state.

The ambivalence of scale

Our research suggests that while, of course, collaboration survives as a multi-faceted set of practices and in pragmatic form, it lost some of its ideological appeal for local and national elites who, through austerity realism and austerity idealism, undermined many of the state-civil society participatory governance mechanisms created in the 1990s and 2000s, as well as longer standing collaborative traditions (Gaynor, 2020a; Davies et al, 2020). This process was reflected partly through rescaling led by national governments and international actors, which eschewed collaboration by imposing scalar re-alignment from the top-down. However, they simultaneously insisted that local states attempt to build collaborative mechanisms to deal with the consequences of offloading responsibility (Anguelov et al, 2018). Coercively imposed collaborative governance was common for harsher austerity regimes. The cases of Dublin and Athens, where the EU prescribed local governance reforms amidst bailout negotiations, point to the multiplicity of fronts on which change was coerced, or even extorted. Scalar politics are therefore closely coupled with mechanisms rolling out and enforcing austerity and neoliberalization, driven by concerted state, quasi-state, supra-state and private interests including credit ratings agencies, and global non-profits pursuing the goals of the super-rich.

Yet, as a social construct, scale is also amenable to reshaping from the bottom-up, in ways that affect the ability of cities and city-regions to determine their futures with respect to austerity. From a boosterish perspective, Chapter 4 recounts how the Nantes Métropole emerged from bottom-up intra-communal collaborations, combined with vigorous city-leadership and state support, lending a relatively small city-region an international profile it might otherwise not have achieved. The Nantes Model is problematic but shows clearly the difference urban and neighbourhood activism can make in determining the political geographies of a city-region and, indeed, a country. Struggles in Baltimore against the racist histories inscribed in the so-called 'City of Neighbourhoods' further exemplify how taken-for-granted cartographies can be challenged. In Barcelona too, neighbourhoods rediscovered assertiveness in their struggles against austerity. At the same time, most respondents there wanted more city-regional collaboration (see Afterword). Consequently, it is important to conceive of scale as a political-geographic relation with complex political implications. Blueprints for metropolitanization – fashionable at the present time – need to be considered politically, as well as in terms of functional efficiencies. The crucial point is that scaling is an active process, which can be influenced, if not radically reconceived, by state actors and activists intent on remapping and reorganizing for a just city. Struggles over scale are a crucial site and determinant of urban futures, and for that reason vital to engage.

Collaboration together with the state?

Collaboration 'together with the state' is, as already suggested, an ambivalent terrain. Austerity cuts and top-down rescaling generate pressure on states to compete for investment resources and mobilize coalitions with business and select civil society actors in pursuit of growth. Hence, in Athens, gestures to partnership building with local civil society organizations were overshadowed by the plethora of state partnerships with business and TNOs developed to revive its economy, change its political culture and cultivate public 'resilience'. In this dimension of state-civil society relations, participatory governance was subsumed by instrumentalized, closed and exclusionary networks constituted by elites – what Chorianopoulos and Tselepi (2020) styled 'elite pluralism'. The problem of elite network capture and closure is by no means new, as Baltimore also attested (Pill, 2020), but austerity amplified these processes, while de-politicized vocabularies of collaboration served to obscure them.

At the same time, as Chapters 5 and 6 demonstrate the proximity of the local state and its officials to public demands means that it remains a key site of political conflict and legitimation/de-legitimation. The tendency for the state to initiate collaboration discourses and agendas highlighted in Chapter 2 was, for that reason, not always a bad thing. For example, Chapter 6 shows how multiculturalism discourses often derive from public policy frameworks and initiatives and can be important in nurturing intercultural solidarities, as a way of welcoming and integrating newcomers and refugees. Chapter 6 depicts a positive role for the local state and public policy in this respect. Although multiculturalism agendas are sometimes criticized for tokenism and failing to address racial inequality, as they were by activists in Leicester, they can overflow official discourse and policy, in the sense of opening spaces in which demands for recognition, cultural and racial equality can be heard. The radicalization of a mainstream discourse is particularly important when the very idea of multiculturalism is under attack from the right.

The Barcelona, Nantes and Québec models further attest to the ambivalence of state-led collaborative discourses and mechanisms. These ways of governing cities emerged organically from earlier generations of struggle in the twentieth century, but they have not been immune to the incremental creep of austere neoliberalism. The occupancy of City Hall by Barcelona en Comú therefore begs the question of how far traditions located in memory of place as well in institutions, urban environments and policies, can be revitalized and perhaps re-envisaged in ways that support new governance strategies and coalitions, particularly in relation to the need for plausible and equitable pandemic recovery measures at the urban scale (Acuto et al, 2020).

One question for civil society organizations considering whether or when to work with the local state – if the local state is amenable – is how to retain political autonomy and avoid mission-drift. This has long been a major theme in international community organizing literatures (for example, Stoecker, 2003). Approaches in our cities varied, from critical engagement with the city council in Barcelona among social movements, to principled rejection and refusal by activists in Athens. Another point of view is that, as Chapter 5 amply demonstrates, the local state is not a singular entity, and tactical alliances with different departments or street level actors might be worthwhile, even when elites are remote or hostile. Chapter 2 also demonstrated that civil society organizations are resourceful in evading and resisting cooptative pressures through robust and politically astute organization. Elements that engage from a position of strength can influence and reshape state-led collaborative governance processes.

However, there are variable degrees of openness within the local state to influence and change. Barcelona and Greater Dandenong provided the best examples. In Dandenong, a functionally de-privileged local authority was able to step in and help sustain momentum when upper tiers lost interest in the revitalization programme. Subtler forms of influence were evident too. We saw in Montréal how street level officials can work under the radar to mitigate austerity in alliance with anti-austerity activists. Political influence is a far greater challenge in cities with 'austerity realist' or 'austerity idealist' governing cultures. In Athens, Dublin and Leicester, dominated by variants of austerity idealism and austerity realism, trust and hope in the local state were breaking down. In Leicester, activists did not accept that the municipality had no alternatives to austerity compliance, highlighting how damaging this form of de-politicization could be (Davies and Thompson, 2016). And, as the example of Nantes cautions, even cities that prioritize participation, sustainability and inclusive growth fall into instrumentalizing practices. This is what Griggs, Howarth and Feandeiro (2020) called the retreat from 'praxis' to 'ideology'.

The two-sided strategic dilemma indicated in Chapter 3 is whether and when those opposing austerity should enter the local state as officials or politicians, and what kind of stance activists and insurgents in civil society should adopt towards different facets of the local state, including the municipalities where social movements have made the transition to City Hall. There are compendious literatures on this question dating back to at least the 1970s (Cockburn, 1977), as well as reflections on the tricky process of moving from resistance into government from activists, for example South Africa in the early 1990s (Klandermans, Roef and Olivier, 1998). We offer no prescription but suggest that anti-austerity forces could usefully place these issues at the forefront of their considerations. Many activists and critics of the municipalist experiment in Spain were doing just this (Blanco et al, 2020).

Collaboration against the state

Barcelona represents the most promising example of a local state transformation programme within the diverse traditions of 'new municipalism', but the research showcases several instances of civil society organizations building coalitions and movements against multi-scalar state policies and bringing new actors onto the political stage. Montréal's *Coalition Main Rouge* played a leading role in uniting unions, community groups and students in struggles against *rigueur* and privatizations, though the potential in this insurgent model of collaboration was undermined by 'corporatist' bargaining traditions prevalent in the trade unions, leaving them trapped within the 'iron cage' of state bureaucracy (Hamel and Autin, 2017). While trade unionism in both old and new forms continues to play an important role in worker struggles, social partnership traditions often left organized workers playing a diminishing and marginal role within urban struggles against austerity.

The most prominent campaign victories encountered during our study occurred with the 'water wars' in Dublin, and the struggle against the airport at Notre-Dame-des-Landes near Nantes. These campaigns demonstrated the power of trenchant anti-austerity and anti-neoliberal mobilizations, and in the case of Dublin, the role of new actors in cultivating community-based solidarities, especially women who were also vocal in criticizing male-dominated union organizing and submissions to austerity. In Nantes, the challenge was to overcome the disconnect between the broad international campaign against the airport and struggles for class and racial equality within the city. Hence, although struggles against the multi-scalar state delivered notable victories against the two-sided coin of austerity and unsustainable development, they continued to pose the question of how to build and sustain solidarity among causes mobilizing different actors, that can talk past each other or pull in different directions. An important message from the research was that innovative struggles, not hidebound by 'corporatist' organizing traditions suited to a more collaborative phase in industrial relations, could indeed challenge the dominance of austere neoliberalism, reconstituting solidarities and asserting demands for sustainable and equitable urban policies. The respondent in Baltimore who intimated that better relations with public officials tended to follow upon conflict highlighted the possibility that anti-austerity struggles can not only deliver on their immediate goals but win longer term influence as well. Another message, therefore, is that trenchant struggles 'against the state' can succeed in building grassroots solidarities and in extracting meaningful concessions from the state, if not in transforming local state agendas, apparatuses and practices. The question posed at the end of Chapter 3 is how these struggles can be scaled up and outwards into international, trans-urban alliances, while continuing to challenge national austerity regimes and invest in strategies to hold complex local state mechanisms more determinedly to that task.

Collaboration despite and without the state

The philosopher Jurgen Habermas (1987) famously argued that a healthy deliberative and democratic culture requires civil society, or what he called the 'lifeworld' to create restraining barriers to protect against the permeation of instrumental reasoning he associated with the political and economic systems of modernity. Our research reaffirms the importance of fostering civil society independence, or autonomy, and the need for healthy scepticism towards collaborating with the state, particularly where this is formalized and contractualized. It also showcased how, in the age of austerity, civil society organizations were often left with little choice but to rely on their own resources.

Chapters 2 and 3 attest to the role of collaborations despite, in the absence of, or in spaces vacated by the state. These endeavours, sometimes aggregated under terms like the 'new urban activisms' (Walliser, 2013), often overlap the functions of subsistence and resistance, as they did in Athens, where anti-austerity activists were heavily involved in dealing with the human emergency, while opposing austerity and seeing voluntary work as a form of resistance. Overlapping resistance in cities like Barcelona, collaborative practices associated with the 'urban commons' were conceived if not as entirely independent, then as part of the process of building active, autonomous civil society alliances capable of acting beyond and sometimes against the state. In Barcelona, these ideas borrowed from and extended cooperative traditions born in the first part of the twentieth century, and reflect the libertarian socialist strand prominent in new municipalist thought with its scepticism towards state-centred or hegemonic politics. Such practices can be double-edged. Whereas in Barcelona, they partly complement new municipalist aspirations, in Athens they left little space or time for building coalitions for change, and risked activists becoming trapped in a charitable mode of activism. Once again, such ambivalent outcomes highlight the difficulty in adequately defining relations between local state mechanisms, movements seeking to transform cities, and actors involved with the provision of necessary social assistance.

More broadly, the chapters demonstrate the importance of building struggles for justice beyond the influence of the state. The Uprising in response to the death of Freddie Gray, and latterly the globalization of the Black Lives Matter movement in the age of COVID-19, both show how rebellions with tangential links to the question of austerity can create new expressions of empowerment and voice, as well as new demands for recognition in the face of harshly authoritarian and racially iniquitous governance. The lessons learned, through fighting racism and leveraging the ambivalent concept of multi-culturalism, are that cities remain vital places for forging intercultural solidarities, taking advantage of their diversity to promote more vibrant, cohesive and democratic societies.

Key messages and suggestions from the research

- In the period since the Global Economic Crisis of 2008–2009, austerity has been very damaging to the prospect for collaborative relationships between municipalities and grassroots civil societies. It has reinforced elite, exclusionary and authoritarian forms of governance, and arguably amplified the devastation wrought by COVID-19.
- However, cities do not have to accept uncritically either 'austerity realism' or 'austerity idealism'. Austerity is a political choice, and there are many ways of subverting it and turning it against its sponsors with or without conflicting with upper tiers and corporate elites. Cities can and do adopt strategies that diverge from those of regional and national governments and can learn from one another in this respect.
- With the COVID-19 pandemic, and global calls for urban-led stimulus and recovery, cities have a unique opportunity to occupy a new political space, rejecting austerity and setting out alternative governing strategies for equality and social justice.
- Despite the widespread repudiation of austerity in international and governmental discourse, it could be smuggled back in surreptitiously and through alternative discourses. The language of *rigueur* in Montréal highlights this possibility. Progressives need to be alert to such risks and become adept at critical discourse framing, as part of wider struggles.
- Like austerity, collaboration is a highly political concept and should therefore be openly politicized. State-led discourses on collaboration can obscure its political character, while sustaining hierarchical relationships and resulting in co-optation.
- Those seeking to resist or mitigate austerity therefore need to be wary of public and managerial discourses and consider strategically whether and when, and with whom, to collaborate in framing and building just and inclusive cities. Our evidence is that collaboration is more effective when the concept itself is problematized and questioned.
- The local state, including the municipality and other governmental agencies, encounters pressures from above and outside, as well as within the city. This means it occupies an ambivalent and sometimes conflictual position with respect to austerity and collaboration. The best of the local state is seen in Barcelona's new municipalist project, the worst in Athens, Baltimore and Dublin.

- Elements of the local state are therefore sometimes to be engaged constructively by civil society actors and activists struggling for equality, sometimes not. Ambivalence and scepticism will be advantageous, coupled with strategic agility in determining which relations to pursue with the local state, when and by what means. The concept of the 'frenemy' might be useful in working through these issues.

- As the city of Barcelona demonstrates, seeking political office can be advantageous for anti-austerity activists, but it is no panacea, even when an electoral platform emerges directly from social movements.

- Resisting tiers of the state and working without or despite the state against austere neoliberalism can be effective, particularly through coalitions of newly active citizens and movements influenced by the progressive values and claims emerging from feminism, environmentalism, anti-capitalism, anti-racism and internationalism.

- Furthermore, although rescaling has often been a vehicle for locking cities into austere neoliberalism, both municipalities and movements are capable of active scale-making and of using scale for alternative agendas. The politicization and problematization of scale is therefore a significant and worthwhile task for urban and local actors.

- Cities have a vital role to play in fighting racism, a struggle which goes hand in hand with resisting austerity and market-led growth. Working to cultivate supportive socio-economic conditions, collaborative political and institutional frameworks and vibrant public spheres can build convivial urban environments, supporting inter-cultural solidarity.

- We emphasize that what happens in cities, suburbs and city-regions matters. They are the theatres in which the major struggles of our time play out, as they have been throughout history. Despite, or even because of COVID-19, urban actors in, against and without the local state have an opportunity to shape a better future than that delivered under austerity.

- As political dynamos, cities harbouring strong commitments to equality and social justice need to forge inter-urban solidarity networks on a global scale to generalize, and more clearly specify the positive messages emerging from anti-austerity struggles and collaborative experiments linked, for example, to the diverse concept of 'new municipalism'.

Conclusion

The spectrum of collaborations capable of influencing the course of cities, in their relationships with austerity, is very diverse. Many of them, particularly where elite coalitions are concerned, serve to entrench and embed austerity with the values, policies and practices associated with decades of neoliberalism and public service retrenchment. However, collaboration is also vital for resisting austerity and reconstituting solidarity, sometimes with the state, and sometimes against or without it. Productive mechanisms span the contingent and cautious relations forged between local states and civil society organizations to mitigate, oppose and transform austerity, as well as micro-solidarities forged within and between communities through struggles for survival, against austerity and for racial equality.

We have seen how cities can invoke collaborative values, institutions and practices to define themselves in the manner of Barcelona, Montréal and Nantes. These 'models' are always precarious and vulnerable to cooption, but at the same time hold out the potential for contention and renewal. The lesson we draw above all is that cities and city-regions have perhaps more capacity than might seem possible at first sight to make meaningful choices about how, and by whom, they are governed and in pursuit of what goals. While urbanists and municipalists should take top-down announcements with a pinch of salt, there is no reason we cannot call upon, and if necessary, subvert or radicalize the OECD's (2020: 3) conception of cities as 'laboratories for bottom-up and innovative recovery strategies' capable of accelerating the 'new urban paradigm towards inclusive, green and smart' futures. Actors capable of critically defining and unsettling the meanings, parameters and objectives of collaboration have much to contribute to realizing better urban futures. Writing in the midst of epochal and multiple crises of public health, ecology and economy, we argue that these strivings must first ensure that humanity exits the COVID-19 pandemic onto a trajectory far removed from the futile privations of austerity.

Afterword: From Austerity to COVID-19 and Beyond

Our research concluded some time before the outbreak of COVID-19, but we suggest that many of the insights drawn from it, about austerity and collaboration, will be useful in considering ways forward from the pandemic. In the first instance, it seems clear that austerity made COVID-19 an even more iniquitous disease than it would in any case have been, with cities and urban peripheries the heart of both contagion and suffering (Biglieri, De Vidovich and Keil, 2020). The disease has unsurprisingly had a multitude of impacts on our cities, often linked to austerity. We therefore conclude further with an Afterword from the eight, including reflections on developments since the end of the research, impacts of COVID-19 and possible signs that it might be possible to 'build back better'.

Athens

The socio-political traits of Athens are changing quickly, influenced by developments in the national economy, as well as by distinct local responses to the aftermath of the sovereign debt crisis. At the national level and after years of austerity, the long-sought balanced budget was eventually attained by the Greek state in 2017. As a result, Greece exited the bailout programme in August 2018, and has hesitantly attempted to borrow in the international bond markets. Post-bailout Greece has gained back a degree of political and financial independence, avoiding the direct *in situ* inspection and authorization of its policies by creditors. More permanent forms of monitoring, however, as well as austerity, are still very much in the picture.

Beyond periodic Eurozone assessment of Greece's public finances, the country is still under 'enhanced surveillance' status (EU, 2017). This form of monitoring will continue for the foreseeable future, or, as stated in the respective documents 'for as long as a minimum of 75% of the financial assistance received from one or several other Member states ... has not be repaid' (EU, 2013). More so, since austerity failed, completely and expectedly, to address the debt strand of public finances, which skyrocketed from 126 per cent in 2010 to 176 per cent in 2017 (Eurostat, 2019). In this light, creditors responded by broadening the austerity canvas. To exit its eight-year bailout programme, Greece committed itself to maintain a primary surplus of 3.5 per cent of GDP until 2022 and 'thereafter a primary surplus of equal to or above but close to 2% of GDP in the period from 2023 to 2060' (Council of the EU, 2017).

The feeling of pessimism that accompanied this development complemented the already dispiriting departure of the SYRIZA government from its anti-austerity agenda, nurturing a climate of political apathy. According to the latest figures, mass anti-austerity demonstrations in Athens are now less frequent and attended by fewer protesters than before, a far cry from the rallies of the early 2010s (Karyotis and Rüdig, 2018). Trade union power has also been steadily diminishing as high unemployment eroded its membership base, while fierce factional strife further undermined the capacity of organized struggle to contest austerity (Papapetros, 2019). Meanwhile, a series of measures introduced by the government reversed some of the unpopular reforms implemented under bailout supervision. The rise of the minimum wage is such an example, undertaken after careful estimation of its impact on national economic targets (Smith, 2019). As formal politics and institutions seem to have surrendered to the stringent economic dogma of the era, aiming at concessions within the commanding framework, what we are witnessing in Greece is a blurry yet detectable conformity with austerity. Austerian realism is holding the national political agenda in check, and its influence is gradually spreading to Athens.

In May 2019, local elections were held in the city. Unlike the previous mayoral contest (2014), however, this time the debate between the lead candidates did not centre on austerity. While there was intense controversy regarding the role of the city in economic development, social policy and policing, the issues of fiscal retrenchment, reduction in force and enhanced responsibilization were not adequately addressed. Apart from for the communist party candidate, arguing that the new mayor should mobilize the citizens to solve the city's problems collectively, the remaining three major political parties conceded to the realignment of the local scale towards an austerity and self-reliance path. More characteristically, election results suggest that the 'common sense' rhetoric that accompanies the neoliberal rescaling ideology, exerts sufficient political influence to divide local civil society (Theodore, 2020).

The winner of the mayoral contest, the new conservative Mayor of Athens, ran a campaign centering on specific 'law and order' promises and schemes, also promoting a further shift in municipal policy, based on an enhanced role for the private sector in service delivery. Increased police activity occurred as soon as the new mayor took office, centering on places with a strong activist record, such as Exarchia, where dozens of squats were evacuated. The local 'law and order' turn has been strongly backed by the new conservative government nationally (2019) and has reached university campuses in the city, where a new police unit is expected to be put soon in place, evicting the 'undesirables'.

In this context, over reliance on policing to address coronavirus restrictions, a public health issue, adds to the narrative of state control over public space, pre-empting responses. This is even more the case, since COVID-19 lockdowns have brought the local economy shuddering to a halt, as recession revisits the city, heightening tensions. Overt policing and the normalization of austerity in Athens seems to be opening a new chapter of struggles over urban space. It remains to be seen whether these developments re-invigorate the somewhat subdued social movements that played such a powerful role in the past decade.

Baltimore

Considering what has happened in Baltimore since fieldwork concluded in 2017 affirms the continuities of (lack of) change: change occurs, which is rapid, but superficial and substantively lacking in terms of democratic empowerment, participatory democracy or political mobilization. The elites, and associated critiques, remain the same, though personnel have been replaced due to scandal and corruption. As of January 2021, the city had its third mayor and fourth police commissioner since the April 2015 uprising. The mayor elected post-uprising was forced to resign when a campaign finance scandal involving payments from one of the city's university medical systems, along with other elite actors, brought Baltimore's political corruption to worldwide attention and ridicule (Broadwater et al, 2019).

Implementation of the federal consent decree to reform the Baltimore Police Department put in place after The Uprising was undermined when officers in a gun trace task force were charged in a federal corruption case, after their three-year campaign of detaining and robbing civilians of cash, property and drugs came to light. This further eroded any remaining community trust (Williams, 2018). In April 2019, the police department was restructured by its latest commissioner, including two newly formed bureaus (of Compliance and Public Integrity) (Anderson, 2019). But these changes are readily critiqued for not tackling the systemic problems, let alone structural underpinnings, of the city's iniquitous governance. For example, a bill to return the police department to local rather than State of Maryland control stalled in part due to fears the city would have to take responsibility for police brutality settlement payouts (Soderberg, 2019). Basic local accountabilities remain lacking, while since 2015 nearly 1,400 city residents have been murdered, part of a spike in homicides that began soon after The Uprising (MacGillis, 2019), related by some to police withdrawal from the city's excluded spaces.

In turn, non-state elite actors in the city's governance retain their power as the 'fiscally squeezed' city government continues to prioritize relationships with those promising economic growth, such as the city's major 'ed and med' anchor institutions like Johns Hopkins University, and the sportswear corporation Under Armour, which continues to anchor the latest waterfront megaproject, and benefits from the biggest financing package in the city's history. Meanwhile, the programme of demolition and site assembly, with displacement of poor, black residents from the city's 'black butterfly' neighbourhoods continues, bolstered by its post-uprising funding boost from the State of Maryland.

Slivers of hope are discernible in the city. For example, the history of occupations by citizen activists demanding justice has continued. After our fieldwork concluded the Tent City occupation (August, 2017) drew attention to Baltimore's homeless. Following clearance of the encampment from the front of City Hall, then Mayor Pugh agreed a $1.5 million housing first programme (Wenger, 2018). But such activisms, which stem from or were shaped by the Uprising, have culminated in incremental, not transformative, change. Does such incrementalism comprise 'steps in the right direction' or an adjusted set of accommodations in line with the same goals and fixes? Another occupation, by Johns Hopkins' student activists to protest the university's plans for a private police force (supported by a state bill in April 2019), has benefited from the support of long-term city activists, but highlights that coercion remains central in the governance repertoire of city elites. In the words of academic-activist Lawrence Brown, the Uprising needs to lead to an upending of how the city is governed.

In Baltimore as elsewhere, the coronavirus pandemic has exacerbated the harsh, racialized socio-spatial inequalities of neoliberal urbanism. Analysis of infections across the US shows that African Americans and Latinos were three times as likely to become infected as their white neighbours and twice as likely to die from the virus (Oppel et al, 2020). The city's unemployment rate doubled from 4.8 to 10.1 per cent (Bureau of Labor Statistics, 2020), accompanied by increased demands for necessities such as food and shelter.

The crisis played out across a country beset by continued racist police violence. In May 2020 the killing of a black man, George Floyd, in Minneapolis triggered Black Lives Matter protests across the US and around the world. But in Baltimore the protests markedly differed from those of 2015. Baltimore was one of the few US cities where mass protests remained peaceful. This may indicate signs of the realization of reform, but certainly indicates a change in policing strategies to de-escalate and contain protest, as encapsulated in police officers taking a symbolic knee to the cheers of protestors in front of City Hall. It also indicates the more strategic understandings of young, black community activists drawing from their experiences of 2015.

The city's political leadership has changed once again and is notably more youthful. Brandon Scott, a 36-year-old, black former council president, took office as Mayor in December 2020. He was elected on a platform of 'working to end gun violence, restore the public's trust in government and change Baltimore for the better', drawing from his 2018 introduction of equity assessment legislation into city policymaking, still being implemented (City of Baltimore, n.d). Thus, our main research findings, which highlight the reinvigoration and importance of young, black citizen activists, still hold. But the pandemic has combined with the city's longstanding austerity urbanism to accelerate the needs of city residents, which continue to outstrip the political and economic resources to address them.

Barcelona

The fieldwork carried out in Barcelona covered the first two years of the Barcelona en Comú government. The research allowed us to observe the tensions between forces of change and continuity, as well as the possibilities and limits of radical political change in cities. The following two years confirmed the importance of these forces, in tension. Some of the main limits to the radical political change sought by Barcelona en Comú were: the limits to local political autonomy; bureaucratic resistance to change; the weight of institutional inertia; the persistent influence of economic elites and the minority nature of the government. However, despite these limits, the government of Barcelona en Comú promoted significant changes in the urban political agenda of Barcelona and managed to lead a municipalist movement on an international scale.

The international recognition of recent political experience in Barcelona contrasted with the loss of internal support in the city. Among other reasons, Barcelona en Comú suffered strongly from the national tensions caused by the independence movement in Catalunya. In the municipal elections of 2019, Barcelona en Comú finished second behind the centre-left independence party Esquerra Republicana de Catalunya (ERC). Esquerra offered Barcelona en Comú a coalition government by exchanging the mayoralty in the middle of the mandate. Barcelona en Comú rejected this offer and opted for a government in coalition with the PSC, which ensured that it would retain the mayor's office for the whole of its mandate. The current government formula provides greater political stability to Ada Colau's government. Its experience in municipal management has significantly increased. During these years, the government has taken important steps in developing a municipalist political agenda that, among other aspects, promotes new forms of urban governance allowing the re-municipalization of previously privatized services, promoting public-community co-production of public services, and strengthening mechanisms for citizen participation. However, the institutional limits of local action remain significant, and hostility towards the government in a context of exacerbated nationalism continues to be particularly intense.

The first months of the COVID-19 pandemic in Spain posed a serious threat to the development of the municipalist project. The declaration of the state of emergency was accompanied by a strong centralization of public decision-making, a significant restriction of the freedom of assembly and demonstration, and a greater role for the armed forces and police. Regional and municipal political autonomy suffered a serious setback in these months. However, outside the institutional sphere, there was a wave of social initiatives of mutual aid in fields as diverse as the care of the elderly, the production and distribution of health material, psychological support, support for vulnerable children, or the distribution of food. These cooperative social initiatives took advantage of the social capital accumulated during the social mobilizations in the face of the 2008 crisis and represent an opportunity for the development and consolidation of new forms of public-community governance in cities.

After the first wave of the pandemic, the political management of the social and health crisis of COVID-19 has been much more decentralized – although the threat of recentralization remains. Regional governments have regained control of health policy and local governments have taken advantage of their political autonomy to promote significant actions in areas such as sustainable mobility, the promotion of culture, social assistance and the promotion of residential alternatives in the face of growing housing evictions (Shea Baird, 2020). The response to this crisis in Spain radically detaches from the principles of austerity and promotes a strong expansion of public spending. Barcelona City Council has led a municipal rebellion to manage its budget surpluses autonomously – a rare instance of political assertiveness and empowerment for local government. Although this represented a notable success for municipalism, the current crisis highlights the profound inequalities in the institutional capacities of the different municipalities, even within the same metropolitan context. Barcelona's institutional capacity to react to a context such as the current one is unmatched in any other municipality in Catalunya. The development of a metropolitan perspective will be one of the great political challenges that the new municipalism will have to face in the coming years.

Greater Dandenong

Australia and the case study city of Greater Dandenong in Melbourne occupy the position of outliers in this comparative study. Despite affirmative remedies being introduced to address social problems in some other cities (for example, rise of the minimum wage in Athens or the targeted housing programme to address homelessness in Baltimore), austerity realism has been further cemented in most places since the end of our study. In fact, recent crises, namely the COVID-19 pandemic, have deepened socio-spatial inequalities and have led to the introduction of further spending controls in some places. While we write this Afterword, northern hemisphere cities are suffering a second wave of the pandemic and associated socio-economic crises. Conversely, in Melbourne no major outbreaks have occurred since the winter outbreak of July–October 2020 and economic recovery has been relatively fast since that episode, for example with national unemployment improving in recent months (down to 6.4 per cent in January 2021).

Administrations at the local, state and national level have had stable and continuous political leadership, and in contrast to some of the other cities, their distinct projects of government have continued to stay the course. In terms of urban governance and policymaking, Central Dandenong, Melbourne offers an 'extreme case' (Flyvbjerg, 2006: 229), a particular microcosm to observe both strengths and weaknesses identified during the research period and amplified by the most recent COVID-19 crisis.

First, enduring basic protections like universal healthcare and minimum rights for workers provided a social safety-net from the beginning of the pandemic. Then, and somewhat predictably from the results of our study, Australia's approach to tackling the pandemic could be contrasted to others following the GEC as interventionist and stimulus led. The Victorian Government (and other state governments across Australia) led the health response to the pandemic, defining restrictions during outbreaks and managing the quarantine programme. One major outbreak occurred in Melbourne during the winter of 2020–2021. Subsequent outbreaks from the hotel quarantine programme were contained quickly and the population's mobility re-established after days or at most weeks, which while disruptive, served to sustain economic activity and allow social interaction. In addition, income support payments were provided, most notably through 'JobSeeker' payments which raised the income of the unemployed and 'JobKeeper' which sustained both businesses and individuals at risk of losing work, along with other kinds of specific support to vulnerable groups (for example housing support for homeless people, rental freezes, bans on eviction like Ireland). Also, stimulus spending has been used to generate jobs and support specific industries, for example infrastructure.

Despite Australia and Melbourne faring relatively well during the pandemic, Central Dandenong was one of the most affected localities in the country during the winter 2020 outbreak. It continues to show signs of slow recovery. This shows that while Australia's response to the virus was generous and effective, the prospects for and pace of recovery are geographically differentiated, especially within the major cities. Firstly, Dandenong continues to be one of the most disadvantaged neighbourhoods in Melbourne and because of this its population was one of the worst affected in the metropolis. The link between disadvantage and COVID-19 outbreaks has been largely attributed to precarious working conditions (Team and Manderson, 2020). The insecure, contracting out model is pervasive in low-wage industries like aged care and security services, where people often work multiple jobs across different parts of the city. As the Secretary of the Australian Council of Trade Unions commented at the time: 'People who are less secure are more likely to go to work if they've got symptoms. They're facing different choices to other people in the pandemic. They're not all equal choices' (Schneiders and Miller, 2020).

According to research conducted by the School of Graduate Studies (SGS) Economics and Planning, commissioned by the Victorian Government's Department of Health and Human Services in mid-2020, Dandenong has the highest concentration of casual workers in Melbourne, is the fifth most disadvantaged locality and had one of the larger clusters of cases during the outbreak (see Figure 8.1). Furthermore, as highlighted in our prior research, women and minority ethnic groups in Dandenong are overrepresented in underemployment, many occupying casualized roles. The COVID-19 crisis has highlighted the socio-spatial inequalities in Melbourne and how the disadvantaged not only live with diminished opportunities but carry the burdens of socio-spatial inequalities, sadly in this crisis by facing heightened exposure to COVID-19 because of their precarious employment conditions, paradoxically, often as 'essential workers.'

Another way that Dandenong was hit particularly hard during the July–October 2020 outbreak was through the closure of many retail businesses. Our research suggested that prior to the pandemic, some of the retail strips in Central Dandenong had lower occupancy than expected as part of the revitalization work. Some small business owners commented that their businesses were struggling, for example because of the cost of carparking for consumers. Despite financial support offered by government, such as the Federal Government's JobKeeper payments for some retail employees, Central Dandenong saw closures of several retail businesses. In general, the public health measures associated with the lockdown over four months in the middle of 2020 contributed to slowing down the revitalization effort, by disproportionately affecting disadvantaged households living in the area and by slowing the activation of public realm improvements.

Given the stalling revitalization effort and disproportionate impact of the pandemic on Central Dandenong, the Victorian Government in collaboration with the municipal government designed a new development initiative in the centre. Through an agreement with developer Capital Alliance, the plan set out to build 'at least 500 new dwellings, community spaces, offices, a hotel

Figure 8.1: Low wage part-time workers (earning less that AUS$25/hour and working between 15–35 hours per week)

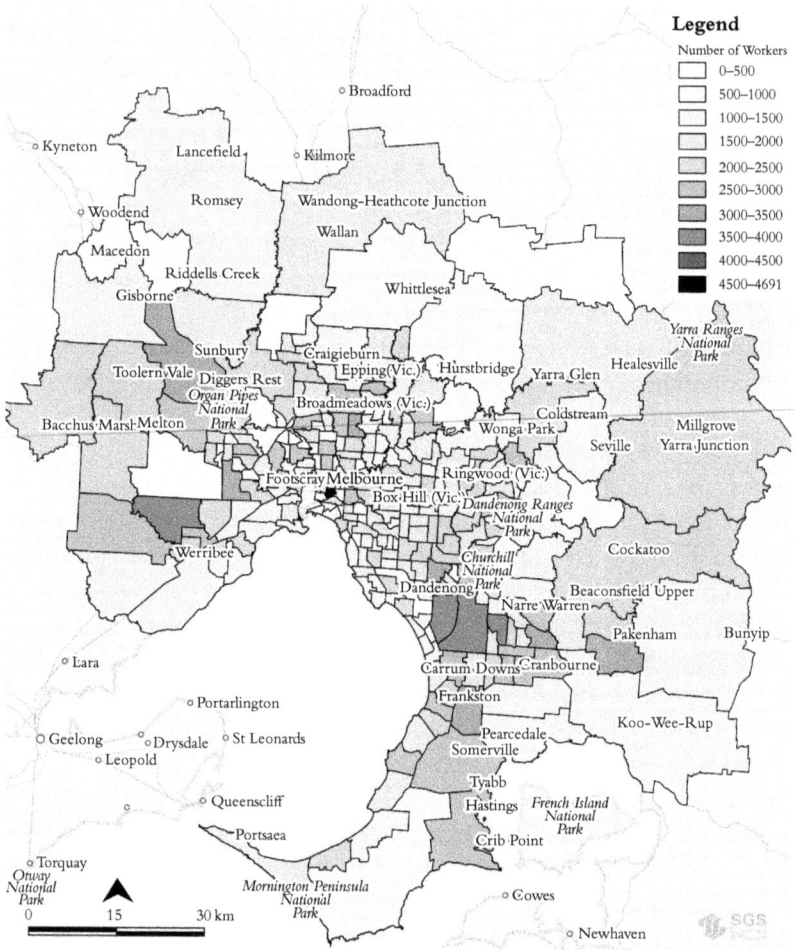

Source: Spiller and Weston, 2020, based on ABS Census data 2016

and conference centre, an urban brewery entertainment district, education facility, retail, medical, a cinema and a contemporary Indian retail and dining precinct' (Victorian Government, 2020). One of the specific aims of the plan is to create jobs during and after construction of the new precinct (5,000 ongoing positions). The first phase of the project is to create a new Little India precinct in Central Dandenong to accommodate existing Indian traders.

While no research has been conducted on the new strategy yet, and it is too early to draw any conclusions, it echoes many of the objectives contained in the original Revitalising Central Dandenong programme. There appears to be a focus on recognizing and retaining cultural diversity particular to the area; however, the relocation of the existing Indian traders would need to occur in a way that provided equal or greater benefits, for example, in terms of locational benefits and affordable rents to ensure the sense of belonging and retail position is enhanced. Also, there is a risk that a concentration of retail activities close to the railway station may detract from the vitality of existing retail strips and market. Given that similar governance structures are in place, we can expect the programme will draw on strengths from experience, including linking up with strong existing collaborative networks, and is likely to face common, perennial issues, such as tensions in the vertical control of local development from the Victorian Government as well as delivering a programme that lacks genuine inclusion of those most disadvantaged in the community (for example, single male households from migrant and low-income backgrounds unable to afford rent, women minority groups excluded from secure work).

Overall, the case of Central Dandenong and the Melbourne experience of dealing the with COVID-19 pandemic strengthened past urban governance dynamics and provides another rebuke to the idea of austerity in the local context. It showed deepening centralized authority, legitimated strong interventions by institutions and revealed the enduring social contract in place, for example with evidence of increased trust in government in Australia (Goldfinch, Taplin and Gauld, 2021) and other institutions, including unions where membership has grown during the crisis. Despite evidence of social democratic principles in action, many of the redistributive and transformative measures in place in 2020 were only temporary, such as free childcare for all, increasing unemployment benefits and suspending homelessness. Central Dandenong, and Melbourne more generally, continue to provide evidence of targeted social spending directed towards improving the quality of life of people living in the community and the vitality of the once flagging centre area. This was complemented by the announcement of a major social housing investment in the state in the 2020 state budget. While clearly an outlier in terms of the strong presence and action of institutions, which overwhelmingly protected residents from the worst impacts of the latest global crisis, COVID-19, there remains questions about the future success of revitalization in the area: both whether the community will flourish following revitalization and, conflictingly, whether the success will be sufficiently nuanced to enable a genuine process of incumbent upgrading.

Dublin

In many ways, although periods of lockdown with the COVID-19 pandemic have left Dublin's streets eerily quiet at times, little appears to have changed in relation to the strategies and patterns of governance within the city. The same strategy of entrepreneurial urbanism dominates planning and investment.

Although the spectre of a no-deal Brexit leading to massive delays at Dublin port loomed large until a deal was finally agreed at the end of December 2020, this has not deterred development plans for the city. As our fieldwork ended in 2018, the government announced plans for a new 'innovation district', complete with a new university campus, in the heart of the Silicon Docks area (Government of Ireland, 2018), and work has now begun on this development (University Times, 2020). Public concerns at the attendant displacement of residents and increased social inequalities across the city appear to be rising however (Lillington, 2019), while Google's decision to abandon its plans to rent offices in the area due to COVID-19 sparked fears that others might follow suit delivering a severe blow to the city council's plans to double the area's workforce in the coming years (Paul, 2020).

The city's associated housing crisis continues. Between 2012 and 2019, rents rose by 100 per cent or more in 15 of Dublin's 25 sub-markets and were up 103 per cent city-wide on average. This has had a knock-on effect on costs nationwide. By the end of 2019 Ireland ranked as the second most expensive country to buy a house in the world (the first being Switzerland) (Clancy, 2020: 1). While public concern and disquiet at these developments was manifest once again through the national election results in February 2020, with left-wing party Sinn Féin emerging as the largest single party in the new parliament, this left-wing surge was not represented in the final coalition government formed some four months later following a protracted period of negotiations and political wrangling. Dublin's neoliberal path seems set to continue with a centre-right coalition government at the helm, although the inclusion of the Green party within the coalition may soften some of its sharper edges.

As all talk of privatization of water services has receded, so too has the anti-water charge movement. Civil society organizations and community-based groups have continued to struggle in the context of the stringent funding cuts meted out both before and during the austerity period (Gaynor, 2020a). While additional public funding has been made available more recently (in 2020), this has been limited to a once-off payment for COVID-19-related frontline services (Government of Ireland, 2020) as the 'cutting, shaping and disciplining of civil society' (Gaynor, 2020b) continues apace. Evidence of independent community resilience continues, notably in the context of the pandemic where acts of neighbourly kindness and generosity abound. Little energy appears to remain however, for the acts of defiance and resistance that characterized the period leading up to and during the early stages of the research.

The Irish state's discourse of 'we're all in this together' in the face of the COVID-19 pandemic mirrors that of its austerity narrative (Gaynor, 2020b) and belies the fact that Dublin's citizens are most certainly not 'all in this together'. The spatial and sectoral distribution of the pandemic's impacts across the city demonstrate how its effects are highly variegated – by income, class and gender. These disproportionate effects are in line with broader socio-spatial inequalities exacerbated, as our research demonstrated, through austerity. The impacts of the housing crisis have become even more acute in the face of repeated phases of lockdowns, remote working and home-schooling where the luxury of a garden and/or a spare room has become critical. While COVID-19 incidences in the relatively affluent neighbourhoods of Dublin's leafy southern suburbs have remained comparatively low, incidences in the more densely populated working-class estates of Dublin North West and Dublin South West have been far higher (McNeice, 2020). Battles to prevent evictions during lockdown have been fiercely fought as new legislation has failed to counteract this (Threshold, 2020), while pandemic outbreaks among some of the cities' most vulnerable, such as asylum seekers forced into overcrowded conditions under the state's much criticized system of Direct Provision, have been common (Gusciute, 2020).

Workers on the frontline and most at risk of infection are largely low paid and already reeling from the impacts of austerity cuts. Seventy per cent of these frontline workers are women (CSO, 2020). While state support remained limited to public statements of gratitude for their sacrifices, embodied as acts of public applause for their 'selfless' service, it was left to workers themselves and their unions to seek the recruitment of additional staff (depleted during austerity); childcare; and access to additional staff and PPE in elder health care facilities (dominated by older women) (Cullen and Murphy, 2020).

In terms of health effects also, the pandemic has not been an egalitarian experience. Women's health and mental well-being has been particularly adversely affected. More women (38.6 per cent) compared with men (26.0 per cent) are reported to be feeling downhearted and depressed, while twice as many women are extremely concerned about maintaining social ties. Left to absorb the care gap brought about by the closure of schools and childcare, women have found the challenges of remote working and social isolation more difficult than men, with men expressing a higher interest in continuing remote working post-pandemic (61 per cent), compared to women (44 per cent) (CSO, 2020). Reflecting global patterns, COVID-19 also coincided with a sharp rise in domestic violence, both within the city and nationally. Calls to one service provider's national helpline increased by 36 per cent while hits on its website increased by 74 per cent (Safe Ireland, 2020), all within a context of 40 per cent austerity cuts in core funding to service providers (Dublin Rape Crisis Centre, 2019).

Overall, therefore, the differential impacts of austerity as documented by the research have now been compounded by the differential impacts of the pandemic, leaving specific groups more marginalized, stressed and vulnerable. With seemingly little change in the overall vision and strategy for the city, there appears little prospect that the growing stresses and inequities will be addressed through its governance mechanisms. Three developments over the pandemic period offer some sliver of hope in this regard, however. First, the states' generous income supports to those who lost their jobs or income because of COVID-19 demonstrates that an austerian economic orthodoxy is not the only show in town. Second, both the temporary rental freeze and ban on evictions (in Spring 2020) and the state and voluntary sector's swift action to house much of the city's vulnerable homeless population show how some of the worst manifestations of the housing crisis can be swiftly tackled when the political will is there (O'Carroll, Duffin and Collins, 2021). And third, the commitment, professionalism and sheer hard work of people in low-paid employment has finally become visible, and its value recognized. These are just some examples of the swift, yet profound changes which have taken place across the city over the last year or so. The extent to which they represent a mere temporary shift in the context of the current pandemic or a more long-term transformation in values, policy and action will determine how equitable, inclusive and liveable Dublin will be in the future.

Leicester

While the internal politics of Leicester itself have, on the face of it, altered little since the research concluded, there have been tectonic shifts in the political economy of the UK. In the first instance, as explained in the conclusion, the discourse of 'austerity' has fallen into abeyance. The Conservative government re-elected in December 2019 now rejects the term, and like other countries in the study, the UK has undertaken massive state spending and stimulus through the pandemic. Yet, many of the practices of austerity remain and there are fears of municipal bankruptcies across the country. In December 2020, Leicester's City Mayor Sir Peter Soulsby made the following comment on the council's finances:

> The budget for 2021 follows 10 years of austerity, in which we have lost over £100million of Government funding. Our difficulties have been compounded by the coronavirus pandemic. We have worked hard to support businesses and vulnerable residents during this time, and do not know how much we will still need to spend. Nor do we know what spending cuts the Government will make in future to repay the extra debt it has incurred. When this is all over, I greatly fear a damaging new round of austerity.[1]

Beyond this reasoned fear of austerity, and sense of uncertainty about the future of local government, we also see signs of real austerity in public service restructuring; for example, the proposed closure of Leicester General

Hospital, which generated substantial public protest. Such instances only reinforce our point about the need to take government discourse shifts with a pinch of salt. The second seismic shift in British political economy was the formalization of Brexit in January 2021. Specific implications for Leicester remain to be seen, though anti-immigration sentiments fuelling aspects of the vote, and the political character of national government, could plausibly impact further upon the multicultural city.

The other major factor, affecting all cities to a greater or lesser extent has been the COVID-19 pandemic. By international comparison, Britain's handling of the pandemic, at least until the vaccination programme, was catastrophic in both public health and economic terms. The character and extent of the catastrophe won't be fully knowable for some time, but it was born of myriad factors, including the legacies of human geography, government incompetence and inertia, and conservative ideological predilections, making the government hesitant in enacting decisive control measures, and zealous in channelling enormous public resources into profit-making entities run by associates of the Tory elite; the so called 'Chumocracy'.

The legacies of poverty, inequality, austerity and the centralized political culture of the UK have intersected with the pandemic in several ways to intensify its impact in Leicester, already a very deprived city in the UK context. In the summer of 2020, months before the far more catastrophic outbreaks marking autumn and the winter of 2020–2021, Leicester became the first UK city subjected to new COVID-19 restrictions, which remained in place until the national lockdown of January–March 2021 began to ease with the vaccination programme and 'roadmap' to supposed normality over spring and summer. The handling of COVID-19 in Leicester generated a multitude of controversies, around the lack of government consultation and information sharing with city leaders, lack of financial support for the council and local businesses, and the sheer cynicism of central government.

The restrictions also brought the city's garment industry to renewed national attention (see Davies et al, 2020 for fuller discussion). For decades, thousands of garment workers in and around Leicester, most from immigrant backgrounds, have had their labour rights systematically violated, earning less than half the national minimum wage. When the city was first subjected to renewed COVID-19 restrictions, it was suggested that the grim working conditions in the garment economy were one possible source of infection, along with other expressions of concentrated poverty in the city. It has been shown how sweatshop labour flourishes in the weak regulatory climate created by the British Conservatives since the dawn of Thatcherism (regulation could be weakened further under right wing visions for Brexit) (Hammer et al, 2015). Rather than taking responsibility, however, the Conservative Home Secretary, Priti Patel MP, blamed the city council claiming that it failed to take enforcement action against the sweatshops, because it feared being branded as racist. Davies (2020), in an article for Municipal Journal suggested that Patel's intervention was 'expedient, inflammatory and false'. He continued,

> The UK government has long known about the sweatshops and done nothing. Only recently, it dismissed recommendations from the 2019 Commons Environmental Audit Committee Report Fixing Fashion. Patel's comments deflect attention from the truth: sweatshops flourish because for decades, government has pursued labour market de-regulation. The Leicester area may have the greatest concentrations, but it is not the only place and apparel is not the only industry breeding barbaric labour practices in Britain.

Davies argued that the government's attempt to manipulate the emerging crisis in Leicester to its own ends should be a 'klaxon warning' that it 'will not hesitate to scapegoat municipalities wherever and whenever it suits'.[2] In short, despite the language-shift and government pledges to 'level up', the first phase of the pandemic appears to have only amplified urban governance characteristics long familiar in the UK: continued fiscal stress with more-or-less egregious austerity, the de-privileging of public services and hostility to elected local government, and the privileging of corporations and cronies. In this environment, the space for collaboration is potentially further squeezed, both vertically in terms of constructive relations between central and local government, and horizontally in terms of participatory governance and partnerships between local government, citizens and civil society groups.

Montréal

Since the end of our survey in 2017, numerous and dramatic changes have been shaping the urban future of Montréal and its metropolitan region in terms of governance discourse and practices of coping with austerity. Our investigation of local politics focused mainly on civil society and reflected the restructuring of interactions between actors that was underway. In fact, we encountered a civil society that had a long tradition of mobilizing and experiencing solidarity. Actors in community organizations were confronted with a new context and they had to adjust. This was done within the organizations, but also through cooperation and conflicts with institutionalized forms of politics and the numerous mechanisms created by formal institutions for promoting citizen participation in the management of public policies and/or the provision of local services.

The outbreak of the COVID-19 pandemic can certainly be considered as a major crisis. And like any major crisis it can serve as a strong analytical device – a cognitive tool – for better highlighting the social contradictions entrenched in the urban fabric. Three elements can be mentioned in that respect. The first one has to do with the trend of economic and urban revitalization in Montréal since the beginning of the 2000s, but more significantly since 2010. The second one is related to the system of public health in relation to social welfare. The third element is converging with the election of a new political party and a new mayor in November 2017, reflecting some of the changes that occurred in Montréal in recent decades.

A fast-growing industrial metropolis at the beginning of the twentieth century, Montréal 'suffered from a westward shift in economic activity combined with a change in economic leadership over the course of the twentieth century' (Bherer and Hamel, 2012: 106). This decline in the twentieth century was in part related to a gradual shift of the economic elite – mainly from English to French-speaking – and the need to rebuild business networks (Higgins, 1986). After the turn of the century, and more specifically over the last decade, several investments – public and private – were made in high-tech sectors as well as in 'ed and med', contributing to a virtuous circle of innovation, business creation, and jobs, this being effective even during the first months of the pandemic according to some (Décarie, 2020). This dynamism has also been visible in the real estate market (Jolin-Dahel, 2020).

But not everyone appears in this rosy picture. In central neighbourhoods the situation gives cause for concern. Griffintown, for example, on the banks of the Lachine Canal close to downtown, experiences high vacancies in its rental apartments due to the absence of students on campus and the absence of tourists who no longer inhabit the pre-pandemic short-term rental housing in the area (Canadian Press, 2020; Dubuc, 2020). There is no doubt that downtown Montréal has been hit hard by the pandemic and, as elsewhere, this is due to the consequences of converging factors: the use of containment to reduce the transmission of virus, the implementation of online work from home in various fields of the economy, the closure of concert halls and other cultural activities like museum and the drastic reduction of usual activities in foodservices, hotels and sector of tourism, for example. For the workers in these sectors, life conditions have been damaged with impacts difficult to assess for the time being.

This reality must be considered in relation to the current public health system and certainly in connection with the solidarity measures prevailing before the pandemic as implemented by the welfare state. It was not far into the first wave of the pandemic that we understood that the weakest link of the health system was the institutional environment of retirement facilities and long-term care homes (LTCs) where elderly people with chronic illnesses were being cared for (Biglieri et al, 2020). As of November 2020, most deaths recorded in Québec were recorded in LTCs or seniors' residences. During the first wave alone, between February and July 2020, 4,000 of the state's 40,000 LTC residents died accounting for 64 per cent of total deaths. While the numbers of infections in LTCs declined during the second wave in the fall of 2020, they remained a concern (Serebrin, 2020).[3] What we have seen is a serious failure of the so called 'Québec model' (Sanfaçon, 2020). In many ways, the pandemic crisis revealed an increase of social inequalities. And most troubling, as mentioned by activists in the community sector, is the return of austerity discourses with the spectre of public service cuts. The possibility of a return of budget cuts and under-investment in public services and social programmes is looming anew (Gibeau et al, 2020), while policing – controversially – remains very generously funded in Montréal.

Finally, as we record in earlier chapters, a major shift occurred in November 2017 with the election of Valérie Plante to the Mayoralty, heading '*Projet Montréal*', with the ambition of improving urban quality of life and promoting sustainable development. Some of the values and social concerns that social movements have been fighting for many decades, like the building of social housing and the improvement of life quality at the neighbourhood scale, were part of Plante's Mayoral discourse. However, while often celebrated outside of Montréal as one of Canada's new progressive mayors, especially in comparison to her conservative Toronto counterpart, John Tory, it is not certain at the time of writing that she will be re-elected. In a recent poll, 42 per cent of Montréalers stated that their opinion that the city had deteriorated since the last election and only 23 per cent believed it had improved (Labbé, 2020).

As is the case elsewhere, people in Montréal ask themselves what urban living will be like after COVID-19 (Scott, 2021)? Utilization of digital technology to get access to services, teleworking, online shopping are all new devices or habits that will impact the urban landscape of neighbourhoods, and more importantly downtown. But on what terms will we define the issues coming with the new behaviours? Will we look at them in terms of social classes, ethnic relations, gender or generational interactions, spatial relations, and/or from an intersectional perspective? One of the main certainties is that economic, social and cultural challenges that were not met before the pandemic will not disappear by themselves.

Nantes

Politically, the French Socialist Party has continued its hold on the municipality of Nantes. Johanna Rolland, the incumbent Mayor, was re-elected in the second round of the municipal elections in June 2020, at the head of a left-green alliance and winning 59.67 per cent of the vote. The second round of the elections was delayed due to the COVID-19 pandemic and turnout out across France was historically low. Centre-left parties, particularly the Greens, did, however, make electoral gains when compared with the 2017 legislative elections, as Macron's party, *La République en Marche*, failed to maintain its inroads in cities and urban areas. In fact, the success of the Greens in key cities across France suggests that there is a potential for a rebalancing of the centre left in future elections.[4]

Political success at the polls for the 'Nantes model' came after a setback to its logic of metropolitanization through the collapse of the project for the international airport at Notre-Dame-des-Landes (NDDL). As explained earlier, the Philippe government summarily abandoned the project on 17 January 2018, putting an end to over 50 years of struggle against the airport (Griggs and Howarth, 2020). Moments of protest have also erupted across the city, punctuated notably by the national movements of the Yellow Vests and the national strike against the Macron pension reform in 2019 and early 2020.

Paradoxically, the collapse of the project for the construction of a new international airport at NDDL has, if anything, accelerated opposition to the Nantes model within the city boundaries, amplifying earlier campaign strategies to position it as part of a broader metropolitan project to transform the city of Nantes and its leadership of the city-region (Griggs and Howarth, 2020). In fact, in the 2020 municipal elections, such opposition to the 'Nantes model' was voiced by *Nantes-en-Commun*, which drew inspiration from Barcelona-en-Comú to promote the model of the urban commons in opposition to what it saw as the neoliberalized city being constructed by the municipal government of Rolland.[5] The list won almost 9 per cent of the vote at the first round of the municipal elections. It decided not to contest the second round having failed to bring together an alliance with the Greens, who joined a list led by Rolland.

France has had one of the highest death rates from COVID-19 in Europe. The response of the national government, like others in Europe, has been criticized for its delay over systematic testing, the difficulties in balancing competing traditions of public health, its budgetary responses, and its over-reliance on top-down centralized measures.[6] In Nantes, a local survey commissioned by Nantes Métropole in November 2020 revealed that the pandemic had rendered more visible and accelerated social inequalities across the metropolitan area, and heightened the ineffectiveness of social protection 'safety nets' for those in temporary, intermittent and short term contract work.[7] Indeed, some 30 per cent of the metropolitan population was deemed to be directly concerned by the effects of the economic crisis following COVID-19 (those fearing short-term threats to their jobs because of COVID-19, those strongly concerned about their current and future chances of getting a job, and those who have had to deal with a fall in income since March 2020). However, this proportion rose to 50 per cent in the poorest households and 47 per cent in priority neighbourhoods.[8]

Such economic and social challenges are no doubt going to put increasing pressures on the Nantes model in the post-COVID-19 environment.

Importantly, Nantes Métropole launched in November 2020, a citizen assembly, which was to report in June 2021 to offer a citizens' diagnostic of the impact of the pandemic and recommendations for change. The space for collaboration continues.

Final reflections: whither collaborative governance after COVID-19?

There is little in the years since our fieldwork concluded to suggest major shifts in the political direction of the eight cities, notwithstanding COVID-19 and changes of political administration (in Athens, Baltimore, Dublin and Montréal). The early experience of governing the pandemic suggests that, in the face of a global crisis of considerably greater scale and intensity than 2008–2009, cities have, for better or worse and with some adjustments, continued with or radicalized existing policies and traditions. Thus, with the electoral defeat of SYRIZA, Athens has seen the intensification of austere neoliberalism, which under the Conservatives has taken on a more authoritarian hue. Barcelona still faces the challenges and dilemmas of the post-2015 period, but has drawn on both insurgent and collaborative traditions to reinforce social protection and solidarity. Montréal has seen a further retreat of the collaborative traditions associated with the Québec Model, in the face of sharpening pandemic inequalities, but it had been in decline for decades. Nantes too, with its citizen assembly, seeks to govern COVID-19 by building on the collaborative traditions of the Nantes game, potentially given a further lease of life with the re-election of Mayor Johanna Rolland in 2020.

Pandemic responses continue to capture the ambivalence we attribute to collaborative governance in the concluding chapter. The UN commented (2020: 4) that the international response to COVID-19 shows how 'society is capable of near overnight transformation'. This is a powerful point, and another useful lesson with respect to austerity. Again, it shows that austerity is a political or ideological choice, not a necessity. However, our Afterword shows that it will take more than a period of stimulus, the return of speculative growth, or the repudiation of austerity as a governing discourse, to dislodge iniquitous ideologies, policies, practices and institutions embedded through the preceding decade, and for many countries, the decades before the GEC. Moves away from austerity can be partial, selective or illusory, as many leaders of local authorities and public services facing retrenchment will attest. Increased government spending does not automatically correlate with reduced inequalities or other expressions of progressivism. What matters is how and to whom resources are allocated, for what purposes, and the capacity of democratic municipalities and quarrelsome civil society organizations to lead struggles for equality. In this respect, the best urban governance traditions portrayed in our study continue to provide useful lessons. Barcelona should not be idealized yet it is no accident that here, we find the most efficacious collaborative practices in response to COVID-19; municipal assertiveness and even defiance, aligned with myriad initiatives from civil society and social movements, building on what was established in previous decades and radicalized in the struggle against austerity after 2008. Even in the face of a calamity like Coronavirus, these cities shows that politics remains open and the future dependent on collaborations and struggles led by urban dwellers across the planet.

Notes

Introduction

[1] See http://cura.our.dmu.ac.uk

[2] Professor Roger Keil framed our research question in these terms at a meeting.

[3] See the introductory chapter in Davies (2021) for a more detailed discussion of methodology.

[4] Available from: https://www.tandfonline.com/toc/ujua20/42/1

[5] https://cura.our.dmu.ac.uk/wp-content/uploads/sites/3/2017/08/Governing-in-and-Against-Austerity-Published-Report-Web.pdf

[6] European Commission, European Capital of Innovation (iCaptial) 2019, at:https://ec.europa.eu/info/research-and-innovation/funding/funding-opportunities/prizes/icapital/icapital-2019_en

Chapter 1

[1] Record of Council Meeting held on 30 November 2017. Here, the City Mayor responds to a question from Councillor Porter. Available from: http://www.cabinet.leicester.gov.uk/%28S%28t1fziw45wvh0zr45gujmstei%29%29/mgAi.aspx?ID=73560

[2] PM Lenihan interviewed on Prime Time, 24 November 2020. Available from: https://www.youtube.com/watch?v=YK7w6fXoYxo

Chapter 2

[1] CMBS is the Municipal Forum of Social Welfare.

Afterword: From Austerity to COVID-19 and Beyond

[1] https://news.leicester.gov.uk/news-articles/2020/december/council-publishes-one-year-stop-gap-budget-plan/

[2] Published 21 July 2020.

[3] These numbers are not unique to Montréal and Québec. As Québec City freelance journalist Nora Loreto has documented, 77 per cent of Canada's almost 17,000 COVID-19 deaths occurred in LTCs and retirement facilities. Loreto documents all infections and deaths through a publicly shared document, updated daily (https://docs.google.com/spreadsheets/d/1M_RzojK0vwF9nAozI7aoyLpPU8EA1JEqO6rq0g1iebU/edit#gid=0)

[4] Margulies, B. (2020) 'What the municipal elections in France told us about the future of the French party system', LSE European Politics and Policy Blog, 3 July, Available from: https://blogs.lse.ac.uk/europpblog/2020/07/03/what-the-french-municipal-elections-can-tell-us-about-the-future-of-the-french-party-system/

[5] See https://www.nantesencommun.org/.

[6] See J-P. Moatti (2020) 'Correspondence: The French Response to COVID-19', *The Lancet Public Health*, 5:5: e255–256; Atlani-Duault, L., Chauvin, F., Yazdanpanah, Y., Lina, B., Benamouzig, D., Bouadma, L., et al (2020) 'France's COVID-19 response', *The Lancet*, 396: 10246, pp 219–221, Available from: https://www.thelancet.com/journals/lancet/article/PIIS0140-6736(20)31599-3/fulltext?dgcid=raven_jbs_etoc_email; Cho, C., Jérôme, T. and Maurice, J. (2020) ' "Whatever it takes": First budgetary responses to the COVID-19 pandemic in France', *Journal of Public Budgeting, Accounting and Financial Management*, Available from: https://doi.org/10.1108/JPBAFM-07-2020-0126; IISS (2020) 'France's response to COVID-19', *Strategic Comments*, 26:5, iv-vi. Doi: 10.1080/13567888.2020.1805910.

[7] TMO Politique Publique (2020) *Nantes Métropole: Enqûete sur les impacts do la crise sanitaire. Rapport. November, No. 6596*, Rennes: TMO Regions, p 15.

[8] TMO Politique Publique (2020), pp 8–9.

References

Acuto, M., Larcom, S., Keil, R., Ghojeh, M., Lindsay, T., Camponeschi, C. and Parnell, S. (2020), 'Seeing COVID-19 through an urban lens', *Nature Sustainability*, 3: 977–978.

Agranoff, R. and McGuire, M. (2003) *Collaborative Public Management: New Strategies For Local Governments in American Governance and Public Policy*, Washington, DC: Georgetown University Press.

Alexander, M. (2017) *Cities and Labour Immigration: Comparing Policy Responses in Amsterdam, Paris, Rome and Tel Aviv*, Abingdon: Routledge.

Amin, A. (2002) 'Ethnicity and the multicultural city: Living with diversity', *Environment and Planning A: Economy and Space*, 34(6): 959–980.

Anderson, J. (2019) 'Baltimore Police Commissioner Michael Harrison thins out command staff, reconfigures organization', *Baltimore Sun*, [online] 15 April, Available from: https://www.baltimoresun.com/news/crime/bs-md-ci-command-staff-changes-20190415-story.html

Anguelov, D., Leitner, H. and Sheppard, E. (2018) 'Engineering the financialization of urban entrpreneurialism: The JESSICA Urban Development Initiative in the European Union', *International Journal of Urban and Regional Research*, 42(4): 573–593.

Ansell, C. and Gash, A. (2007) 'Collaborative governance in theory and practice', *Journal of Public Administration Research and Theory*, 18(4): 543–571.

Ansell, C., Doberstein, C., Henderson, H., Siddiki, S. and 't Hart, P. (2020) 'Understanding inclusion in collaborative governance: A mixed methods approach', *Policy and Society*, 39(4): 570–591.

Arampatzi, A. (2017) 'The spatiality of counter-austerity politics in Athens, Greece: Emerging urban solidarity spaces', *Urban Studies*, 54(9): 2155–2171.

Arapoglou, V.P. (2012) 'Diversity, inequality and urban change', *European Urban and Regional Studies*, 19(3): 223–237.

Arbaci, S. and Tapada-Berteli, T. (2012) 'Social inequality and urban regeneration in Barcelona city centre: Reconsidering success', *European Urban and Regional Studies*, 19(3): 287–311.

Autin, G. (2016) *Governing Austerity in Montreal*, [online] 12 July, Available from: https://cura.our.dmu.ac.uk/2016/07/12/governing-austerity-in-montreal/

Barnett, C. (2014) 'What do cities have to do with democracy?', *International Journal of Urban and Regional Research*, 38(5): 1625–1643.

Bauman, Z. (1995) *Postmodernity and its Discontents*, London: Wiley.

Bauman, Z. and Bordoni, C. (2014) *State of Crisis*, Cambridge: Polity Press.

Beck, U. and Beck-Gernsheim, E. (2001) *Individualization*, London: Sage.

Berry, C. and Giovannini, A. (eds) (2018) *Developing England's North: The Political Economy of the Northern Powerhouse*, London: Palgrave Macmillan.

Bherer, L. and P. Hamel. (2012) 'Overcoming adversity, or public action in the face of new urban problems: The example of Montreal', in M. Horak and R. Young (eds) *Sites of Governance: Multilevel Governance and Policy Making in Canada's Big Cities*, Montreal and Kingston: McGill-Queen's University Press, pp 104–135.

Biglieri, S., De Vidovich, L. and Keil, R. (2020) 'City as the core of contagion? Repositioning COVID-19 at the social and spatial periphery of urban society', *Cities & Health*. DOI: 10.1080/23748834.2020.1788320.

Blanco, I. (2015a) 'Between democratic network governance and neoliberalism: A regime-theoretical analysis of collaboration in Barcelona', *Cities: The International Journal of Urban Policy and Planning*, 44: 123–130.

Blanco, I. and Gomà, R. (2020) 'New Municipalism', in A. Kobayashi (ed), *International Encyclopaedia of Human Geography*, London: Elsevier, 2nd edition, vol. 9, pp 393–398.

Blanco, I. and León, M. (2017) 'Social innovation, reciprocity and contentious politics: Facing the socio-urban crisis in Ciutat Meridiana, Barcelona', *Urban Studies*, 54(9): 2172–2188.

Blanco, I., Salazar Y. and Bianchi, I. (2020) 'Urban governance and political change under a radical left government: The case of Barcelona', *Journal of Urban Affairs*, 42(2): 18–38.

Borraz, O. and Le Galès, P. (2010) 'Urban governance in Europe: The government of what?', *Pôle Sud: Revue de science politique de l'Europe méridionale*, 32(1): 137–152.

Brenner, N. (2004) *New State Spaces: Urban Governance and the Rescaling of Statehood*, New York: Oxford University Press.

Brenner, N. (2009) 'A thousand leaves: Notes of the geographies of uneven spatial development', in R. Mahon and R. Keil (eds) *Leviathan Undone? Towards a Political Economy of Scale,* Vancouver: UBC Press, pp 27–49.

Brenner, N. and Schmid, C. (2015) 'Towards a new epistemology of the urban'?, *City*, 19(2–3): 151–182.

Brenner, N. and Theodore, N. (2002) 'Cities and the geographies of "actually existing neoliberalism"', *Antipode*, 34(3): 349–379.

Brenner, N., Peck, J. and Theodore, N. (2010) 'Variegated neoliberalization: Geographies, modalities, pathways', *Global Networks*, 10(2): 182–222.

Broadwater, L., Duncan. I. and Marbella, J. (2019) 'Baltimore Mayor Pugh resigns amid growing children's book scandal', *Baltimore Sun*, [online] 2 May, Available from: https://www.baltimoresun.com/maryland/baltimore-city/bs-md-pugh-resigns-20190502-story.html

Bruff, I. and Starnes, K. (2019) 'Framing the neoliberal canon: Resisting the market myth via literary inquiry', *Globalizations*, 16(3): 245–259.

Brunet-Jailly, E. and Martin, J.F. (2010) 'Local government in a global world: Comparing findings and conclusions', in E. Brunet-Jailly and J.F. Martin, (eds) *Local Government in a Global World: Australia and Canada in Comparative Perspective*, Toronto: University of Toronto Press, pp 238–252.

Bureau of Labor Statistics. (2020) *Baltimore area Economic Summary*, [online] December, Available from: https://www.bls.gov/regions/mid-atlantic/summary/blssummary_baltimore.pdf

Callanan, M. (2020) 'Europe and the rescaling of domestic territorial governance in Ireland', *Regional & Federal Studies*, 30(2): 175–193.

Canadian Press. (2020) *COVID-19 Pandemic Prompts Urbanites to Rethink 'Grand Bargain' of Dense City Living*, [online] 10 May, Available from: https://chatnewstoday.ca/2020/05/10/covid-19-pandemic-prompts-urbanites-to-rethink-grand-bargain-of-dense-city-living/

Castells, M. (1983) *The City and the Grassroots: A Cross-Cultural Theory of Urban Social Movements*, London: Edward Arnold.

Castells, M. (2012) *Networks of Outrage and Hope: Social Movements in the Internet Age*, Cambridge: Polity Press.

CEC (1992) *Urbanisation and the Functions of Cities in the European Community*, Luxembourg: Office for Official Publications of the European Communities.

CEC (1993) *Growth, Competitiveness, Employment. The Challenges and Ways Forward into the 21st Century — White Paper*, Brussels: Office for Official Publications of the European Communities.

CEC (2012) *Memorandum of Understanding between the European Commission and Spain: European Commission,* Brussels: Office for Official Publications of the European Communities.

CEC (2014) *The European Code of Conduct on Partnership (ECCP) in the Framework of the European Structural and Investment Funds*, Luxembourg: Office for Official Publications of the European Communities.

Central Statistics Office (CSO) (2020) *Employment and Life Effects of Covid-19*, Available from: https://www.cso.ie/en/releasesandpublications/er/elec19/employmentandlifeeffectsofcovid-19/

Cerny, P. (2006) 'Restructuring the state in a globalizing world: Capital accumulation, tangled hierarchies and the search for a new spatio-temporal fix', *Review of International Political Economy*, 13(4): 679–695.

Childe, V.G. (1950) 'The urban revolution', *The Town Planning Review*, 21(1): 3–17.

Chorianopoulos, I. (2002) 'Urban restructuring and governance: North-south differences in Europe and the EU URBAN initiative', *Urban Studies*, 39(4): 705–726.

Chorianopoulos, I. (2012) 'State spatial restructuring in Greece: Forced rescaling, unresponsive localities', *European Urban and Regional Studies*, 19(4): 331–348.

Chorianopoulos, I. and Tselepi, N. (2019) 'Austerity urbanism: Rescaling and collaborative governance policies in Athens', *European Urban and Regional Studies*, 26(1): 80–96.

Chorianopoulos, I. and Tselepi, N. (2020) 'Austerity governance and bifurcated civil society: The changing matrices of urban politics in Athens', *Journal of Urban Affairs*, 42(1): 39–55.

City of Baltimore (n.d.) *Mayor Brandon M. Scott*, Available from: https://mayor.baltimorecity.gov/#:~:text=Scott,Brandon%20M.,his%20colleagues%20in%20May%202019

Cladera, J.R. and Burns, M.C. (2000) 'The liberalization of the land market in Spain: The 1998 reform of urban planning legislation', *European Planning Studies*, 8(5): 547–564.

Clancy, M. (2020) 'Tourism, financialization, and short-term rentals: The political economy of Dublin's housing crisis', *Current Issues in Tourism*, First published 3 July, Available at: https://doi.org/10.1080/13683500.2020.1786027

Clarke, S. (1990) 'The crisis of Fordism and the crisis of capitalism', *Telos*, 83: 71–98.

Cockburn, C. (1977) *The Local State: Management of Cities and People*, London: Pluto Press.

Cohen, J.L. and Arato, A. (1992) *Civil Society and Political Theory*, Cambridge: The MIT Press.

Coq-Huelva, D. (2013) 'Urbanisation and financialisation in the context of a rescaling state: The case of Spain', *Antipode*, 45(5): 1213–1231.

CoR (2009) *Mission Statement, Brussels: Committee of the Regions*, Available from: https://cor.europa.eu/en/about/Documents/About/CoR%20mission%20statement/EN.pdf

Council of the EU (2017) *Eurogroup Statement on Greece: 375/17. Brussels: The General Secretariat of the Council*, Available from: https://www.consilium.europa.eu/en/press/press-releases/2017/06/15/eurogroup-statement-greece/

Cucca, R. and Ranci, C. (2017) *Unequal Cities: The Challenge of Post-Industrial Transition in Times of Austerity*, London: Routledge.

Cullen, P. and Murphy, M.P. (2020) 'Responses to the COVID-19 crisis in Ireland: From feminized to feminist', *Gender, Work & Organisation*, first published 4 December, Available from: https://doi.org/10.1111/gwao.12596

Davidoff, P. (1965) 'Advocacy and pluralism in planning', *Journal of the American Institute of Planners*, 31(4): 331–338.

Davidson, M. and Ward, K. (2018) 'Introduction', in M. Davidson and K. Ward (eds), *Cities Under Austerity: Restructuring the US Metropolis*, Albany: SUNY Press, pp 1–26.

Davies, J.S. (2007) 'The limits of partnership: An exit-action strategy for local democratic inclusion', *Political Studies*, 55(4): 779–800.

Davies, J.S. (2011) *Challenging Governance Theory: From Networks to Hegemony*, Bristol: Policy Press.

Davies, J.S. (2017) *Governing in and against austerity: International lessons from eight cities*, Leicester: De Montfort University, Available from: https://cura.our.dmu.ac.uk/2017/08/16/dissemination-report-governing-in-and-against-austerity/

Davies, J.S. (2020) 'Leicester's politicised lockdown: A warning to local government', *Municipal Journal*, [online] 21 July, Available from: https://www.themj.co.uk/Leicesters-Politicised-Lockdown-A-warning-to-local-government/218209#

Davies, J.S. (2021) *Between Realism and Revolt: Governing Cities in the Crisis of Neoliberal Globalism*, Bristol: Bristol University Press.

Davies, J.S. and Thompson, E. (2016) 'Austerity realism and the governance of Leicester', in M. Bevir and R.A.W. Rhodes (eds), *Rethinking Governance: Ruling, Rationalities and Resistance*, Oxford: Routledge, pp 144–161.

Davies, J.S. and Blanco, I. (2017) 'Austerity urbanism: Patterns of neoliberalisation and resistance in six cities of Spain and the UK', *Environment and Planning A: Economy and Space*, 49(7): 1517–1536.

Davies, J.S., Bua, A., Cortina-Oriol, M. and Thompson E. (2020) 'Why is austerity governable? A Gramscian urban regime analysis of Leicester, UK', *Journal of Urban Affairs*, 42(1): 56–74.

Décarie, J.-P. (2020) 'Grande entrevue: Les filiales étrangères comme moteur de la relance', *La Presse*, [online] 5 August, Available from: https://www.lapresse.ca/affaires/2020-08-05/grande-entrevue-les-filiales-etrangeres-comme-moteur-de-relance.php

De la Porte C. (2017) 'EU governance of welfare states and labour markets', in P. Kennett and N. Lendvai-Bainton (eds) *Handbook of European Social Policy*, Cheltenham: Edward Elgar, pp 141–154.

della Porta D., Fernandez, J., Kouki, H. and Mosca, L. (2017) *Movement Parties against Austerity*, Cambridge: Polity Press.

Department of Environment, Community and Local Government (DECLG) (2012) *Putting People First: Action Programme for Effective Local Government. Dublin: Department of Environment, Community and Local Government*, Available from: https://www.gov.ie/en/publication/e9037-putting-people-first-action-programme-for-effective-local-government/

Department of Environment, Community and Local Government (DECLG) (2014) *Press release for the Local Government Reform Act 2014*, Available from: http://www.environ.ie/en/LocalGovernment/LocalGovernmentReform/

de Souza, M.L. (2006) Social movements as 'critical urban planning' agents, *City*, 10(3), 327–342. DOI:10.1080/13604810600982347.

Devisme, L., with Bossé, A., Dèbre, C., Garat, I., Nicolas, A., Ouvrard, P. and Roy, E. (2013) 'Conclusion générale' in A. Bossé, C. Dèbre, L. Devisme, I. Garat, A. Nicolas, P. Ouvrard, and E. Roy (eds), *POPSU²-Nantes. Rapport final #2*, Nantes: POPSU, pp 191–196.

Dickinson, H. and Sullivan, H. (2014) 'Towards a general theory of collaborative performance: The importance of efficacy and agency', *Public Administration*, 92(1): 161–177.

Dikeç, M. (2006) 'Two decades of French urban policy: From social development of neighbourhoods to the republican penal state', *Antipode*, 38(1): 59–81.

Dikeç, M. (2017) *Urban Rage: The Revolt of the Excluded*, New Haven: Yale University Press.

Dollery, B., Crase L. and Byrnes J. (2006) 'Local government failure: Why does Australian local government experience permanent financial austerity?', *Australian Journal of Political Science*, 41(3): 339–353.

Dublin Rape Crisis Centre (2019) *Annual Report*, Available from: https://www.drcc.ie/news-resources/resources/drcc-annual-report-2019/

Dubuc, A. (2020) 'La pandémie boulverse le marché dan Griffintown', *La Presse*, [online] 6 November, Available from: https://www.lapresse.ca/affaires/economie/2020-11-06/immobilier-residentiel/la-pandemie-bouleverse-le-marche-dans-griffintowOVn.php

Enwright, T. and Rossi, U. (eds) (2018) *The Urban Political: Ambivalent Spaces of Late Neoliberalism*, Basingstoke: Palgrave Macmillan.

Esping-Andersen, G. (1990) *The Three Worlds of Welfare Capitalism*, Princeton: Princeton University Press.

EU (2013) 'Regulation (EU) No 472/2013 of the European Parliament and the Council of 21 May 2013 on the strengthening of economic and budgetary surveillance of Member States in the euro area experiencing or threatened with serious difficulties with respect to their financial stability', *Official Journal of the European Union*, L 140: 1–10.

EU (2017) 'Commission Implementing Decision (EU) 2018/1192 of 11 July 2018 on the activation of enhanced surveillance for Greece', *Official Journal of the European Union*, L 211: 1–4.

Eurostat (2019) *General Government Gross Debt: Percentage of Gross Domestic Product (GDP)*, Available from: https://ec.europa.eu/eurostat/tgm/refreshTableAction.do?tab=table&plugin=1&pcode=sdg_17_40&language=en

Fainstein, S.S. (2005) 'Cities and diversity: Should we want it? Can we plan for it?', *Urban Affairs Review*, 41(1): 3–19.

Farías, I. and Blok, A. (2016) 'Technical democracy as a challenge to urban studies', *City*, 20(4): 539–548.

Farrell, C.R. and Lee, B.A. (2011) 'Racial diversity and change in metropolitan neighborhoods', *Social Science Research*, 40(4): 1108–1123.

Fincher, R. and Iveson, K. (2008) *Planning and Diversity in the City: Redistribution, Recognition and Encounter*, Basingstoke: Palgrave Macmillan.

Fincher, R., Pardy, M. and Shaw, K. (2016) 'Place-making or place-masking? The everyday political economy of "making place"', *Planning Theory & Practice*, 17(4): 516–536.

Flyvbjerg, B. (2006) 'Five misunderstandings about case-study research', *Qualitative Inquiry*, 12(2): 219–245.

Fong, E. and Shibuya, K. (2005) 'Multiethnic cities in North America', *Annual Review of Sociology*, 31(1): 285–304.

Galimberti, D. and Pinson, G. (2017) 'Place equality regime(s) in French city regions', in J.M. Sellers, M. Arretche, D. Kübler and E. Razin (eds), *Inequality and Governance in the Metropolis: Place Equality Regimes and Fiscal Choices in Eleven Countries*, London: Palgrave Macmillan, pp 201–218.

Gamble, A. (1994) *The Free Economy and the Strong State*, Basingstoke: Macmillan, 2nd edition.

García, M.S. (2010) 'The breakdown of Spanish urban growth model: Social and territorial effects of the global crisis', *International Journal of Urban and Regional Research*, 34(4): 967–980.

Gaspar, J. (1984) 'Urbanisation: Growth, problems and policies', in A. Williams (ed), *Southern Europe Transformed: Political and Economic Change in Greece, Italy, Portugal and Spain*, London: Harper and Row Publishers, pp 208–235.

Gaynor, N. (2020a) 'Governing austerity in Dublin: Rationalization, resilience, and resistance', *Journal of Urban Affairs*, 42(1): 75–90.

Gaynor, N. (2020b) 'Neoliberalism, deliberation and dissent: Critical reflections on the "community activation" turn in Ireland's community development programme', *Community Development Journal*, 55(4): 645–661.

Giannakourou, G. (2012) 'The Europeanization of national planning: Explaining the causes and potentials of change', *Planning Practice and Research*, 27(1): 117–135.

Gibeau, É., Laflamme, V., Begley, J. and Lacoursière, B. (2020) 'Il faut redoubler d'ardeur contre les inégalités sociales', *Le Devoir*, [online] 14 September, Available from: https://www.ledevoir.com/opinion/libre-opinion/585894/il-faut-redoubler-d-ardeur-contre-les-inegalites-sociales

Gleeson, B., Dodson, J., and Spiller, M. (2010) *Metropolitan Governance for the Australian City: The Case for Reform*, Griffith University Urban Research Program (Issue Paper 12).

Godrej, D. (2019) 'Whose city?', *New Internationalist*, [online] 24 July, Available from: https://newint.org/immersive/2019/07/24/whose-city

Goh, K. (2021) *Form and Flow: The Spatial Politics of Urban Resilience and Climate Justice*, Cambridge: The MIT Press.

Goldfinch, S., Taplin, R. and Gauld, R. (2021) 'Trust in government increased during the Covid-19 pandemic in Australia and New Zealand', *Australian Journal of Public Administration*, 1–9. DOI: 10.1111/1467-8500.

Gough, J. (2002) 'Neoliberalism and socialisation in the contemporary city: Opposites, complements and instabilities', *Antipode*, 34(3): 405–426.

Government of Ireland (2018) 'Taoiseach launches plans to develop new Grand Canal Innovation District', *Merrion Street*, [online] 12 July, Available from: https://merrionstreet.ie/en/news-room/news/taoiseach_launches_plans_to_develop_new_grand_canal_innovation_district.html

Government of Ireland (2020*) COVID-19 Stability Fund for Community and Voluntary, Charity and Social Enterprises*, [online] 7 December, Available from: https://www.gov.ie/en/publication/b1a7b9-covid-19-community-voluntary-charity-and-social-enterprise/#scheme-details

Graeber, D. (2015) *The Utopia of Rules: On Technology, Stupidity, and the Secret Joys of Bureaucracy*, New Jersey: Bowker Books.

Griggs, S. and Howarth, D. (2020) 'Two images of Nantes as a "Green Model" of urban planning and governance: The "collaborative city" versus the "slow city"', *Town Planning Review*, 94(4): 415–436.

Griggs, S., Howarth, D. and Feandeiro A. (2020) 'The logics and limits of "collaborative governance" in Nantes: Myth, ideology, and the politics of new urban regimes', *Journal of Urban Affairs*, 42(1): 91–108.

Guinan, J. and O'Neill, M. (2020) *The Case for Community Wealth Building*, Cambridge: Polity Press.

Gusciute, E. (2020) 'Leaving the most vulnerable behind: Reflection on the Covid-19 pandemic and Direct Provision in Ireland', *Irish Journal of Sociology*, Available from: https://doi.org/10.1177%2F0791603520940145

Habermas, J. (1987) *The Philosophical Discourse of Modernity*, Cambridge: MIT Press.

Hajer, M. and Versteeg, W. (2008) *The Limits to Deliberative Democracy: Paper to be presented at the Annual Meeting of the American Political Science Association Conference*, Boston, August 28–31.

Hamel, P. (2006) 'Institutional changes and metropolitan governance: Can de-amalgamation be amalgamation? The case of Montreal', in E. Razin and P.J. Smith (eds), *Metropolitan Governing: Canadian Cases, Comparative Lessons*, Jerusalem: The Hebrew University Magnes Press, pp 95–120.

Hamel. P. (2014) 'Urban social movements', in H-A. van der Heijden (ed), *The Handbook of Political Citizenship and Social Movements*, Cheltenham: Edward Elgar, pp 464–492.

Hamel, P. and Autin, G. (2017) 'Austerity governance and the welfare crisis in Montreal', *Alternate Routes*, 28(1): 165–188.

Hamel, P. and Keil, R. (2020) ' "La coopération, c'est clé: Montreal's urban governance in times of austerity', *Journal of Urban Affairs*, 42(1): 109–124.

Hammer, N., Plugor, R., Nolan, P. and Clark, I. (2015) *New Industry on a Skewed Playing Field: Supply Chain Relations and Working Conditions in UK Garment Manufacturing*, Available from: https://www2.le.ac.uk/offices/press/for-journalists/media-resources/Leicester%20Report%20-%20Final%20-to%20publish.pdf/

Harvey, D. (1989) 'From managerialism to entrepreneurialism: The transformation in urban governance in late capitalism', *Geografiska Annaler, Series B: Human Geography*, 71(1): 3–17.

Hastings, A., Bailey, N., Bramley, G. and Gannon, M. (2017) 'Austerity urbanism in England: The "regressive redistribution" of local government services and the impact on the poor and marginalised', *Environment and Planning A: Economy and Space*, 49(9): 2007–2024.

Hatherley, O. (2020) *Red Metropolis: Socialism and the Government of London*, London: Repeater Books.

Hearn, R., Boyle, M. and Kobayashi, A. (2020) 'Taking liberties with democracy? On the origins, meaning and implications of the Irish water wars' *Geoforum*, 110: 232–241.

Henderson, H., Sullivan, H. and Gleeson, B. (2020) 'Variations on a collaborative theme: Conservatism, pluralism, and place-based urban policy in Central Dandenong, Melbourne', *Journal of Urban Affairs*, 42(1): 125–142.

Higgins, B. (1986) *The Rise and Fall? of Montreal: A Case Study of Urban Growth: Regional Economic Expansion and National Development*, Moncton: Canadian Institute for Research on Regional Development.

Hinkley, S.M. (2015) *Governing the Broke City: Fiscal Crisis and the Remaking of Urban Governance*, Unpublished doctoral dissertation, University of California, Berkeley. Available from: http://digitalassets.lib.berkeley.edu/etd/ucb/text/Hinkley_berkeley_0028E_15039.pdf

Hlepas, N.K. (2020) 'Checking the mechanics of Europeanization in a centralist state: The case of Greece', *Regional & Federal Studies*, 30(2): 243–261.

Jessop, B. (1999) 'The changing governance of welfare: Recent trends in its primary functions, scale, and modes of coordination', *Social Policy & Administration*, 33(4): 348–359.

John, P. (2009) 'Why study urban politics?', in J. Davies and D. Imbroscio (eds), *Theories of Urban Politics*, London: Sage, pp 17–23, 2nd edition.

Jolin-Dahel, L. (2020) 'Un marché immobilier dynamique malgré la pandémie, *Le Devoir*, [online] 7 November, Available from: https://www.ledevoir.com/vivre/habitation/588611/immobilier-un-marche-dynamique-malgre-la-pandemie

Jones, S.H. (2014) 'The "metropolis of dissent": Muslim participation in Leicester and the "failure" of multiculturalism in Britain', *Ethnic and Racial Studies*, 38(11): 1969–1985.

Kandylis, G., Maloutas, T. and Sayas, J. (2012) 'Immigration, inequality and diversity: socio-ethnic hierarchy and spatial organization in Athens, Greece', *European Urban and Regional Studies*, 19(3): 267–286.

Karyotis, G. and Rüdig, W. (2018) 'The three waves of anti-austerity protest in Greece, 2010–2015', *Political Studies Review*, 16(2): 158–169.

Keil, R. (2002) '"Common Sense" neoliberalism: Progressive conservative urbanism in Toronto, Canada', *Antipode*, 34(3): 578–601.

Keil, R. (2009) 'The urban politics of roll-with-it neoliberalization', *City*, 13(2/3): 231–245.

Klandermans, B., Roef, M. and Olivier, J. (1998) 'A movement takes office', in S. Tarrow and D.S. Meyer (eds), *The Social Movement Society: Contentious Politics for a New Century*, Lanham: Rowman and Littlefield, pp 173–194.

Koehler, S. and König, T. (2015) 'Fiscal governance in the Eurozone: How effectively does the Stability and Growth Pact limit governmental debt in the Euro countries?', *Political Science Research and Methods*, 3(2): 329–351.

Konzelmann, S.J. (2014) 'The political economics of austerity', *Cambridge Journal of Economics*, 38(4): 701–741.

Koontz, T.M., Thomas, C.W., Carmin, J. and Moseley, C. (2010) *Collaborative Environmental Management: What Roles for Government?*, London: Routledge.

Labbé, J. (2020) 'Montréal: l'électorat de Valérie Plante se fragilise', *Site de Radio-Canada*, [online] 26 October, Available from: https://ici.radio-canada.ca/nouvelle/1743385/sondage-intentions-vote-satisfaction-montrealais-elections-mairie-2021

La Mauvaise Troupe Collective and Ross, K. (2018) *The Zad and NoTAV: Territorial Struggles and the Making of a New Political Intelligence*, London: Verso.

Lammert, C. and Vormann, B. (2017) *Die Krise der Demokratie udn wie wir sie überwinden*, Berlin: Aufbau Verlag.

Laroche, M. and Barré, P. (2012) 'Concertation sociale et négociation collective au Québec en temps de crise Restructurations et découplage', *Travail et Emploi*, 132: 65–77.

Lefèvre, C. (1998) 'Metropolitan government and governance in western countries: a critical review', *International Journal of Urban and Regional Research*, 22(1): 9–25.

Lefèvre, C. (2003) 'Paris – Île -de-France region', in W. Salet, A. Thornley, and A. Kreukels (eds), *Metropolitan Governance and Spatial Planning*, London: Spon, pp 287–300.

Lefèvre, C. (2007) 'France: Metropolitan areas and the new "Reference territories" for public policies', in L. van den Berg, E. Braun, and J. van der Meer (eds), *National Policy Responses to Urban Challenges in Europe*, Aldershot: Ashgate, pp 145–168.

Le Galès, P. (1995) 'Du gouvernement des villes à la gouvernance urbaine', *Revue française de science politique*, 45(1): 57–95.

Lillington, K. (2019) 'How Silicon Docks is killing Dublin, *The Irish Times*, [online] 4 July, Available from: https://www.irishtimes.com/business/technology/how-silicon-docks-is-killing-dublin-1.3945722

Leontidou, L. (1990) *The Mediterranean City in Transition: Social Change and Urban Development*, Cambridge: Cambridge University Press.

Levy, J.M. (2016) *Contemporary Urban Planning*, Abingdon: Routledge.

Lobo, M. (2010) 'Interethnic understanding and belonging in suburban Melbourne', *Urban Policy and Research,* 28(1): 85–99.

MacGillis, A. (2019) 'The tragedy of Baltimore', *New York Times Magazine*, [online] 12 March, Available from: https://www.nytimes.com/2019/03/12/magazine/baltimore-tragedy-crime.html

MacPherson, D. (2014) 'Philippe Couillard warns Quebecers to get used to austerity', *Montreal Gazette*, [online] 8 December, Available from: https://montrealgazette.com/news/quebec/don-macpherson-philippe-couillard-warns-quebecers-to-get-used-to-austerity

Magnusson, W. (2015) *Local Self-Government and the Right to the City*, Montreal and Kingston: McGill-Queen's University Press.

Maly, M.T. (2005) *Beyond Segregation: Multiracial and Multiethnic Neighborhoods in the United States*, Philadelphia: Temple University Press.

Marcuse, P. (2015) 'Depoliticizing urban discourse: How "we" write', *Cities*, 44: 152–156.

Martí-Costa, M. and Tomàs, M. (2017) 'Urban governance in Spain: From democratic transition to austerity policies', *Urban Studies*, 54(9): 2107–2122.

Matthijs, M. and McNamara K. (2015) 'The Euro crisis' theory effect: Northern saints, southern sinners, and the demise of the Eurobond', *Journal of European Integration*, 37(2): 229–245.

Mayer, M. (2016) 'Urban social movements in times of austerity politics', in B. Schönig and S. Schipper (eds), *Urban Austerity*, Berlin: Theater der Zeit, pp 219–241.

McGuirk, P. (2000) 'Power and policy networks in urban governance: Local government and property-led regeneration in Dublin', *Urban Studies*, 37(4): 651–672.

McNeice, S. (2020) 'Significant differences in COVID-19 rates across Dublin, latest figures show', *Newstalk*, [online] 16 September, Available from: https://www.newstalk.com/news/significant-differences-covid-19-rates-across-dublin-latest-figures-show-1076928

Miller, B. (2009) 'Is scale a chaotic concept? Notes on processes of scale production', in R. Keil and R. Mahon (eds), *Leviathan Undone? Towards a Political Economy of Scale*, Vancouver and Toronto: UBC Press, pp 51–66.

Moini, G. (2011) 'How participation has become a hegemonic discursive resource: Towards an interpretivist research agenda', *Critical Policy Studies*, 5(2): 149–168.

Monkkonen, E.H. (1998) *America Becomes Urban: The Development of US Cities and Towns – 1780–1980*, Berkeley: University of California Press.

Moody's Investor Service (2012) *Rating Action: Moody's Assigns Baa3 Issuer Rating to the City of Barcelona; Outlook Negative*, Available from: https://www.moodys.com/research/Moodys-assigns-Baa3-issuer-rating-to-the-City-of-Barcelona--PR_261350

Moody's Investor Service (2014) *Announcement: Moody's: Montreal's Focus on Cutting Labour and Pension Costs is Credit Positive*, Available from: https://www.moodys.com/research/Moodys-Montreals-focus-on-cutting-labour-and-pension-costs-is--PR_310094

Moody's Investor Service (2018) *Rating Action: Moody's assigns Aaa to Maryland's $525M 2018 First Series GO Bonds; Outlook Stable*, Available from: https://www.moodys.com/research/Moodys-assigns-Aaa-to-Marylands-525M-2018-First-Series-GO--PR_904475049

Moody's Public Sector Europe (2018a) *Rating Action: Moody's Upgrades City of Athens' Rating to B3; Maintains Positive Outlook*, Available from: https://www.moodys.com/research/Moodys-upgrades-City-of-Athens-rating-to-B3-maintains-positive--PR_379374

Moody's Public Sector Europe (2018b) *Rating Action: Moody's Upgrades Ratings of 15 Spanish Sub-sovereigns; Outlooks Unchanged*, Available from: https://www.moodys.com/research/Moodys-upgrades-ratings-of-15-Spanish-sub-sovereigns-outlooks-unchanged--PR_381627

Nelles, J. and Durand, F. (2012) 'Political rescaling and metropolitan governance in cross-border regions: Comparing the cross-border metropolitan areas of Lille and Luxembourg', *European Urban and Regional Studies*, 21(1): 104–122.

Newman, P. and Thornley, A. (2002) *Urban Panning in Europe: International Competition, National Systems and Planning Projects*, London: Routledge.

Nyden, P., Maly, M. and Lukehart, J. (1997) 'The emergence of stable racially and ethnically diverse urban communities: A case study of nine US cities' *Housing Policy Debate*, 8(2): 491–534.

O'Carroll, A., Duffin, T. and Collins, J. (2021) 'Harm reduction in the time of COVID-19: Case study of homelessness and drug use in Dublin, Ireland', *International Journal of Drug Policy*, 87, Available from: https://doi.org/10.1016/j.drugpo.2020.102966

OECD. (2020) *COVID-19 and Cities: Impact, Lessons learned and Recovery Strategies*, OECD, Available from: https://www.oecd.org/coronavirus/policy-responses/cities-policy-responses-fd1053ff/

Offe, C. (1985) 'New social movements: Challenging the boundaries of institutional politics', *Social Research*, 52(4): 817–868.

OJEU (2013) 'Regulation (EU) No 1303/2013 of the European Parliament and of the Council', *Official Journal of the European Union*, 56: 320–469.

Oppel R. Jr, Gebeloff, R., Lai, K., Wright, W. and Smith, M. (2020) 'The fullest look yet at the racial inequity of coronavirus', *New York Times*, [online] 5 July, Available from: https://www.nytimes.com/interactive/2020/07/05/us/coronavirus-latinos-african-americans-cdc-data.html

Papapetros, S. (2019) 'Early morning clashes at Rhodes hotel where trade union umbrella group general assembly was due to open', *Naftemporiki*, [online] 4 April, Available from: https://www.naftemporiki.gr/story/1461256/early-morning-clashes-at-rhodes-hotel-where-trade-union-umbrella-group-general-assembly-was-due-to-open

Park, R.E. (1928) 'Human migration and the marginal man', *American Journal of Sociology*, 33(6): 881–893.

Parker, O. and Tsarouhas, D. (2018) 'Causes and consequences of crisis in the Eurozone periphery', in O. Parker and D. Tsarouhas (eds), *Crisis in the Eurozone Periphery: The Political Economies of Greece, Spain, Ireland and Portugal*, London: Palgrave Macmillan, pp 1–28.

Paul, M. (2020) 'Silicon Docks: Where the streets have no people', *The Irish Times*, [online] 11 September, Available from: https://www.irishtimes.com/business/technology/silicon-docks-where-the-streets-have-no-people-1.4351558

Peck, J. (2012) 'Austerity urbanism', *City: Analysis of Urban Trends, Culture, Theory, Policy*, 16(1): 626–655.

Peck, J. (2018) 'Preface: Situating Austerity Urbanism', in M. Davidson and K. Ward (eds), *Cities Under Austerity: Restructuring the US Metropolis*, Albany: SUNY Press, pp xi–xxxviii.

Peck, J. and Whiteside, H. (2016) 'Financializing the entrepreneurial city', in B. Schönig and S. Schipper (eds), *Urban Austerity: Impacts of the Global Financial Crisis on Cities in Europe*, Berlin: Theater de Zeit, pp 21–39.

Pelkonen, A. (2013) 'Rescaling and urban-regional restructuring in Finland and in the Helsinki region', *European Urban and Regional Studies*, 23(2): 149–166.

Perrons, D. (2004) *Globalization and Social Change: People and Places in a Divided World*, London: Routledge.

Petzold, T. (2018) *Austerity Forever?! Die Normalisierung der Austerität in der BRD*, Münster: Westfälisches Dampfboot.

Piattoni, S. (2010) *The Theory of Multi-level Governance. Conceptual, Empirical, and Normative Challenges*, Oxford: Oxford University Press.

Pierson, P. and Skocpol, T. (2002) 'Historical institutionalism in contemporary political science', in I. Katznelson and H. Milner (eds), *Political Science: The State of the Discipline*, New York: W.W. Norton, pp 693–721.

Pike, A., Coombes, M., O'Brien, P. and Tomaney, J. (2018) 'Austerity states, institutional dismantling and the governance of sub-national economic development: The demise of the regional development agencies in England', *Territory, Politics, Governance*, 6(1): 118–144.

Pill, M.C. (2020) 'The austerity governance of Baltimore's neighborhoods: "The conversation may have changed but the systems aren't changing"', *Journal of Urban Affairs*, 42(1): 143–158.

Pinson, G. (2015) 'Gouvernance et sociologie de l'action organisée. Action publique, coordination et théorie de l'État', *L'année Sociologique*, 65(2): 483–519.

Pinson, G. and Le Galès, P. (2005) 'State restructuring and decentralisation dynamics in France: Politics is the driving force', *Cahier Européen numéro 07/05 du Pôle Ville/Metropolis/Cosmopolis*, Centre d'Etudes Européennes de Sciences Po Paris.

Pithouse, R. (2008) 'A politics of the poor: Shack dwellers' struggles in Durban', *Journal of Asian and African Studies*, 43(1): 63–94.

Rhodes, R.A.W. (1997) *Understanding Governance: Policy Networks, Governance, Reflexivity, and Accountability*, Buckingham: Open University Press.

Rhodes, R.A.W. (2012) 'Waves of Governance', in D. Levi-Faur (ed), *The Oxford Handbook of Governance*, Oxford: Oxford University Press, pp 33–48.

Robinson, D. (2010) 'The neighbourhood effects of new immigration', *Environment and Planning A*, 42(10): 2451–2466.

Roodbol-Mekkes, P.H. and den Brink, A. van. (2015) 'Rescaling spatial planning: spatial planning reforms in Denmark, England, and the Netherlands', *Environment and Planning C: Government and Policy*, 33(1): 184–198.

Rosenberg, J. (2000) *The Follies of Globalization Theory*, London: Verso.

Rothstein, R. (2015) 'From Ferguson to Baltimore: The fruits of government-sponsored segregation', *Journal of Affordable Housing & Community Development Law*, 24(2): 205–210.

Roussos, K. (2019) 'Grassroots collective action within and beyond institutional and state solutions: the (re-)politicisation of everyday life in crisis-ridden Greece', *Social Movement Studies*, 18(3): 265–283.

Ruddick, S.L., Peake, G.S, Tanyildiz, G. and D. Patrick. (2018) 'Planetary urbanization: An urban theory for our time?', *Environment and Planning D: Society and Space*, 36(3): 387–404.

Russell, B. (2019) 'Beyond the local trap: New municipalism and the rise of the fearless cities', *Antipode*, 51(3): 989–1010.

Safe Ireland (2020) *Programme for Government Submission – Global Pandemic, National Epidemic – Working to end Domestic Abuse & Coercive Control*, Available from: https://www.safeireland.ie/policy-publications

Sandford, M. (2006) *The New Governance of the English Regions*, Basingstoke: Palgrave.

Sanfaçon, J.-R. (2020) 'Le 'modèle' prend l'eau, *Le Devoir*, [online] 8 June, Available from: https://www.ledevoir.com/opinion/editoriaux/580370/services-publics-le-modele-prend-l-eau

Schipper, S., Pohl, L., Petzold, T. Mullis, D. and Belina B. (2018) 'Blockupy fights back: global city formation in Frankfurt am Main after the financial crisis', in X. Ren and R. Keil (eds), *The Globalizing Cities Reader*, London: Routledge, pp 325–332.

Schneiders, B. and Millar, R. (2020) 'A city divided: COVID-19 finds a weakness in Melbourne's social fault lines' *The Age*, [online] 8 August, Available from: https://www.theage.com.au/national/victoria/a-city-divided-covid-19-finds-a-weakness-in-melbourne-s-social-fault-lines-20200807-p55ji2.html

Scott, M. (2021) 'How will the pandemic reshape Montreal? A look at 2021's challenges: Will our beloved metropolis ever go back to the way it was?', *Montreal Gazette*, [online] 2 January, Available from: https://montrealgazette.com/news/local-news/the-post-covid-city

Serebrin, J. (2020) 'Long-term care homes in Quebec better protected during second COVID-19 wave', *Canadian Press, Global News*, [online] 17 December, Available from: https://globalnews.ca/news/7529166/long-term-care-homes-in-quebec-better-protected-during-second-covid-19-wave-report/

Shea-Baird, K. (2020) 'A municipalist response to COVID-19', *Trademark Belfast*, [online] 28 August, Available from: http://trademarkbelfast.com/a-municipalist-response-to-covid-19/

Simmel, G. (1908) *Soziologie*, Leipzig: Duncker & Humblot.

Sinclair, T.J. (2005) *The New Masters of Capital: American Bond Rating Agencies and the Politics of Creditworthiness*, Ithaca: Cornell University Press.

Singh, G. (2003) 'Multiculturalism in contemporary Britain: Reflections on the "Leicester Model"', *International Journal on Multi-Cultural Societies*, 5(1): 40–54.

Smith, H. (2019) 'Greece moves towards ending austerity with rise in minimum wage', [online] 28 January, Available from: https://www.theguardian.com/world/2019/jan/28/greece-moves-towards-ending-austerity-with-rise-to-minimum-wage

Soderberg, B. (2019) 'The Baltimore uprising: four years later the real news', [online] 19 April, Available from: https://therealnews.com/columns/baltimore-uprising-four-years-later

Sørensen, E. and Torfing, J. (2018) 'Governance on a bumpy road from enfant terrible to mature paradigm', *Critical Policy Studies*, 12(3): 350–359.

Spiller, M. and Weston, R. (2020) 'Casualisation and COVID-19: New analysis reveals tears in Melbourne's social fabric', *SGS Economics & Planning*, [online] 10 August, Available from: https://www.sgsep.com.au/publications/insights/casualisation-and-covid-19

Stoecker, R. (2003) 'Understanding the development-organizing dialectic', *Journal of Urban Affairs*, 25(4): 493–512.

Sullivan, H., Henderson, H. and Gleeson, B. (2019) *Central Dandenong: Australia's Comeback City? Lessons about Revitalisation for Diverse Places*, The University of Melbourne, Available from: https://sustainable.unimelb.edu.au/__data/assets/pdf_file/0011/3227267/Dandenong_final_web_26112019.pdf

Swyngedouw, E. (2018) 'CO_2 as neoliberal fetish: The love of crisis and the depoliticized immuno-biopolitics of climate change governance', in D. Cahill, M. Cooper, M. Martijn Konings and D. Primrose (eds), *The SAGE Handbook of Neoliberalism*, London: SAGE, pp 295–307.

Team, V. and Manderson, L. (2020) 'How COVID-19 reveals structures of vulnerability', *Medical Anthropology*, 39(8): 671–674.

Theodore, N. (2020) 'Governing through austerity: (Il)logics of neoliberal urbanism after the global financial crisis', *Journal of Urban Affairs*, 42(1): 1–17.

Thomas, W.I. and Znaniecki, F. (1918) *The Polish Peasant in Europe and America*, Vol. 1–5, New York: Alfred A. Knop.

Thompson, M. (2020) 'What's so new about New Municipalism?', *Progress in Human Geography*, First published 9 March. Doi: 10.1177/0309132520909480.

Threshold (2020) 'Threshold deals with over 100 illegal evictions despite moratorium', *Threshold*, [online] 10 December 10, Available from: https://www.threshold.ie/news/2020/12/10/threshold-deals-with-over-100-illegal-evictions-de/

Todd, E. (2017) *Où en Sommes-Nous? Une Esquisse de L'histoire Humaine*, Paris: Éditions du Seuil.

United Nations (2020) *COVID-19 in an Urban World*, Available from: https://www.un.org/sites/un2.un.org/files/sg_policy_brief_covid_urban_world_july_2020.pdf

University Times (2020) 'Trinity initiates first phase of Grand Canal Innovation District', *University Times*, [online] 20 November, Available from: http://www.universitytimes.ie/2020/11/first-phase-grand-canal-innovation-district/

Victorian Government (2020) *A Game Changer for Central Dandenong*, [online] 18 December, Available from: https://www.premier.vic.gov.au/game-changer-central-dandenong

Vink, M. (2017) 'Comparing citizenship regimes', in A. Shachar, I. Bloemraad, M. Vink, and R. Bauboeck (eds), *The Oxford Handbook of Citizenship*, Oxford: Oxford University Press, pp 221–244.

Walliser, A. (2013) 'New urban activisms in Spain: Reclaiming public space in the face of crises', *Policy & Politics*, 41(3): 329–350.

Welsh, J. (2016) *The Return of History: Conflict, Migration, and Geopolitics in the Twenty-First Century*, Toronto: House of Anansi Press.

Wenger, Y. (2018) 'I got hope today: Program moves former Baltimore homeless-camp residents into permanent housing', *Baltimore Sun*, [online] 29 May, Available from: https://www.baltimoresun.com/maryland/baltimore-city/bs-md-ci-encampment-homeless-20180510-story.html

Williams, T. (2018) 'In Baltimore, brazen officers took every chance to rob and cheat', *New York Times*, [online] 6 February, Available from: https://www.nytimes.com/2018/02/06/us/baltimore-police-corruption.html

Wissel, J. and Wolff, S. (2017) 'Political regulation and the strategic production of space: The European Union as a post-Fordist state spatial project', *Antipode*, 49(1): 231–248.

Yarram, S.R., Dollery, B. and Tran, C. (2020) 'The impact of rate capping on local government expenditure', *Policy & Politics*, https://doi.org/10.1332/030557320X15910206974407

Zolberg. A. (2000) 'Preface', in S. Body-Gendrot and M. Martiniello (eds), *Minorities in European Cities*, London: Macmillan, pp xiv–xvii.

Bibliography of Working Papers

Blanco, I. (2015b) *Working Paper 4: Collaborative Governance in Barcelona*, Unpublished.

Blanco, I. (2017) *Working Paper 21: Barcelona Final Case Study Report*, Unpublished.

Blanco, I. (2016) *Working Paper 12: Austerity Governance and Contestation in Barcelona*, Unpublished.

Chorianopoulos, I. (2015) *Working Paper 2: Austerity and Rescaling: The Emergence of Collaborative Governance Structures in Athens*, Unpublished.

Chorianopoulos, I. (2016) *Working Paper 10: Austerity and Collaborative Governance in Athens*, Unpublished.

Chorianopoulos, I. (2017) *Working Paper 19: Athens Final Case Study Report*, Unpublished.

Davies, J.S. (2015) *Working Paper 1: Scoping the Project*, Unpublished.

Davies, J.S. (2015) *Working Paper 6: Collaborative Governance in Leicester*, Unpublished.

Davies, J.S. (2017) *Working Paper 18: Notes for Comparative Analysis*, Unpublished.

Davies, J.S. and Bua, A. (2016) *Working Paper 14: Austerity Governance and Welfare in Leicester*, Unpublished.

Davies, J.S., Bua, A. and Cortina-Oriol, M. (2017) *Working Paper 23: Final Report of the Leicester Case Study*, Unpublished.

Gaynor, N. (2015) *Working Paper 5: Collaborative governance in Dublin: Centralisation and Protest*, Unpublished.

Gaynor, N. (2016) *Working Paper 13: Governing Austerity in Dublin*, Unpublished.

Gaynor, N. (2017) *Working Paper 22: Dublin Final Case Study Report*, Unpublished.

Gleeson, B., Henderson, H. and Sullivan H. (2015) *Working Paper 7: ESRC Austerity Governance Project. Melbourne Case Literature Review*, Unpublished.

Griggs, S. and Howarth, D. (2015) *Working Paper 9: Nantes Case Study Literature Review*, Unpublished.

Griggs, S. and Howarth, D. (2016) *Working Paper 17: Collaborative Governance Under Austerity*, Unpublished.

Griggs, S., Howarth, D. and Feandeiro A. (2018) *Working Paper 26: Collaborative Governance Under Austerity, Final Report: City of Nantes*, Unpublished.

Hamel, P. and Keil, R. (2015) *Working Paper 8: Facing Austerity while Undergoing Industrial and Post- Industrial Restructuring: the Montreal Case*, Unpublished.

Hamel, P. and Keil, R. (2016) *Working Paper 16: Austerity Governance and Welfare in Montreal*, Unpublished.

Hamel, P. and Keil, R. (2018) *Working Paper 25: Montreal Case Study Final Report*, Unpublished.

Henderson, H., Gleeson, B. and Sullivan, H. (2016) *Working Paper 15: Melbourne Exploratory Research Paper*, Unpublished.

Henderson, H., Gleeson, B. and Sullivan, H. (2017) *Working Paper 24: Final Report of the Melbourne Case Study: Revitalisation in Central Dandenong, Melbourne*, Unpublished.

Pill, M.C. (2015) *Working Paper 3: Baltimore Literature Review*, Unpublished.

Pill, M.C. (2016) *Working Paper 11: Baltimore Exploratory Research*, Unpublished.

Pill, M.C. (2017) *Working Paper 20: Baltimore Final Case Study Report*, Unpublished.

Index

www.ingramcontent.com/pod-product-compliance
Lightning Source LLC
Chambersburg PA
CBHW070625030426
42337CB00020B/3920